AMERICAN PHILOSOPHY AND RUDOLF STEINER

Rudolf Steiner

AMERICAN PHILOSOPHY AND RUDOLF STEINER

EMERSON • THOREAU • PEIRCE • JAMES
ROYCE • DEWEY • WHITEHEAD • FEMINISM

Rebecca Kneale Gould
David Ray Griffin
Gertrude Reif Hughes
Robert McDermott
Dan McKanan
Frank M. Oppenheim, S.J.
Douglas Sloan

EDITED AND INTRODUCED BY
ROBERT MCDERMOTT

LINDISFARNE BOOKS | 2012

2012
LINDISFARNE BOOKS
AN IMPRINT OF STEINERBOOKS / ANTHROPOSOPHIC PRESS, INC.
PO Box 749, Great Barrington, MA 01230
www.steinerbooks.org

Copyright 2012 © by Robert A. McDermott All rights reserved. No part of this publication may be reproduced, stored in a retrieval system, or transmitted, in any form or by any means, electronic, mechanical, photocopying, recording, or otherwise, without the prior written permission of the publisher.

BOOK & COVER DESIGN: WILLIAM JENS JENSEN

LIBRARY OF CONGRESS CATALOGING-IN-PUBLICATION DATA

American philosophy and Rudolf Steiner : Emerson, Thoreau, Peirce, James, Royce, Dewey, Whitehead, feminism / edited by Robert McDermott.
   p. cm.
Includes bibliographical references (p. 247).
ISBN 978-1-58420-137-3 (pbk.)—ISBN 978-1-58420-138-0 (ebook)
1. Philosophy, American. 2. Steiner, Rudolf, 1861–1925.
I. McDermott, Robert A.
B893.A44 2012
191—dc23

2012033841

Contents

	Preface by Robert McDermott	vii
	Foreword by Dan McKanan	ix
	Introduction by Robert McDermott	xxiii
1.	Hearing Steiner's Anthroposophy in Emerson's Prophetic Voice by Gertrude Reif Hughes	1
2.	Deliberate Lives, Deliberate Living: Thoreau and Steiner in Conversation by Rebecca Kneale Gould	19
3.	William James and Rudolf Steiner by Robert McDermott	51
4.	Charles Sanders Peirce and Rudolf Steiner: Prophetic Philosophers by Robert McDermott	65
5.	Josiah Royce and Rudolf Steiner: A Comparison and Contrast by Frank M. Oppenheim, S. J.	89
6.	Steiner's Anthroposophy and Whitehead's Philosophy by David Ray Griffin	135
7.	John Dewey's Project for "Saving the Appearances": Exploring Some of Its Implications for Education and Ethics by Douglas Sloan	183
8.	Rudolf Steiner's Activist Epistemology and Feminist Thought in America by Gertrude Reif Hughes	227
	Bibliography	251
	About the Contributors	259

For

John J. McDermott and Frank M. Oppenheim, S. J.,

scholars and proponents of classical American thought

and for

Gertrude Reif Hughes, Douglas Sloan, and Arthur Zajonc,

scholars and exemplars of Rudolf Steiner's Anthroposophy

PREFACE

Robert McDermott

Five of the articles in this volume were written as part of a seminar on Rudolf Steiner and American Thought as part of a Project for the Renewal of Philosophy, Science, and Education sponsored by Laurance S. Rockefeller. These essays—by David Ray Griffin, Gertrude Reif Hughes, Frank M. Oppenheim, S. J., Douglas Sloan, and myself were first published in *ReVision: A Journal of Consciousness and Transformation* (spring and summer 1991). I am grateful to Jurgen Kremer, editor of *ReVision*, and to The Society for the Study of Shamanism, Healing, and Transformation, for permission to republish these essays. In spring 1992 a second seminar, directed by Arthur Zajonc, met to discuss Goethean science. The proceedings of the third seminar, directed by Douglas Sloan, and devoted to society and education, were published in *ReVision* (1993).

I invited to this seminar eleven professors who I knew would be able to explore collaboratively the relationship between the Anthroposophy of Rudolf Steiner and major American thinkers, including: five professors and authors committed to Anthroposophy—Gertrude Reif Hughes, Robert Sardello, Douglas Sloan, and Arthur Zajonc, and six colleagues well-schooled in American thought—David Ray Griffin, Patrick Hill, Frank M. Oppenheim, S. J., Richard Tarnas, Frances Vaughan, Roger Walsh. I also invited Georg Locher, a distinguished teacher of Waldorf teachers, to lead the group in artistic exercises each afternoon. I served as facilitator. All thirteen participants read several books by Steiner and by American philosophers.

The group took time on several occasions during the seminar to discuss and regret the first American attack on Iraq that took place during our week together. The group was grateful to participate in a Mass offered for us by Frank Oppenheim, S.J. Except for Patrick Hill, who died in 2008, all thirteen participants are still working on behalf of the topics that brought us to Rye, NY in 1991.

When Gene Gollogly, publisher of SteinerBooks, agreed to my recommendation that we republish the *ReVision* double issue, *Rudolf Steiner and American Thought,* as a Lindisfarne book, I immediately recognized the need for several additions. They are: an essay on Steiner and Emerson, contributed by Gertrude Reif Hughes, professor emerita at Wesleyan University; an essay on Steiner and Henry David Thoreau contributed by Becky Gould, professor of religion and ecology at Middlebury College; and a foreword by Dan McKanan, Ralph Waldo Emerson Unitarian-Universalist Professor, Harvard Divinity School. I am grateful to Matthew David Segall, a gifted CIIS doctoral student, for correcting typographical errors and improving infelicitous expressions throughout this volume.

San Francisco, CA
October 2012

FOREWORD

Dan McKanan

Few thinkers from outside the United States have touched American culture in as many ways as Rudolf Steiner. Agriculture, education, spirituality, and medicine—or more precisely, alternative practices in these fields—all bear clear marks of his influence, for those with eyes to see. Yet the very breadth of Steiner's impact has perhaps made him harder, not easier, for observers of American culture to notice. The terms *Waldorf education* and *biodynamic agriculture* are more widely recognized than are Rudolf Steiner and Anthroposophy. Anthroposophic initiatives are commonly understood in relation to parallel initiatives with different spiritual roots, rather than in relation to the rich fabric of Steiner's worldview. Americans typically imagine biodynamic agriculture as a more intense form of organics and Waldorf schools as "like Montessori schools only more so." When I describe the Camphill movement, most interlocutors respond with "Is that like the L'Arche movement?" And thousands of shoppers at health food cooperatives and Whole Foods supermarkets purchase Weleda skin lotion, diaper cream, or homeopathic remedies with little sense of connection to Steiner's vision of spirit active in the world.

This situation is not catastrophic. People can benefit from the fruits of Steiner's insight without knowing his name, and many who have been helped by a specific anthroposophic initiative ultimately find their way to others. Still, Steiner's relative invisibility in the United States is problematic for at least three reasons. First, obviously, is that many people who have been helped by a specific anthroposophic initiative do *not* find their way to others, even to those others that might be most relevant to their own life situation. Second is that certain aspects of Steiner's vision that might be highly relevant to the American situation are virtually unknown beyond committed members of the Anthroposophical Society. I think particularly of his theory of the threefold social order. It has the potential to reconcile the libertarian current that is so strong in American politics with equally strong traditions of egalitarian social reform, yet its lack of an institutional base comparable to Waldorf schools has rendered it virtually unknown. Third, when people fail to perceive the full spiritual context of Waldorf or biodynamics or Weleda, they are less able to assess them critically and thus to embrace or reject them in freedom. A significant minority of parents who have sent their children to Waldorf schools, for example, have been troubled by what they perceive as a lack of transparency about Waldorf's spiritual roots. Roman Catholic schools and hospitals do not face this particular challenge, simply because the Catholic worldview is fully a part of the broader American conversation.

This collection aspires to raise Steiner's profile by digging into just one field of inquiry: philosophy. Before he became known to the world as a transmitter of clairvoyant wisdom, Steiner was an academic philosopher, editor of the scientific writings of Johann Wolfgang von Goethe and the author of a foundational work in philosophy, *The Philosophy of Freedom: The Basis for a Modern World Conception*, published in 1894. *Philosophy of Freedom* expressed in philosophical terms many of the ideas that would later emerge as integral to the spiritual science of Anthroposophy.[1] In that early work, Steiner chose not to make mention of his own extraordinary spiritual experiences, making his case in

---

1. Steiner, *Intuitive Thinking as a Spiritual Path: A Philosophy of Freedom*. Many of the titles of Steiner's works have been rendered into English very differently in different translations. This particular work is best known as *The Philosophy of Freedom*. Readers who are new to Steiner's work will benefit from McDermott (ed.), *The New Essential Steiner*, and Lachman, *Rudolf Steiner: An Introduction to His Life and Work*. *The New Essential Steiner* includes a "Guide to Further Reading." Hundreds of volumes by and about Steiner's life, thought, and work are thoroughly described in the Steinerbooks complete catalog (Steinerbooks.org).

terms that would be readily accessible to any reader with philosophical training. For this reason, it figures prominently in most of the essays presented here, and readers might consider having a copy close by as they work their way through this volume.

Both the affinities and the tensions between Steiner and American philosophy can, perhaps, be traced to a single, perplexing word: *pragmatism*. In a loose sense, this word designates a concern for results, for effectiveness, for worldly transformation. The Puritanism of seventeenth-century New England, the republicanism of the eighteenth century, and both capitalist industry and social reforming energy in the nineteenth and twentieth centuries are "pragmatist" in this sense. Steiner resonates with this tendency because, more than most spiritual teachers, he was deeply concerned with what we might call "applied spirituality"—with using spiritual insights to inform education, medicine, agriculture, and the arts.

In a narrower sense, *pragmatism* designates a specific school of American philosophy that reached its heyday in the early decades of the twentieth century, when it was promoted in slightly different forms by William James, John Dewey, and Charles Sanders Peirce. The founding idea of this school was articulated by Peirce: "Consider the practical effects of the objects of your conception. Then, your conception of those effects is the whole of your conception of the object."[2] From the perspective of this "pragmatic maxim," both traditional idealism and traditional materialism fell short—the former because it was not grounded in experience and the latter because it arbitrarily reduced experience to the interplay of atomistic sensations and particles, failing to see how meanings are built up from interconnections. The pragmatists aspired to be "radically empiricist"—attentive exclusively to experience, but open to its full richness and variety.

Steiner certainly shared the pragmatists' yearning for a third way between idealism and materialism. But the pragmatists

---

2. After William James embraced and popularized the term "pragmatism," Peirce himself began using "pragmaticism" to underscore some differences between his position and that of James.

likely would have rejected Steiner's philosophical approach on the grounds that it tilted too close to the idealist stance. Like the nineteenth-century Transcendentalists, Steiner believed that the practice of *intuition*, or thinking about thinking, allows us to transcend the opposition of subject and object, building a bridge between our individuality and universal spirit. (This position is elaborated in greater detail in the essays by Robert McDermott and Gertrude Reif Hughes.) His stress on intuition echoed the idealism of Immanuel Kant, but Steiner insisted that Kant had erred in concluding that intuitive knowledge could offer no direct knowledge of "things in themselves." Indeed, as Steiner made clear in his later works, the practice of intuition as a spiritual discipline could open the individual to ever-expanding knowledge of reality, extending even to the "Akashic Record," or the repository of all consciousness. From Steiner's perspective, this constituted a move from pure idealism to a third way. For him, intuition was not something apart from experience; rather, intuition was the form of experience that unlocked all others. But given the pragmatists' affinity for experimental science, they likely would have regarded it as a move even deeper into idealism and away from experience. Still, the tensions between Steiner and classical pragmatism only highlight the potential for dialogue.

The essays in this volume connect Steiner to pragmatism in both the loose and the narrow senses. The first two address Transcendentalism, one of the American philosophical traditions that was emphatically "pragmatic" in its concern for results, yet far friendlier to idealism than were Peirce, James, and Dewey. The affinities between Transcendentalism and Steiner's philosophy are extensive, and this should be no surprise. Steiner and the Transcendentalists drew on some important common sources, most notably the work of Johann Wolfgang von Goethe. The Transcendentalist movement began, arguably, when a precocious teenager named Frederic Henry Hedge was sent by his father for four years of study in Germany before entering Harvard College. Eighteen years later, the Transcendentalist or "Hedge" club began to meet whenever Hedge travelled from his pastorate in Maine to visit with friends in Boston and Concord. Hedge introduced American thinkers to the German philosophical and literary traditions of idealism and Romanticism. With his childhood friend Margaret Fuller, Hedge had a special affinity for Goethe, whose *Faust* and *Letters from Switzerland* and *Travels in Italy* he edited late in life. Transcendentalism thus brought some of the Goethean spirit into American thought, just as Steiner never lost his reverence for Goethe as a key source of the intellectual and methodological foundations of Anthroposophy. Similarly, most of the Transcendentalists were influenced by Emanuel Swedenborg, an esoteric visionary whose influence in the nineteenth century was as wide-ranging as Steiner's in the twentieth. Goethe and Swedenborg helped point the Transcendentalists toward what we might call a "spiritual pragmatism"—a conviction that the best way to achieve transformation in the world was to open oneself to what Swedenborg called the "influx" of divine spirit, by means of intuitive practices.

In this volume, Gertrude Reif Hughes illumines the connections between Steiner and Transcendentalism by examining the central philosopher of the Transcendentalist circle, Ralph Waldo Emerson. Tellingly, she begins by noting Steiner's veneration for Emerson's *Representative Men*, a collection of essays that includes chapters on both Goethe ("the writer") and Swedenborg ("the mystic"). Both Emerson and Steiner, Hughes explains, overcome the dualism of spirit and matter by insisting that spirit is "the source of all realities, including material ones." This implies, of course, that "spirit has primacy for both men"—an important point of tension with the twentieth-century pragmatists for whom experience, not spirit, was the philosophical starting point. Though Emerson and Steiner expressed their insights in very different vocabularies, Hughes argues, those insights were essentially the same. She notes the close parallel between Emerson's emphasis on "self-reliance" and Steiner's insight that intuitive thinking about thinking opens a door to knowledge that does not rely on any external authority. When intuition leads to action, it thus provides the basis for a morality that is genuinely free. By reading Emerson and Steiner together, Hughes demonstrates, one can discover a Steiner who is "more American than might otherwise be expected"—and one can also discover a model of American freedom that is not narrowly consumerist but oriented to "evolving soul capacities."

This point echoes in Rebecca Kneale Gould's essay on Steiner and Thoreau, which identifies a "passion for the pursuit of freedom" as the first of several similarities between the builder of the Goetheanum and the sage of Walden Pond. Both men were true originals capable of generating unforgettable impressions on others; both were also passionate educators who sought to give others the tools to compose their own lives. Steiner and Thoreau, Gould shows, promoted a worldly spirituality, looking especially to natural phenomena for insights into spiritual realities. And both contributed to the "re-enchantment of the world" that was the hallmark of Romanticism. Indeed, Gould uses their shared Romanticism to explain their different relationships to Christianity. Thoreau broke from the Puritan Christianity he had inherited, even as he preserved the Puritans' tendency to find "types" of the spirit within nature. Steiner, by contrast, broke with the Eastern spirituality of the Theosophical Society—whose roots included Thoreau's study of Eastern scriptures—when he oriented his esotericism to the mystery of Christ. Gould also highlights the very different personal energies of the two men. Thoreau was "centripetal," deepening his contemplation in the company of just a few people and places, while Steiner was "centrifugal," spinning out new forms of worldly spirituality in multiple arenas of human endeavor. Yet both offered a spiritual therapy that continues to heal and enrich lives today.

A second set of essays center on the three thinkers who defined "pragmatism" as a coherent philosophical school rather than (as previously) a tendency or emphasis in American thought. Here there is no escaping the real tensions. Though James, Peirce, and Dewey rejected the materialist dogmatism of many individual scientists, they fully embraced the findings of experimental science, while Steiner thoroughly reinterpreted

Darwin's theory of evolution and, indeed, all scientific conclusions derived from an experimental method that abstracted subject from the object of knowledge.

Douglas Sloan takes on the toughest challenge of this volume, putting Steiner in dialogue with John Dewey, generally regarded as the most "secular" of the pragmatists. He does not deny the tension between his two figures, but instead highlights Dewey's indebtedness to the scientific positivism of Auguste Comte—a materialist philosopher whose views are diametrically opposed to those of Steiner. Dewey, Sloan concludes, was two thirds of a Comtean. He held that "science is the only method for attaining true knowledge of any kind," but departed from classical positivism in his refusal to accept that science can provide a comprehensive and self-sufficient worldview. Dewey sought to overcome the modern divide between fact and value by attending both to the insights gained from scientific experimentation *and* to "meaningful, value-laden experience." The instrumental reason of science, Dewey insisted, can exist only within a larger experiential context that is qualitative, holistic, participatory, and value-laden.

But Dewey also insisted that this context was always precognitive: it could be felt but not known. And here, Sloan argues, lay his fatal mistake. By narrowing the scope of "knowledge" to the scientific, Dewey unwittingly contributed to the contemporary dominance of value-free science over value-laden experience. The antidote, for Sloan, lies in Rudolf Steiner's philosophy of freedom, particularly as implemented in the Waldorf system of education. A truly qualitative form of knowing, capable of keeping scientific knowledge within its proper limits, can emerge if children are not "hothoused" into developing abstract, conceptual ways of knowing too early. When children are allowed to develop within "a socially, an aesthetically, and a morally rich and nourishing 'field of experience,'" they will gain "the tacit knowing necessary to truly powerful, creative cognition later on." This is what Waldorf education seeks to achieve—and Sloan's essay nicely demonstrates why the Waldorf tradition has appealed to so many

American educators seeking to advance the Deweyan vision of progressive education.

Robert McDermott's task in the essay on William James is somewhat easier than Douglas Sloan's, because his conversation partner had a deep and abiding interest in spirituality, inherited in part from his father's Swedenborgian commitments. Still, McDermott does not shy away from the differences. James wrote about spiritual experience as a curious, sympathetic, but still skeptical outsider; Steiner spoke with the authority of his own spiritual experience. What the two men shared was a desire to find a third way between the positivist dogma of modern science and the anti-empiricist dogmas of traditional theology and idealism. For James, this third way was an open-ended pluralism, persistently curious about evidences for "Something More"; for Steiner, it was a practice of "highly disciplined, individual spiritual effort" culminating in a harmony between individual selfhood and universal spirit. McDermott astutely notes that the Jamesian path was characteristically both American and Protestant: American in its "show-me" skepticism; Protestant in its assumption that whatever spiritual experience may come will be largely unbidden, the result of grace rather than practice. The implication is clear: American philosophers in the tradition of James might do well to try the sort of disciplined spiritual practices involved in Steiner's path, which McDermott aptly describes as "transformational" rather than "pragmatic."

McDermott's essay on Charles Sanders Peirce is a latecomer to this volume, added only as the book was nearing final production. Peirce was originally neglected because there is no obvious point of connection between his work and Steiner's—nothing comparable to Dewey's intense interest in education and James's lifelong fascination with spirituality. While philosophical inquiry absorbed a relatively modest share of Steiner's attention, Peirce was a pure philosopher whose extraordinarily technical writings have found few readers outside of philosophy departments. McDermott thus begins by acknowledging these and other differences, while meditating on some of the parallels in the biographies of the two men. Gradually, though,

McDermott comes around to the startling observation that what set the mature Peirce apart from his pragmatist brethren was his attempt to combine the pragmatist (now pragmaticist) emphasis on consequences with the philosophical realism of Plato and Aristotle. Unlike the nominalists Dewey and James, Peirce believed the universal ideals were real and not merely convenient "names." So, too, did Steiner; indeed, he understood universal ideals as spiritual agents, describing them in terms whose concreteness might have embarrassed Peirce. If the ultra-realist Steiner, who also cared deeply about the consequences of spiritual ideals, could have been a pragmatist, he surely would have been one along the lines expressed in Peirce's turgid prose and *not* the lines articulated so brilliantly and accessibly by James and Dewey. Thus, Peirce emerges as the linchpin of any attempt to reconcile Anthroposophy with American pragmatism.

Even so, some anthroposophists might conclude that none of the pragmatists hold as much promise as conversation partners as Emerson, or as those twentieth century American philosophers who hewed more closely to Emersonian idealism. Two of the most important of these thinkers, Josiah Royce and Alfred North Whitehead, are the subjects of the most extensive essays in this collection. David Ray Griffin's comment about Steiner and Whitehead applies equally to Royce: all three offered "all-embracing interpretations of the universe" of a sort that "have been out of fashion for most of this century."

Frank Oppenheim's essay on Josiah Royce offers a comprehensive account of the most important "idealist" in conversation with the pragmatists. Both Steiner and Royce, he demonstrates, understood the universe to be rooted in spirit, and both came to see the Paschal Mystery as the key to a spiritual understanding of reality. Common influences, such as Fichte and Schelling, led them to similar epistemologies and emphases on education. Oppenheim also identifies areas of divergence, suggesting that Steiner ultimately placed first stress on the individual, and thus on freedom, while Royce privileged loyalty to community. Given the recent renewal of interest in Royce's notion of "beloved community," this is a point well worth further exploration. It may be that close attention to Steiner's vision for the Anthroposophical Society, and the ongoing work of the Camphill movement and Christian Community, would reveal even greater affinity between Steiner and Royce.

Though the essays included cover a wide range of topics, most share an elegiac tone. The authors see great potential for dialogue between Steiner and the great American philosophers of the nineteenth and early twentieth centuries, but they have not yet attempted a similarly optimistic dialogue with more recent philosophical traditions. Many contributors either imply or state outright that American philosophy took a wrong turn in the middle of the twentieth century, when pragmatism gave way to a tradition of analytical philosophy that eschewed metaphysics as inherently meaningless and focused on the coherence or incoherence of linguistic structures. This narrowing of the scope of philosophy drastically curtailed its capacity to transform the world. The contributors to this volume are anguished about this narrowing, and I suspect that much of the anguish reflects the fact that most were writing in 1991, when the analytic tradition still dominated most academic departments of philosophy in the United States. Much has changed since then, creating many new sites of potential dialogue between Steiner and American philosophy.

Gertrude Reif Hughes's second essay highlights one of those dialogue partners: the feminist movement that revived itself in the second half of the twentieth century and gradually gained a foothold in philosophy departments and in academia more generally. Hughes suggests that feminism has real affinities with what she calls the "activist epistemology" of Rudolf Steiner. Steiner's spiritual exercises were, she astutely notes, a form of "consciousness raising"—practices capable of transforming and not merely interpreting reality. Anthroposophy can thus join feminism in challenging the "universalizing" claims of "male-stream thinking," even as it invites feminists to consider that a deeply contextual practice of individual thinking may offer an authentic point of contact with universal realities.

Foreword

Quite a few other recent impulses in philosophy offer similar prospects for dialogue. Here I will mention a few. I invite the reader to explore these—and the publisher to consider devoting a second volume of essays to their elucidation.

Most noteworthy is the rise of a significant "neopragmatist" philosophical tradition. In its most influential articulation, that of Richard Rorty, neopragmatism retains enough traces of Rorty's background in analytical philosophy that it is probably a less appealing conversation partner than Dewey himself, to say nothing of James.[3] But other leading neopragmatists, notably Cornel West and Jeffrey Stout, are trained as philosophers of religion and thus have worked assiduously to make space for spirituality within the Deweyan framework.[4] An even more intriguing conversation partner is Robert Corrington, whose "ecstatic naturalism" is influenced both by his early grounding in Peirce's pragmatism and by his theosophical commitments.[5]

Another cluster of recent American philosophers, drawing on European philosophies of practice, have revitalized the ancient Greek understanding of philosophy as a form of spiritual practice intended to transform the self of the practitioner. Thus, Judith Butler has offered transformative challenges to currently hegemonic constructions of both sex and gender, while Alasdair MacIntyre has revitalized the Thomistic tradition of virtue ethics.[6] The sharp ethical and political differences between Butler

---

3. Rorty, *Philosophy and the Mirror of Nature*; Rorty, *Contingency, Irony, and Solidarity*; Rorty, *An Ethics for Today: Finding Common Ground Between Philosophy and Religion*; Saatkamp, ed., *Rorty and Pragmatism: The Philosopher Responds to His Critics*.
4. Stout, *Democracy and Tradition*; West, *The American Evasion of Philosophy: A Genealogy of Pragmatism*; West, *Keeping Faith: Philosophy and Race in America*; Anderson, *Pragmatic Theology: Negotiating the Intersections of an American Philosophy of Religion and Public Theology*.
5. Corrington, *An Introduction to C. S. Peirce: Philosopher, Semiotician, and Ecstatic Naturalist*; and Corrington, *Ecstatic Naturalism: Signs of the World*.
6. Butler, *Gender Trouble: Feminism and the Subversion of Identity*; Salih (ed.), *The Judith Butler Reader*; MacIntyre, *After Virtue: A Study in Moral Theory*. For Butler and MacIntyre's European sources, see

and MacIntyre suggest that there may be room in this dialogue for Steiner's equally distinctive understanding of the transformative power of spiritual exercises, especially as these are outlined in *How to Know Higher Worlds*. From a very different direction, recent engagements with cognitive neuroscience by philosophers, theologians, and scholars of religion might raise intriguing questions about Steiner's spiritual exercises.[7]

Other recent philosophical traditions might enter into dialogue with still other portions of Steiner's corpus. The tradition of anthroposophical medicine, with its emphasis on the healing *relationship* between doctor and patient, has close affinities with the feminist "ethics of care" proposed by Sara Ruddick, Nel Noddings, and Eva Feder Kittay. All of these theorists propose a contextual emphasis on vulnerability and interdependence, in contrast to the Kantian stress on universal principles and free agency. Kittay's work on ethical responsibility to persons with intellectual disabilities is particularly relevant for those associated with the Camphill movement, social therapy, and curative education.[8]

Likewise, the rapidly growing tradition of ecophilosophy, with its sharp critique of mechanistic and instrumental understandings of the natural world, has a natural affinity with Steiner's theory of biodynamic agriculture, as well as with the holism that informs his thought as a whole. At the same time, different strands of the environmental movement might challenge specific aspects of Steiner's thought. Those who are

---

Rabinow and Rose (eds.), *The Essential Foucault*; and Hadot, *Philosophy as a Way of Life: Spiritual Exercises from Socrates to Foucault*.

7. Bennett, Dennett, Hacker, and Searle, *Neuroscience and Philosophy: Brain, Mind, and Language*; Taves, *Religious Experience Reconsidered: A Building-Block Approach to the Study of Religion and Other Special Things*; Thandeka, "Future Designs for American Liberal Theology," *American Journal of Theology & Philosophy* 30 (January 2009): 72–100.

8. Gilligan; Ruddick, *Maternal Thinking: Toward a Politics of Peace*; Noddings, *Caring: A Feminine Approach to Ethics and Moral Education*; Feder Kittay and Feder, *The Subject of Care: Feminist Perspectives on Dependency*; Feder Kittay and Carlson (eds.), *Cognitive Disability and its Challenge to Moral Philosophy*.

fully committed to the experimental methods of modern science would, of course, challenge those aspects of biodynamics that are not subject to experimental verification. Steiner offers a salutary challenge to environmentalists who assume that any distinction between "spirit" and "body" is inherently hierarchical and thus inimical to genuine care for material realities, but those environmentalists might well ask if a (perhaps unnecessary) element of hierarchy still exists within Steiner's nuanced understanding of spirit, soul, and body. Finally, the "ecosophy" proposed by some within the deep ecology movement has a prima facie tension with Steiner's "Anthroposophy," that may or may not be reconcilable on the grounds that there is an underlying correspondence between the human form and the ecosystem.[9]

These suggestions are just the beginning. There is much work to be done, and much still to be learned, from this dialogue between Rudolf Steiner and American philosophy.

---

9. Drengson and Inoue, *The Deep Ecology Movement: An Introductory Anthology*; Naess, *Ecology, Community, and Lifestyle: Outline of an Ecosophy*; Warren (ed.), *Ecofeminism: Women, Culture, Nature*.

INTRODUCTION

By Robert McDermott

The articles in this 1991 issue of *ReVision* were originally written for a seminar on Rudolf Steiner and American Philosophy which took place as part of the "Project for the Renewal of Thinking in Philosophy, Science, and Education" (made possible by a generous grant by Laurance S. Rockefeller). This weeklong invitational seminar, which met at Wainwright House, in Rye, New York, in January 1991, explored the relevance of Rudolf Steiner's thought for the American philosophical tradition and for contemporary American thought and culture.

Because the important themes creatively developed in the classical American philosophical tradition, from Jonathan Edwards and Ralph Waldo Emerson to John Dewey and the later (metaphysical) thought of A. N. Whitehead, have not been significantly advanced in the second half of the twentieth century, it is productive and provocative to juxtapose salient characteristics of that illustrious tradition with the heretofore neglected but remarkably prescient thought of Rudolf Steiner.

In *The Spirit of American Philosophy* (1963), John E. Smith offers "three dominant or focal beliefs through which our philosophic spirit can be articulated":

> First, the belief that thinking is primarily an activity in response to a concrete situation and that this activity is aimed at solving problems. Second, the belief that ideas and theories must have a "cutting edge" or must *make a difference* in the conduct of people who hold them and in the situations in which they live. Third, the belief that the earth [i.e., the natural and human, in contrast to the divine] can be civilized and obstacles to progress overcome by the application of knowledge. Taken together, these beliefs define a basically humanistic outlook. In the end,

the spirit of philosophical thinking in America represents another outcropping of that ancient tradition established by the reflective genius of Socrates and Plato in which the Good is the dominant category. From this perspective all things derive their value from the contribution they make to the founding and securing of the good life. (p. 188)

On all three of these counts, Steiner is at least as consistent and consequential as the representatives of the American philosophical tradition from Jonathan Edwards to John Dewey and more than any American philosopher since Dewey's philosophic influence was eclipsed in mid-century by logical positivism and linguistic analysis. Here is a brief summary of Steiner's philosophy according to Smith's three features:

1. The intent of Steiner's philosophy could not be more practical: he aims at nothing less than the transformation of the individual and, thereby, the culture. Steiner's first two philosophical works, *Truth and Knowledge* ([1892]2007) and *The Philosophy of Freedom* ([1894]2012) aim to show that thinking can and must be developed as a liberating activity, one that grasps the most immediate particular by penetrating to its essential/spiritual core. Steiner strives to lead the thinker to the experience of the practical and transformative power of original thinking in relation to the empirical world.

2. Steiner is second to none in his insistence that ideas—one's own ideas generated by thinking freed of convention—make all the difference. For Steiner, the ills of the world are largely attributable to the failure of human beings to achieve a mode of thinking that is suffused with heart and will, which he refers to synonymously as free or spiritual. For Steiner, the hope for a truly humane world depends entirely on the deep and widespread cultivation of a method of thinking that reunites the thinking, feeling, and willing faculties, thereby producing ideas that are at once individual and universally sharable.

3. As Steiner has a highly articulated account of the Earth as such, he would not use the term *earth*, as Smith does in his third point, to refer to the human or natural as earthly,

and as such distinct from the divine. But in Smith's sense of the term—the earth, nature and the human—Steiner obviously is committed to civilizing "the earth" by thinking that is transformed by disciplined cultivation of feeling and willing. The path to true civility is to intuit and act on ideals in the service of the artistic, scientific, and the educative. To a degree at least equal to Dewey, and to a greater extent than any other American thinker, Steiner offers a detailed *paideia*—comprehensive ideals for the creation of an entire culture and criticisms of the obstacles to realization of these ideals.

As Smith's three points clearly indicate, the American philosophical tradition is characterized by a commitment to a rugged conception of experience and the practical import of philosophic reflection. As noted earlier, this tradition runs from Jonathan Edwards in the eighteenth century through Emerson in the nineteenth century to the classic period at the turn of the twentieth century, represented by C. S. Peirce, Josiah Royce, and William James. This tradition culminates in two of the major philosophical options of the twentieth century, the philosophy of John Dewey, which dominated American intellectual life throughout the second quarter of the twentieth century, and the metaphysics that Alfred North Whitehead developed during his years at Harvard (1924-47) and articulated primarily in his *Process and Reality* ([1929]1978).

It is important to regard Rudolf Steiner, an esoteric and spiritual teacher, in terms basically sympathetic to the American pragmatic emphasis on the problem-solving function of philosophy. James invariably asked, not only of a possible philosophical response but equally of a philosophical question, what difference does it make in a lived experience? It is in his last work, the posthumously published *Pluralistic Universe* ([1909]1977) that James insists that the single most important fact about a person is his (or her) vision.

In addition to the three characteristics cited by Smith, Steiner also shares with James—as with all of the American thinkers except Dewey—a consistent and deep concern for the transformative power of religious experience. James and Royce, despite the difference in the degree to which their writings issue from their own religious experience, stand together more or less at the center between their profoundly religious predecessors, Edwards and Emerson, and their successors, Dewey and Whitehead.

Steiner worked from the same sense of urgency that characterizes the classical American philosophical tradition, most forcefully articulated by Dewey's insistence that the task of philosophy is to solve the problems of ordinary human beings, not the technical problems of philosophers. Yet even Dewey, the most practical-minded of philosophers, recognized that in the long run, there is no more practical problem, or set of answers, than one's philosophy—and in this respect, he was as committed as Steiner to philosophy as transformation. Steiner and Dewey are at opposite ends of the spectrum—with James, Royce and Whitehead in the middle—with respect to the sources and appropriate methodology for transformation. Steiner's method represents the possibility of attaining another level of insight and transformation, one that is unabashedly spiritual but not reducible to conventional religious belief systems. In this respect, Steiner exemplifies and advocates individual and cultural transformation on a far greater scale than that envisioned by any American philosopher.

However different their linguistic expression and cultural mood, Steiner and the American philosophical tradition represent essentially complementary methods and intent. Steiner's work can rightly be regarded as an adventuresome version of some of the philosophic aspirations that remained largely unfulfilled at mid-century, when the American tradition came to the end of its creative course. It would seem, then, potentially enriching to introduce to that tradition some of the powerful contributions of Steiner's philosophy.

Although Steiner obviously worked with late-nineteenth-century intellectual materials—drawing heavily on the natural philosophy of J. W. von Goethe and the idealist epistemology of J. G. Fichte—his radical commitment to experience and to the

Introduction

solution of cultural problems encourages a comparison between his philosophic and religious ideas and the philosophic and religious thought of the classical American philosophic tradition.

The essays in this book focus primarily on Steiner's exoteric and particularly on his philosophic works. Except for the middle section of David Ray Griffin's article, the rest generally ignore his esoteric disclosures on such topics as the evolution of consciousness, karma and rebirth, diverse sciences and arts, and the inner life of the child (which forms the basis of the Waldorf approach to education).

Of the five articles in this issue originally published in *ReVision*, those by Gertrude Reif Hughes, Douglas Sloan, and me offer comparisons influenced by long and sympathetic association with Steiner's thought; the articles by Frank M. Oppenheim and David Ray Griffin view Steiner from perspectives that reveal at least as much contrast as similarity with Steiner's.

My chapter "William James and Rudolf Steiner" offers a comparison between the philosophic method and religious thought of Steiner and William James. Hughes's "Rudolf Steiner's Activist Epistemology and Its Relation to Feminist Thought in America" explains the significance for feminist thought of Steiner's activist epistemology, his concepts of "philosophy of freedom" and "spiritual activity" and the exploitative relations of power. "John Dewey's Project for 'Saving the Appearances': Exploring Some of Its Implications for Education and Ethics," by Sloan, explores the significance and limitations of John Dewey's attempt to overcome the dualism of science and values. Oppenheim's "Josiah Royce and Rudolf Steiner: A Comparison and Contrast" examines the similarities and differences between Steiner and Josiah Royce (1855–1916), specifically Steiner and the "mature" phase (1912–1916) of Royce's religious and ethical thought. In "Steiner's Anthroposophy and Whitehead's Philosophy," by Griffin, a brief summary of fourteen similarities between the positions of Steiner and Whitehead is given. The chapter goes on to show "that Whitehead supported some of that side of Steiner that is probably most responsible for the widespread neglect and rejections of his thought—his concern with 'occult' realities." The article concludes by commending to Whiteheadians Steiner's method of spiritual discipline, particularly his emphasis on the intensity of thought, feeling and desire.

The overall import of these five articles from quite dissimilar perspectives would seem to be that Steiner's thought is worth being mined for a variety of contemporary individual and cultural needs. His writings can make a contribution at least comparable to the singular contributions of each of the great American thinkers. He offers a spiritual technology at least as experiential and as observant as that of Jonathan Edwards, a wisdom philosophy continuous with and more contemporary than that of Emerson. His epistemology and psychology of the spiritual would seem more authoritative, and surely more comprehensive, than that of James. It remains to be argued whether a full account of his social thought would compare with the empirically precise social philosophy of Dewey, but there is little doubt that his approach to education (which is the source of the worldwide Waldorf school movement) is more detailed, multilayered, and has proven more influential, than the courageous and largely untried pedagogy of Dewey. Finally, Steiner offers an account of history and civilization, including the interplay of sciences and the arts that awaits full comparison with the grand synthesis of the scientific and the imaginative found in the later writings of A. N. Whitehead.

Although Steiner offers an epistemology rather than a metaphysics comparable to the systems articulated in Royce's *The World and the Individual* (1899–1901) or Whitehead's *Process and Reality,* he generated an astonishing number of observations about diverse realities to be included in any complete ontology; for example, on the evolution of the cosmos, on subtle bodies, life forces, and on the relation of beings to the widest range of consciousness. The difficulty with Steiner's disclosures from the perspective of a more conventional philosophical position is simply that he bequeathed too much information and particularly too much that runs against, or falls outside, our usual ways of knowing. In this respect, all of the thinkers with whom Steiner is compared in these articles are more accessible and, on average,

Introduction

less troublesome than Steiner's overwhelming legacy of insights in a dozen fields.

Steiner's Spiritual Science or Anthroposophy nevertheless seems to offer a promising method, with altogether positive consequences (artistic, scientific, and practical as well as philosophical) by which to lead the American philosophical tradition out of its present impasse. It might be that American philosophy and religious thought can be better lifted and advanced by Steiner's spiritual-scientific philosophy than by conventional contemporary American intellectual and religious assumptions or, simply, than by the dominant intellectual paradigm.

Steiner offers a comprehensive case for the kinds of experiences, particularly for a spiritual-scientific way of thinking, that complement the interests of the major American philosophical and religious thinkers from Edwards and Emerson, to Royce and especially to James, but not beyond. James and Royce, at the turn of the century, were the last two major American philosophers to take seriously extraordinary and exceptional states of consciousness. Since the second half of the twentieth century, the dominant schools of American philosophical and religious thought have continued to generate analyses and arguments on the same level of thinking as gave rise to the general poverty of contemporary Western thought.

Ralph Waldo Emerson

I.

HEARING STEINER'S ANTHROPOSOPHY IN EMERSON'S PROPHETIC VOICE

By Gertrude Reif Hughes

According to American anthroposophists, Rudolf Steiner is supposed to have said that everything Emerson taught in his lectures could serve as a foundation for Anthroposophy. Steiner's remark is widely believed though not verified, as far as I know. In the 1964 issue of *The Golden Blade,* a well-regarded, long-standing British annual devoted to Anthroposophy, the American journalist, poet, biographer, and anthroposophist, Virginia Moore (1903–1993), mentions Steiner's appreciation of Emerson's thought.[1]

Moore says that Steiner "called Emerson's *Representative Men* 'one of the greatest achievements of the spiritual striving of humankind.'" (He owned a copy and you can see it with penciled marks in the margins at the Goetheanum in Dornach Switzerland where his library is archived.) Moore speaks of Emerson as "noble" and as "one of the greatest spirits of the nineteenth century" and she corroborates the belief that Emerson and Anthroposophy overlap, saying in her somewhat airy style, "Steiner once remarked (as reported on excellent authority) that...the whole of Anthroposophy could be built up" on the essays Emerson created out of the lecture courses that originated from his journals."[2] Moore closes her essay with a quotation from the ending of Emer-

---

1. Virginia Moore, "Emerson, Rudolf Steiner, and the Fire in the West," in *The Golden Blade,* 1964, 93.
2. Virginia Moore, *Ibid.* See also John Gardner, *American Heralds of the Spirit: Emerson Whitman, Melville,* Appendix C, pp. 298–299.

son's "Divinity School Address" (1838) in which he longs to find a teacher of spirituality:

> I look for the new Teacher who shall follow so far these shining laws [of the spirit] that he shall see them come full circle...; shall see the world to be the mirror of the soul; shall see the identity of the law of gravitation with purity of heart; and shall show that the Ought...is one with Science, with Beauty and with Joy. [3]

Closing her article, Moore comments on Emerson's description of the teacher he yearns for: "There are other ways of describing Rudolf Steiner, but this would serve.... We can leave it there."

In the following pages, I would like to "leave it there" by integrating Emerson's prophetic voice with "Spiritual Science," a term Steiner frequently used for Anthroposophy. The integration I have in mind will illustrate how both men emphatically trust human thinking for its intuitive nature and how they both perceive matter as having its source in spirit, which means among other things, that they perceive matter and spirit able to exist as a unity not, ultimately, in opposition to one another. Finally, both Emerson and Steiner see freedom as a matter of self-reliance and see selfhood as the seed from which community, rather than isolation, can develop when the "I" in any one of us becomes conscious of the "I" in others.

Spirit has primacy for both men. That said, however, the qualities of each man's writing (as distinct from their views) differ sharply. Where Emerson's writing is literary and lyrical, Steiner's is ontological and scientific. Steiner's writings and lectures serve the cultural mission of his life: to clarify the scope and nature of spirit, showing that spirit existence—its being—lives in matter as well as in infinity. Spirit substance, like spirit science, is not an oxymoron. Rather, it consists of cognitive experiences encountered by an evolving, human consciousness that can understand the invisible as ultimately visible, find infinity intimately present, and recognize macrocosmic lawfulness in its microcosmic form.

---

3. See Whicher, Stephen E., ed. *Selections from Ralph Waldo Emerson: an Organic Anthology*, pp. 115–16.

Steiner's books and lectures teach by planting a thought seed that will awaken his readers, one by one, to the commonality of their individuality. Emerson writes journal entries, lectures, and essays to behold and explore his own thought by transforming it into writing.

An affinity for oratory lives in Emerson's writing. He experiences writing as utterance—that which makes inner outer. Through writing, Emerson makes his own thought real for himself as much as for his readers. That feature brings to his journals, correspondence, lectures and essays the dynamic mix of intensity and surprise that characterizes them. The "speaker" in Emerson's essays is almost always seeking how to regard, appreciate, and perhaps apprehend more deeply what he called "questions of whence and whither"—those questions that we ask in our hunger to know what, where, and why we are. For both men, an abiding focus on spirit as source of all realities, including material ones, forms the foundation of their work. Immersed in questions of whence and whither, their speeches and writings aim to engage their audiences in those mysteries. Emerson is performing, through language, his inner life of thought, feeling, and desire, while Steiner offers his audiences representative thoughts he selects from his vast contemplative inquiry—his meditative research—so that the thought he chooses ripens in his readers, preparing them to experience for themselves how a subtle but real presence of spirit lives in their own inner being. Fundamental themes shared by both men make Emerson's Americanism clearly, if implicitly, part of Steiner's own thought and suggest that Steiner's is perhaps more American than might otherwise be expected or noticed. In short, listen to Emerson's prophetic voice and you hear Steiner's Anthroposophy.

Freedom and Individuality

America: land of the free, home of the brave, where individuality rules, not class or tribe. Once the land of endless frontiers and eternal hope, America, it was expected, would provide opportunity for all who seek it, and protection for all who need it. Of course this American dream has not yet materialized. As a dream it inspired generations of pioneers, immigrants, and refugees, but few thinking people today believe that the dream has power any more. The dream has gone; its ideals have failed. Equal opportunity has degenerated into a bureaucratic legalism eager to erase "difference," the hallmark of individuality. At the same time, rugged individualism has been replaced by an arrogant, even ruthless, individualism, which disregards community life and has no feeling for social justice. As for Yankee ingenuity, no longer is it expected to make a better mousetrap and create prosperity. It survives now only as caricature of itself in the consumerist culture that America exports by marketing to adolescents of all ages fads of every kind—sex, sneakers, celebrities, phobias.

The rampant, impoverished American culture at home and worldwide reveals a mistake, but not a failure. The mistake happened when a sense of entitlement to physical comfort, ease, and security corrupted the original idealism in America. At its best the American dream is a vision of evolving soul capacities that can and will belong to human beings anywhere in the world who can summon the strength to desire and claim them. Such capacities are those of an evolving consciousness in the souls of modern human beings—modern, that is, since the European renaissance according to Steiner's spiritual research. Steiner (1861–1925) speaks of "the consciousness soul" as an important metamorphosis in humanity's ability to cognize the mystery of the "I" and even to use such cognizing for creating a new metamorphosis in human souls, which Steiner speaks of as Spirit Self.[4] Similarly, from his early thirties until ageing dimmed his intellect in the 1860s, Emerson (1803–1882) heralded the desire to awaken and become active in the experiment of transforming soul life.

If one wants to revisit the "American" ideals to try to understand them and begin to practice them creatively, Emerson's

---

4. On the "I" and the consciousness soul, see Rudolf Steiner, *Theosophy: An introduction to the Spiritual Processes in Human life and in the Cosmos*, pp. 31–62. Note: The chapter is easily accessible in Robert McDermott, ed., *The New Essential Steiner: An Introduction to Rudolf Steiner in the 21st Century*. See the chapter, "Anthropos: Body, Soul, and Spirit," especially pp. 124–131.

prophetic voice can guide that search worthily. But his guidance depends on readers and listeners who are able to receive his words as life-giving speech. In the tradition of prophets and poets, Emerson has to be read *esoterically*, not just *exoterically*. He said as much himself in "Circles" (*circa* 1840), his essay about orienting toward the future rather than the past:

> There are degrees in idealism. We learn first to play with it academically, as the magnet was once a toy. Then we see in the heyday of youth...that it may be true, that it is true in gleams and fragments. Then its countenance waxes stern and grand, and we see that it must be true. It now shows itself ethical and practical.[5]

The "stern and grand" countenance of his demanding optimism calls us to think grandly about our potential but sternly about our current status. In the above lines from "Circles" for example, the exoteric and the esoteric balance one another: At the start, attention catches glimpses of a truth. Then the fragmental glimpses solidify to the point of grandeur. At that point, the "ethical and practical" of everyday life balances the grandeur and at the same time confirms its truth.

On the subject of mental health, for another example, Emerson always insisted that individuals are healthiest, most themselves and *at the same time* most fully human when they are most completely attuned to the cosmos:

> The height of culture, the highest behavior, consists in the identification of the Ego [usually he calls it "Self"] with the universe; so that when a man says, I hope, I find, I think, he might properly say, The human race thinks or finds, or hopes.

Then, lest his audience misunderstand his quasi-imperialistic assertions, Emerson immediately adds,

> And meantime he shall be able continually to keep sight of his biographical Ego—I have a desk, I have an office, I am

---

5. Emerson, "Circles" in *The Complete Works of Ralph Waldo Emerson*, Centenary Edition, introductions and notes by Edward Waldo Emerson; hereinafter cited as "CW"; CW, vol. 2, p. 309.

hungry...as offset to his grand spiritual Ego without...confounding them.⁶

Intuitive Selfhood

Emerson really had only one topic, the self and its essentially intuitive character. To perceive your own self, or anyone else's, you have to intuit it. "Absolute life," he often calls it, as in the following passage from an 1837 journal.⁷ He is pondering "the infinitude of the private man," his favorite paradox, which holds that the one way all humans are alike is that each of us is unique. "I could not be" he writes in his journal, "but that absolute life circulated in me; and I could not think this without being that absolute life." To "think this" meant, of course, to intuit this.

Intuitive understanding underlies Emerson's whole principle of Self-Reliance, the radical individualism for which he is most famous. The very first paragraph of his essay on self-reliance (1839–1840) says that your own thinking is the unobserved element in your life of thought and that this deficiency needs correction. You should learn to notice your own thinking and give yourself credit for it:

> A man should learn to detect and watch that gleam of light which flashes across his mind from within, more than the luster of the firmament of bards and sages. Yet he dismisses without notice his thought, *because it is his*.⁸

---

6. From "Powers and Laws of Thought" in the lecture cycle "Natural History of Intellect," which Emerson gave numerous times in various forms from the mid-1840s until the mid-1860s but never edited for publication. Included in the Centenary edition of Emerson's *Complete Works,* edited by his son Edward W. Emerson (vol. 12, p. 62). This passage, which exists in Emerson's notebooks, is excluded in other editions of the cycle. For the history of the twenty folders that Emerson intended to turn into essay form but did not manage to do before he became too old, and for the contents of those folders, see Ralph Waldo Emerson, *Natural History of the Intellect,* preface by the editors, Maurice York and Rick Spaulding, pp. i–xix.
7. See Stephen E. Whicher, ed. *Selections,* p. 81.
8. Emerson, "Self-Reliance," *CW, Essays* vol. 2, p. 43, emphasis added.

About fifty-five years later Steiner would say the same and would elaborate the significance of this simple and virtually universal mistake of failing to notice your own thought as a process *because it is your own.* Steiner showed that ordinary thinking can discover its own intuitive nature—Emerson's "light which flashes...from within." Once ordinary thinking discovers that the thinking process can notice its own existence, a fundamental capacity awakens in the thinker. Steiner elaborates, saying that the awakened thinking lives "within" as a body-free thinking; in that form it can begin to fan intuition's spark-like power until eventually the capacity for intuition strengthens and can reliably motivate decisions that have been freely found or made.

Steiner describes these key discoveries in a well-known passage in chapter 9 of his *Philosophy of Freedom* (1894).[9] His brilliant description shows first that *true thinking* (not the ordinary kind) is body-free; second, that it observes itself through the thinking experience; and third, that humans' body-free, essential thinking exemplifies intuition, the same intuitive ability that Emerson views as necessary for knowing oneself and for performing self-reliance. Emerson held that one can develop one's own intuition (which is nothing less than one's own self) so fully that one can rely on it, and only it, to authorize moral deeds. In his *Intuitive Thinking as a Spiritual Path: A Philosophy of Freedom,* Steiner affirms that when human beings enact a free deed they do so out of an evolved "ethical individualism."

Ethical Individualism and Free Deeds

Continuing now with Steiner's anthroposophic version of self-reliance, consider first his spiritual scientific discovery that thinking is a "self-supporting entity"; it needs no explanation from outside itself. Thinking sustains itself *and* observes itself, needing

---

9. The following passages are taken from the American version of Steiner's *Philosophie Der Freiheit,* called *Intuitive Thinking as a Spiritual Path: A Philosophy of Freedom,* trans. Michael Lipson, introduction by Gertrude Reif Hughes. Note: The English-language editions of this book have several titles, *The Philosophy of Freedom* being the most frequently used.

nothing but itself to notice its own processes. Steiner describes the phenomenon this way:

> Those who find it necessary to explain thinking as such by appealing to something else—such as physical processes in the brain or unconscious mental processes lying behind observed, conscious thinking—misunderstand what the unprejudiced observation of thinking provides. To observe thinking is to live, during the observation, immediately within the weaving of a self-supporting spiritual entity.... We shall then see in what appears in consciousness as thinking, not a shadowy copy of reality but a spiritual essence that sustains itself. Of this spiritual essence we can say that it becomes present to our consciousness through intuition. *Intuition is the conscious experience, within what is purely spiritual, of a purely spiritual content. The essence of thinking can be grasped only through intuition.*[10]

Steiner's careful, scientific observation and analysis shows that thinking observes itself without any other process being involved. With that experience, Steiner uncovers a core characteristic of the human thinking process: it is in itself body-free. That is why its essence can be "grasped only through intuition"—the same thought quality that Emerson ranks high in his views of both thinking and selfhood.

Later in chapter 9 of *Intuitive Thinking as a Spiritual Path*, Steiner develops his form of self-reliance. He calls it "Ethical Individualism," a phrase that many readers find difficult to understand even in the original German. Probably, the difficulty arises because readers tend to expect that by "ethical" or "moral" Steiner means some sort of obedience to a code of agreed-upon, moral actions and standards. Not so. He means exactly the opposite! For Steiner, as for Emerson, morality has nothing to do with authority coming from another person, community, code, or scripture. By "ethical individuality" Anthroposophy means a freely chosen deed executed by one's self, and intended toward the good as judged by one's own inner understandings of, and intuitions about, moral concepts and possibilities. Such an ethical

---

10. Ibid., pp. 136–137, emphasis added.

deed issues from the self, because the self trusts its ability to perceive the rightness of the deed in question.

If you didn't know better you could think that Steiner is elaborating Emerson's "Self-Reliance" when he speaks about trust here, so completely do both men focus on motivation as the interesting problems of "self-reliance" and "ethical individualism." Indeed, in this regard the two phrases share a single meaning; they both point to the same capacity—the ability to trust yourself without permission from others. In cases of real authority Anthroposophy's individuality-based morality relies on no authority other than the self, from whom the deed will issue and who is the same self that views the deed as truly moral in that situation—no matter whether others may view the deed as good, or necessary, or even view it at all.

Anthroposophically speaking, then, there can be moral deeds that an individual is able to perceive and authorize as moral, right, and free—a deed that he or she knows to be not wrong, or at least not merely self-indulgent. Here is the famous paragraph in which Steiner names the capacity he has described. (Notice that Steiner connects intuitive convictions to the acting individual's particular situation, but *has nothing to say about the situation itself or about how it is viewed generally.* In other words Steiner is not implying that the circumstances themselves are somehow creating or shaping the free deed):

> The sum of ideas active within us, the real content of our intuitions, constitutes what is individual in each of us, notwithstanding the universality of the world of ideas. To the extent that the intuitive content turns into action, it is the ethical content of the individual. Allowing this intuitive content to live itself out fully is the highest driving force of morality. At the same time, it is the highest motive of those who realize that, in the end, all other moral principles unite within it. We can call this standpoint, *ethical individualism*.[11]

---

11. See ibid, chap. 9, pp. 149–150. The remainder of the chapter offers important arguments and descriptions that address predictable questions about anarchy and so forth. In doing so, those pages offer a feast of Steiner's delicate, suggestive, and brilliantly articulated reasoning about what constitutes a free deed—a content that reassures and

Trust in Intuitive Thinking

The 1894 preface of his book on the nature of freedom declared Steiner's interest in, and intentions for, the new thinking and the vital spiritual knowledge that new thinking could bring to human lives and cultures. Emerson's trust in the constellation of selfhood, freedom, and participatory receptivity resides almost audibly in the following words of Steiner's, as he begins the Preface: [12]

> Truth that comes to us from without always bears about it the stamp of uncertainty. We want to believe only what appears to each of us inwardly as truth.... We no longer want merely to *believe*; we want to *know*.

Steiner continues in this manifesto-like style to articulate the kind of knowing he seeks, which he expects his readers to recognize as justified and as desirable to identify or cultivate in their own knowing:

> Belief demands the recognition of truths that we do not quite understand. But whatever we do not completely comprehend goes against the individual element in us that wants to experience everything in its deepest inner core. The only knowing that satisfies us is the kind that submits to no outer norm, but springs from the inner life of the personality.
>
> Nor do we want the kind of knowing that has become frozen once and for all in academic rules preserved in encyclopedias valid for all time. We consider ourselves justified in proceeding from our intimate experiences, our immediate life, and ascending from there to apprehension of the whole universe. We strive for certainty in knowledge, each of us in our own way....
>
> Today, no one should be compelled to understand. We expect neither recognition nor agreement from those who are not driven to a given opinion by their own particular, individual needs.[13]

---

perhaps clarifies the definitive paragraph quoted here.
12. Steiner, *Intuitive Thinking as a Spiritual Path*, appendix 2, the 1894 Preface, pp. 254–255.
13. Ibid.

Hearing Steiner's Anthroposophy in Emerson's Prophetic Voice

Practitioner Consciousness: From True to Valid

The 1894 preface articulates Steiner's expectations by speaking of truth as a spiritual capacity that sparks a further capacity in those who are ready to respond. His treatment of truth implies that something like a practitioner consciousness needs to stir within the reader if the truth Steiner is describing is to become valid. That is, before the spiritual truths could become spiritual realities they need to be received consciously by human individuals. By perceiving the potency of truth with their own receptive, self-reliant knowing, those individuals would become the veritable practitioners of truth's spiritual power and would thus generate the power of that reality in fellow human beings and perhaps other earthly beings.

Steiner frequently said that *The Philosophy of Freedom* (1894), which had begun as his doctorate dissertation *Truth and Knowledge* (1892), would be read long after the rest of his approximately forty written books had been forgotten along with the volumes of his lecture courses (containing some six thousand lectures). He hoped that individuals with a certain heartfelt thirst would find and absorb his Anthroposophy when they met it in his foundational book about freedom, under its various titles. Such readers would be individuals whose selfhood was not isolated but open and transporting, like a big cup or a chalice.

In the way that Emerson longed for a teacher who could validate his hopes and help him elaborate his trusting but—he felt—insufficiently developed insights, Steiner longed for an audience who would be inclined and ready for the new science of the spirit he knew he could instill in their heartfelt thoughts. In the twenty-six years since that first edition in 1984, Steiner had seen in his readers too little of the kind of active reading and thinking he had envisioned they would achieve. Precisely for that reason he wanted to continue printing the 1894 preface in later editions of the book where he had first presented his intentions and the orientations that would guide his readers toward the new view of spirit they needed and sought. In his Preface Steiner concedes that only a few of his readers understand his book, what with deadly stereotyping in the surrounding culture and a rampant "automatism, devoid of individuality" (how readily Emerson would have welcomed this diction). Still, Steiner recognizes warmly that some do absorb the book's message and want to rise toward its requirements. His heart lives in this early book of his. Against odds and with strong hope, he entrusts it to those who are ready for it. His tone is more candid than hopeful, but it is also generous, even a kind of blessing: not just truth but grace *and* truth:

> I am under no illusion... how much, [in] my time, automatism devoid of individuality, prevails. But I am also just as aware that many of my contemporaries seek to orient their lives in the direction that I have suggested here. I would like to dedicate this book to them. It is not supposed to give "the only possible" path to the truth, but to *describe* the path taken by one for whom truth is central.[14]

Intuition: Building with Knowledge

In Emerson's view, intuition is actually the indwelling divinity of each human being. We are made of it and so is the world. Intuition is the life that pulses through self and world as "absolute life." It lives *in* us as thinking or "perception" and *around* us as world. Circumstances were real to Emerson but never primary and never final. Circumstances were no more or less than an expression of the divine human that made them and could therefore also change them. If your circumstances are bothering you, he says in the Journal entry about the absolute life, "as fast as you can, break off your association with your personality and identify yourself with the Universe."[15] That is, as fast as you can, ignore your merely biographical self and claim your Universal one. Excellent advice if one can manage to follow it.

About two decades later, in his great essay on "Fate," the first piece in *The Conduct of Life (1860)*, which was the last book collection Emerson made of his essays, he describes fate as the self in disguise. He calls this self in disguise "the secret of the world," and describes it as "the tie between person and event."

---

14. Ibid., p. xiv.
15. Whicher, ed. *Selections*, p.81.

¹⁶ He urges his audience to penetrate that secret connection; if they did, he says, they would perceive that they and their circumstances were not two but one. "A man will see his character emitted in the events that seem to meet [him], but which [actually] exude from and accompany him."¹⁷ When you achieve this self-reliant insight, you transform something alien and limiting into something known and supporting. You accept it, own it. You recognize your circumstance as your self, your fate as your destiny. He urges his audience to penetrate that secret connection. Then they would perceive that they and their circumstances were not two but one.

Emerson's approach to self as the divine and reliable soul-spiritual core in each one of us forms the basis for his wisdom and his optimism. He found, as Steiner also did,¹⁸ that optimism gives a more realistic evaluation of life than pessimism. Just as reductive thinking accepts individuality as egotistic but misses its subtle yet strong powers for creating and serving community, so one can make the mistake of viewing Emerson's optimism (and Steiner's) as a wishful outlook that lacks truth, realism, and depth. In the same way, perceiving Emerson's prophetic voice and outlook esoterically instead of exoterically produces a deeper and wider standpoint from which to value his affirmations and wise pronouncements.

In fact, lack of esotericism in the bourgeois Protestantism of his time made Emerson resign, only two years after his ordination, from the Unitarian Church in Boston where he served as a minister. It was 1832, he was twenty-nine years old. In a famous Address delivered at the Harvard Divinity School, he explained why he could no longer celebrate the sacrament of communion. He had been reading what for him was modern philosophy—especially Coleridge who led him to the "amazing revelation" that a god dwelt in his own heart. To the Divinity School students, Emerson said:

---

16. Emerson, CW, *The Conduct of Life (1860),* "Fate," pp. 3–49, esp. p. 39.
17. Ibid, 42.
18. See *Intuitive Thinking as a Spiritual Path,* chap. 13, "The Value of Life: Pessimism and Optimism."

Jesus Christ...saw with open eye the mystery of the soul....
He saw that God incarnates himself in man and evermore
goes forth anew to take possession of his World. He said, "I
am divine. Through me, God acts; through me, speaks. Would
you see God, see me; or see thee, when thou also thinks as I
now think."[19]

Emerson deplored what exoteric Christianity had made of this message. "In the next age," he continues, they "caught this high chant from the poet's lips, but then said"—and here Emerson ventriloquizes the exoteric corrupters: "This was Jehovah come down out of heaven. I will kill you, if you say he was a man." With bold strokes Emerson satirizes the clannish treatment of Christ's birth, death, and resurrection. For him, passive response from congregations to the "high chant" of the original message scorns its grandeur and the strength of its blessing. Such lazy, indeed corrupted, reduction of religious thought and discourse angered Emerson. It lacked sufficient reverence, wonder, and gratitude. He wanted his audience to see how only an *esoteric* understanding could perceive that Christ's divinity had entered humanity and had become the indwelling divinity of each human individual and of the Earth itself.[20]

With a now famous accusation, Emerson drove home the difference between the two views: "That which shows God in me, fortifies me. That which shows God out of me, makes me a wart and a wen." The first claim fortifies him as had the "amazing revelation" he had learned from Coleridge, when reading him taught Emerson that God dwells in his own heart. The second claim belongs to the dualistic pronouncements and ruthless pieties that distressed Emerson because they distorted fundamentally the full implications of esoteric Christianity. By mistakenly receiving Christianity's truths as dogma, Emerson said, the ordinary thinking of the congregation (and many of their preachers) turned an essentially miraculous event into a merely freakish one:

---

19. See CW vol. 1, p. 129, and the entire "Divinity School Address," [119]–131.
20. For views on "esoteric" and "exoteric" consult http://www.kheper.net/topics/esotericism/esoteric_and_exoteric.htm.

The word *miracle*, as pronounced by Christian churches gives a false impression; it is Monster. It is not one with the blowing clover and the falling rain."[21]

By means of its dichotomizing logic, institutional Christianity had made miracles an exception instead of perceiving and presenting miracles as integral to earth's and humanity's ever-transforming life and as merging earth into unity with heaven. Emerson himself, however, refused to operate within a dualism that was content to make the human being a wart on the divine existence when in fact human beings are endowed with the potential capacity to receive divinity's life-giving presence.

In short, transcendence is *immanent* for Emerson, "not somewhere else but here," to borrow a phrase from the poet, Adrienne Rich.[22] The paradox of immanent transcendence characterizes Emerson's esotericism and his entire quest as an American Romantic. His optimism, his individualism, and his allegedly ahistorical conviction that each one of us is entitled to "enjoy an original relation to the universe"[23]—these three intertwined principles of Emerson's are not so much goals as givens. He experiences these given certainties as real, and he does not expect his audience to look to him for assurance of their truth. Rather, he seeks audiences who can experience that the given contains potential capacities belonging to each one of them, to be developed and used creatively.

Emerson designed his prose to challenge and hearten. It does not stoop to persuade. It offers neither exemplary narratives of how to live nor systematic proofs. Although every essay announces some form of his lifelong belief in each individual's access to the universally available power that he sometimes called the "Over-Soul," he constructed each essay and lecture to

---

21. CW, vol. 1, "Divinity School Address," 132.
22. Adrienne Rich, *The Dream of Common Language: Poems 1974–1977*. The words constitute the title of Part Three of her three-part book; they also serve as the title of the first poem in that part (40–45), and they are used near its end: "...lives that must be lived not somewhere else / but here (45).
23. CW, vol. 1, *Nature* [1] –77; see the opening paragraph of "Introduction," [3].

invigorate rather than convince his audience, because "the one thing in the world, of value, is the active soul," not assent or dissent ("American Scholar," 1837).[24] This is why we should listen to him, not to be won over to some position he has established but to join him and others like him in a search for the kind of truth that lives and constructs realities.

Emerson can activate our souls. He knew and loved the "thoughts that always find us young and keep us so" ("The Over-Soul" 1838),[25] bringing with their revelation both astonishment and a surge of vitality. Such American love of youthfulness can be called immature, but only in caricature. Like Steiner, he loved the new because he was devoted to the future. He cultivated intuition because it was and is the way to perceive the individuality of all humans, born and unborn. Each of us is a divine earthling, Emerson knew, and the Earth itself is the planet where we receive the modern version of an initiation by learning to know our selves, our planet, and our cosmic status ever more realistically. A modern and futuristic view of everyday life as initiation is similarly central to Steiner's thought. His *How To Know Higher Worlds* (1904–05)[26] gives a thorough example of Steiner's practical yet profoundly esoteric chapters on meditative exercises, cultivating reverence and humility, and the cognitive aspects of human consciousness as it develops.

If we as human beings dare to accept and cultivate the possibilities that Emerson and Steiner present us with, we can let Emerson's austere yet worshipful vision of our role in the Earth's future inspire us to rely, despite all our insufficiencies, on developing our own evolving capacities:[27]

> And so I think that the last lesson of life, the choral song which rises from all elements and all angels, is a voluntary obedience,

---

24. Ibid "The American Scholar," 90.
25. CW 2, p. 272.
26. Rudolf Steiner, *How To Know Higher Worlds: A Modern Path of Initiation*, tr., Christopher Bamford, foreword and afterword by Arthur Zajonc.
27. See CW 3, *Conduct of Life*, "Worship," p. 240.

a necessitated freedom. Man is made of the same atoms as the world is, he shares the same impressions, predispositions, and destiny. When his mind is illuminated, when his heart is kind, he throws himself joyfully into the sublime order, and does, with knowledge, what the stones do by structure.

Henry David Thoreau

2.

DELIBERATE LIVES, DELIBERATE LIVING
THOREAU AND STEINER IN CONVERSATION

Rebecca Kneale Gould

When I am eager to know whether a student really "gets" the complex ideas of various thinkers we are reading in a seminar, I often make the suggestion that they imagine a dialogue between the persons in question. What if Gandhi traveled to Kentucky and visited Father Thomas Merton in his hermitage above Gethsemane Abbey? What if Dorothy Day and Thich Nhat Hanh took a slow walk together through the streets and alleyways of Manhattan's Lower East Side?[1] What would these spiritually grounded social change agents *say* to each other and how would they say it? Would the conversation generate the crackly excitement of a newly sparked friendship rooted in shared inclinations of the intellect and the heart? Or would there be snippy words, awkward pauses and a parting of ways? What would we learn and how might we benefit if we imagined certain thinkers crossing over the boundaries of time and place to genuine conversation partners?

Not surprisingly then, when I began to think about this essay on "Steiner and Thoreau," I found myself taking some of my own advice—imagining first, not so much what I have to say about *them*, but what *they* might say (and not say) to each other. Perhaps Thoreau would row Steiner out to the middle of Walden Pond—where

---

1. Some of these kinds of meetings actually *have* occurred, including a meeting between Thomas Merton and His Holiness the Dalai Lama in Bangkok (1968) and between Martin Luther King and Thich Nhat Hanh in the context of King's growing criticism of the Vietnam War.

it appears to be bottomless and speak to him of how the pond is "God's Drop" or "the Earth's Eye," mystical renderings that Steiner would appreciate.[2] Or maybe Steiner would ask Thoreau to take him to the bean field. They might discuss the significance of Thoreau's question in *Walden*: "What do I know of beans or beans of me?"[3] Or, once asked, Steiner might kneel down, run the soil through his fingers and give Thoreau some biodynamic tips. Certainly, Steiner would agree with Thoreau's rhetorical query, "Am I not partly leaves and vegetable mould myself?"[4]

Now Steiner might encourage me to continue to spin out the dialogue in this imagined scene—and then go on to stage it! Thoreau, by contrast, would likely prefer a more philosophical, intellectual approach: a confluence of observation, analysis, and some pleasurable musing. Because I am a Thoreau scholar and more of an "enthusiastic intruder" into the world of Steiner and Steiner scholarship, I will adopt a more Thoreauvian style of inquiry. But as Steiner himself often remarked about teaching, lecturing, and artistic production, I approach this task with a certain degree of humility.

My rendering of Steiner here is through my own particular lenses: the lens of a scholar of American religion and culture, the lens of a writer dedicated to exploring the myriad connections among spiritual orientations and attendant commitments to ecological flourishing, and the lens of a college professor deeply committed to "integral education" as Thoreau, Steiner, Dewey and others have variously articulated it from the nineteenth century forward.[5]

---

2. *Walden*, 187. The foremost edition of *Walden* is, in my view, the annotated edition edited by Jeffrey S. Cramer: *Walden: A Fully Annotated Edition*. All pages numbers cited in this essay are given from the Cramer edition. For historical purposes, the original citation for the first edition of *Walden* is as follows: Henry David Thoreau, *Walden*.
3. *Walden*, 150.
4. *Walden*, 134.
5. The current most articulate, reform-minded supporters of integral education include a wonderful cluster of mentors and friends, especially Arthur Zajonc, Sharon Parks, Parker Palmer, and Robert McDermott—to whom I am indebted for the inspiration behind this essay and much else!

Finally, I embark on this pursuit of Steiner and Thoreau's overlapping, and yet distinct cultural-literary projects, as a writer and thinker who shares Steiner's and Thoreau's intellectual curiosity. As with these intellectual ancestors, my curiosity is driven not only by intellectual hunger for its own sake, but also by my own desire to question the prevailing culture of the West—a culture increasingly grounded in materialism, consumerism, uncritical "scientism" and the compartmentalization of life and work. Of course, these challenges of our own time have their particular twenty-first-century forms of expression, but the concerns that enliven my current interest in Thoreau and Steiner are ultimately the same kinds of concerns that earlier motivated Steiner's and Thoreau's own transformative writing and teaching. So let us begin the adventure!

The Streams They Go "a-Fishing In":
Thoreau, Steiner, and the History of Ideas

When we imagine Thoreau and Steiner in conversation, we might discover several important themes and assumptions that bind them together. Most prominent among them is their shared belief in freedom as the basis for human flourishing and expression. In reading the early Steiner, we can see how the significance and shape of his concept of freedom is grounded in a long-standing fascination with Goethe's thinking and writing, particularly with respect to Goethe's notions of individual capacities of spiritual perception. Steiner later married his Goethean ideas to ongoing explorations in Theosophy, theology, world religions, science, social sciences, pedagogy, and the arts. All of these myriad inquiries became most visibly expressed in his thousands of lectures and essays and the organizational and architectural institutionalization of his ideas in the Anthroposophical Society (founded in 1913) and the Goetheanum (begun in 1913, completed in 1920, destroyed by arson in 1922, and rebuilt after Steiner's death). Steiner shares Thoreau's conviction that humanity (by which they both commonly meant Euro-Americans) has lost a previously inherent, authentic way of engaging with the world, what Emerson famously called "an original relation to the Universe."

With their mutual commitment to freedom as an essential starting point, Steiner and Thoreau also share the basic assumption that knowledge is much more than merely rational, scientific thought. Correspondingly, the "knower" has an inborn capacity for spiritual knowledge, which includes not only wisdom in a general sense, but also specific "spiritual facts" about the nature of reality. This spiritual knowledge is acquired most obviously through recognizably "spiritual" sources: concepts of God, heaven, salvation, and the afterlife. More subtly, but also more importantly, Thoreau and Steiner advance the notion that spiritual content is often "hidden" in the material/natural world and requires certain kinds of "seers" (among whom they count themselves) to perceive it and to share this perception with others.

As Steiner puts it in his "Individuality and Genus," a chapter of his *Intuitive Thinking as a Spiritual Path:* "Cognition consists in linking a concept with a precept through thinking. For all other objects [such as humans and nature] the observer must penetrate to the concept by means of his or her own intuition," to which he adds several paragraphs later, "Only the part of our action that springs from our *intuitions* has moral value in the true sense. And what we have in the way of moral instincts through inheritance of social instincts becomes something ethical through our taking it up into our *intuitions*" (emphasis added).[6] Steiner is arguing here that cognition, in the way he has defined it, is a specific and circumscribed way of knowing, while the use of intuition is a more authentic way to know other people, the natural world, and even the unfolding of history.

In addition to being authentic and "free" (not dependent on "generic" assumptions about either the knower or the thing to be known), intuitive knowledge has a moral dimension that, while it may *reflect* social norms, is not a result *of* them. For Steiner, intuitive knowledge is an expression of ethical instincts that are nurtured from within, rather than defined from without. Finally, as becomes more clear elsewhere in Steiner's writing,

---

6. Steiner, from *Intuitive Thinking as a Spiritual Path* in *The New Essential Steiner*, Robert McDermott, ed., p. 99.

individual intuition is distinct from what a contemporary reader might call "cultural construction." While, in Steiner's view, individuals have both free will and tremendous untapped capacities to develop their souls, there *is* such thing as Truth that stands behind free will and individual capabilities. In this sense, Steiner is very much a modernist who is committed to the search for universal principles and ideas, rather than a postmodernist who questions the very notion of a universal and unifying Truth and instead calls attention to the ways in which "truths" are actually quite fluid and are expressed differently in various distinct cultures and historical periods.[7]

For Thoreau and Steiner, discerning "the spiritual," is less about looking in places where it is customarily found—"above and beyond" the physical world, especially in the Christian context—and *more* about cultivating the ability to discover "spirit" in the natural world and within humanity. In this sense, both Steiner and Thoreau argue for *a way of perceiving nature* that

---

7. As Steiner puts it: "In grasping the truth, the soul links up with something that possesses intrinsic value, a value that neither appears nor disappears with the soul's perception of it. The real truth neither comes into being nor passes away; its significance cannot be destroyed," *The New Essential Steiner*, 119. Nevertheless, my distinction here between Steiner's modernism and the postmodernism of recent decades deserves further nuance. In our conversations about Steiner, Robert McDermott has pointed out that Steiner was attuned to particularity and cultural-historical difference and did understand various "truth claims" to be partial and contingent, depending upon the historical and cultural location of the thinker, as well as his or her "karmic configuration." What keeps Steiner from being a "postmodernist" in the classical sense, McDermott remarks, is that "Steiner thinks that all perspectives, if intuitively based, no matter how different they appear, are ultimately compatible—and this is because there is a spiritual realm where true ideas and ideals are real and accessible to the intuitive thinker." Personal communication with Robert McDermott, April 2, 2012. Finally, it is worth noting that a postmodernist might point out that Steiner's very assertion of Truth as being "wholly independent in itself" is itself a cultural expression of English and Continental post-Enlightenment thought and particularly representative of Romanticism and Idealism. My point here, however, is not to argue for my own understanding of the distinctions between Truth and "truth," but to represent what I understand to be Steiner's perspective.

reflects Emerson's own Transcendentalist "recipe" as he outlines it in his first book, *Nature*:

> Words are signs of natural facts.
> Particular natural facts are signs of particular spiritual facts.
> Nature is the symbol of spirit.[8]

In terms of American religious history and literature, Emerson's proclamation that "natural facts are signs of spiritual facts" (which we gain access to through "words" that are read or written) is itself a kind of cultural product worth examining further. By "cultural product" I mean that Emerson's ways of reading nature for spiritual messages come down to us through a particular Puritan legacy of reading nature "typologically" for signs of God's pleasure or anger toward individuals or communities.

Originally, "typology" began as a way for Christians to read the Hebrew Bible as an "Old Testament" whose main purpose was to explain, make way for, and predict the "Good News" of the New Testament. For instance, clergy (and, by extension, lay people) would interpret the story of Jonah spending three days "in the belly of the whale" as being simply a "type" (symbol) of the later story of Jesus' burial in the tomb, followed by his resurrection three days later. Through much of Western history, this specifically Christian typological approach to the "Book of Scripture" provides an interpretation of the "Old Testament" (Hebrew Bible) primarily in symbolic terms that anticipate the events of Christ's life, death and resurrection in the "New Testament." Especially in colonial Puritan discourse, this language of "types" was heavily used.

At the same time, the Puritans also revived and made prominent a parallel Christian view of the physical world in which the "Book of Nature" could (and should) *also* be read typologically. For Puritans, the dramas of the Bible were deeply interwoven into their own lived experience. Especially in the "New World," scanning the natural world for "types" and symbols was

---

8. Ralph Waldo Emerson, *Nature* in *Nature/Walking*, 22. Emerson's *Nature* was originally published in 1836.

a common practice. A sighting of a rainbow would reassure villagers that they remained in good standing with respect to God's covenant, while crop-destroying storms or babies born with birth defects were not merely "natural" tragedies in their own right, but were indications of God's displeasure—"afflictions"—that were feared, but also cautiously welcomed as reminders from the Divine that individuals and the community need to recommit to pure Christian living.

Thus, while the Puritans are often vilified in ecological hindsight as destroyers of wilderness and indigenous cultures, it is also true that they appreciated and attended to the natural world because of what God might say through nature about their own spiritual destiny.[9] This kind of theological attentiveness, in fact, led the way for a corresponding development of scientific attentiveness as an extension of the quest "to know the mind of God." Ultimately, in the context of Transcendentalist critiques of Enlightenment rationalism (about which more below), this practice of "reading" nature for spiritual lessons gained new traction among the Romantics and Transcendentalists. A new and significant difference, however, is that in Romantic and Transcendentalist writing, the content of these symbolic lessons is no longer Biblical, nor often even generically Christian. In other words, typological habits of mind (especially in terms of "reading" Nature) continue to be clearly evident in the works of the Transcendentalists even while Emerson and Thoreau (even more so) have clearly left even liberal Christian theology behind.[10]

In terms of their personal and spiritual development, then, we may speak of Thoreau and Emerson as "post-Christian" in that they were both steeped in—and in Emerson's case, briefly

---

9. For an overview of the Puritan way of "reading" nature typologically, see Perry Miller, "From Edwards to Emerson," chap. 8, in *Errand Into the Wilderness*, and David D. Hall, *Worlds of Wonder: Days of Judgment: Popular Religious Belief in Early New England*.
10. A concise discussion of the "Book of Nature" idea and its ongoing expression within Transcendentalism in general and the work of Thoreau in particular, see my three overview essays on these topics: Rebecca Kneale Gould, "The Book of Nature" (pp. 210–211, vol. 1), "Thoreau" (1634–1636, vol. 2), and "Transcendentalism" (1652–1654, vol. 2) in Bron Taylor, Ed., *The Encyclopedia of Religion and Nature*.

employed by—Unitarian institutions in Massachusetts, the most liberal of Christian contexts in the mid-nineteenth century. But for both, even Christianity in its most liberal forms, ultimately interfered with, rather than led them toward, a deeper spiritual life. While they continued to use "God-language" here and there in their works, they saw themselves as having grown out of Christianity's restrictions and "superstitions" and in search of spirituality in nature, other people, literature and in the Good, the True and the Beautiful wherever it might be found.

Unlike Emerson and Thoreau, Steiner followed a path of spiritual growth that drew him far away from the Catholic Church of his youth, but ultimately took an explicitly Christian turn, albeit a nontraditional, esoteric and "pluralistic" one. For Steiner, an esoteric experience (occurring in 1899) of finding himself "standing in the spiritual presence of the Mystery of Golgotha" helped him to emerge from a deep, spiritual crisis. From then on, the Mystery of Christ was the touchstone of Steiner's spiritual self-understanding.[11] Nevertheless, this mystical place and time was transformed by Steiner as something wide, expansive, and—at least in theory—accessible to all, Easterners and Westerners, atheists and believers. For Steiner, one did not have to *be* a Christian to have access to the spiritual wisdom embodied in the Mystery of Christ (a claim he could easily make, but that others might not so easily take up!). At the same time, however, Steiner insisted that alternative esoteric approaches, such as those of the Eastern-oriented Theosophists were not intended for the West and would therefore not gain traction in the Euro-American context.

---

11. Steiner's sudden Christian turn first struck me as unexpected and rather inexplicable except for the fact that returning—but in a new way—to a tradition in which one was originally raised is not unusual *per se*. Beyond the influence of individual biography, however, is another possibility. It seems to me that the draw toward discerning the spiritual in the material world (which both Steiner and Thoreau actively promote with respect to the natural world) is not inconsistent with—indeed, is potentially in accordance with—Christian theology. Indeed, the story of the Incarnation of Christ is a profound example of the spiritual (God) being "hidden" (embodied) in the material (Jesus) until finally revealed as the Christ.

Much of the difference between Steiner and Thoreau's spiritual development turns on the absence or presence of particular languages and metaphors. These metaphors are explicitly Christian and also "trans-religious" for Steiner, explicitly non-Christian, nature-oriented and also, at times, "trans-religious" for Thoreau, who knew what little there was to know in the 1840's about Hinduism and Buddhism.[12] In other words, Thoreau and Steiner share the underlying epistemology of being able to "read" nature (and other humans) for spiritual lessons—although these lessons are often understood and expressed in different ways. Moreover, Thoreau and Steiner were both energetically engaged in a larger intellectual and cultural conversation that questioned *both* doctrinal Christianity (even in its liberal, Christian Unitarian forms) *and* the positivistic legacies of those Enlightenment efforts that sought completely to overcome Christian "superstition."

To understand Thoreau and Steiner in their broader cultural contexts, it is worth remembering that German Romantics, the English Romantics, the American Transcendentalists and later, the Anthroposophists—along with their various cultural "kin"—were all committed to a certain kind of "Natural Supernaturalism," a phrase coined by the literary scholar M.H. Abrams to describe this conceptual relocation of spirit into the everyday world of nature and human experience.[13] What is sig-

---

12. Thoreau and Emerson were interested in what we now call "world religions," especially Hinduism and Buddhism. They published their own English translations of French translations of sacred texts in their Transcendentalist journal, *The Dial*, in a series entitled "Ethnical Scriptures." While the French translations naturally reflected the biases of looking at Hinduism and Buddhism through a European lens (the very term "Hinduism" is a Western, collective concept for a very broad range of beliefs, practices and visions of the divine), they were an important means by which knowledge and appreciation of world religions entered into the religiously liberal contexts of American culture. Not surprisingly, the Transcendentalists enthusiastically supported learning about other religious traditions, while traditional Christians' knowledge of these traditions developed primarily in the context of missionizing.
13. See M. H. Abrams, *Natural Supernaturalism: Tradition and Revolution in Romantic Literature.*

nificant in the writings of Goethe, Coleridge, Emerson, Thoreau, and Steiner—all of whom expressed these sentiments in their own distinctive ways—is that they were not advocating for a "new" vision of human nature and epistemology (although scholars interpret this movement as "new" historically); rather, they were arguing for the *recovery* of what they perceived to have been lost in the fray of recent cultural developments, as well as in their own, personal biographies. These thinkers and writers all held to the view that our inborn capacities for nonscientific, "intuitive" ways of knowing are commonly "educated out of us" in the name of civilization, "progress" and the elevation of rational thinking to the exclusion of all other modes of knowledge-seeking and attainment. They emphatically rejected John Locke's theory of the mind as a *tabula rasa* on which sense experience inscribes all forms of knowing and insisted on an inherent way of knowing—often called Reason—that is easily accessible to children and can be reclaimed and cultivated by adults.[14]

Although the precise timing of the appearance and salience of these ideas varied from country to country, it is clear that Goethe, Emerson, Thoreau, and Steiner were all engaged in the broader movement of intellectual (and often, political) critical responses to Enlightenment rationalism that we usually call—with all of its potential conceptual pitfalls—"Romanticism." For Steiner, Goethe was the original catalyst for his thinking, while for Emerson, Coleridge and Carlyle were his strongest inspirations. But the essential message of these intellectual ancestors was understood by Emerson and Steiner as being roughly the

---

14. The term *Reason* can be confusing for the contemporary reader because it often calls to mind "rationality." In the Romantic lexicon, however, "Reason" is the exact opposite of rationality (especially Lockean Empiricism). In turn, "Understanding" was seen as equivalent to rationality—knowledge coming through cognition and sense experience. As Emerson puts it in the "Idealism" chapter of *Nature*, "The animal eye [the eye of Understanding] sees, with wonderful accuracy, sharp outlines and colored surfaces. When the eye of Reason opens, to outline and surface are at once added, grace and expression. These proceed from imagination and affection, and abate somewhat of the angular distinctness of objects." Emerson, *Nature*, 43.

same: 1) to trust Intuition ("Reason") as well as—and even more than—rationalism ("Understanding"), 2) to turn to the biophysical world ("Nature") as the source of spiritual insight and experience, 3) to shed the world of "progress" and "the market" in favor of a return to childlike innocence and wonder and, finally, 4) to convey—usually through poetry, essays, lectures and teaching—the insights gathered from these pursuits in the hope of individual and cultural reform—a reform of thought, action and the life of the spirit.

In the context of describing these broad themes and cultural movements, it is worth noting that Thoreau himself pays less explicit attention to the matter of influence, although he certainly had many intellectual debts to pay. For Thoreau, it is important to avoid naming any primary intellectual influences (even though he benefitted from such), but rather to take hints from the Romantics' actual encounters with nature and culture and to prepare the ground for his own direct experiences.[15] This is not to say that Emerson and Steiner did not themselves seek to craft their own ways of responding to (or better, "against") their dominant cultures, but rather to point out that Emerson and Steiner were both attentive to their places in the continuum of intellectual and religious history. Although Emerson called for readers to create and enjoy an "original relation" to the universe, he knew that his own response was not *only* thus. Thoreau, by contrast, was keen to minimize the impact of his intellectual ancestors (except, perhaps, for the Greeks) and to present himself as thoroughly "original," a posture that played a role in his friendship with Emerson as well as his later (temporary) falling out with him

---

15. This stance of Thoreau's is captured well in *Walden* when he rails against the idea of having mentors: "I have lived some thirty years on this planet, and I have yet to hear the first syllable of valuable or even earnest advice from my seniors. They have told me nothing, and probably cannot tell me anything" (*Walden*, p. 9). Of course, his contemporary readers knew that Thoreau had plenty of intellectual and "real life" mentors, as do current scholars. In my estimation, Thoreau is being intentionally contradictory and provocative here, in order emphatically to convey his message of originality—his own and that which he hopes his readers will acquire.

Of course, neither Thoreau nor Steiner sought to overturn the achievements of the Enlightenment. Indeed, in many ways, they stood on the shoulders of those such as Locke, Hume, Diderot, and Rousseau who sought to overcome "Christian superstition," to champion the "rights of man," to develop rational social contracts, and to gather and systematize scientific knowledge. What the Romantics worried about was not the Enlightenment as such, but the excesses, unintended consequences and problematic legacies of the Enlightenment, what Max Weber presciently termed "the disenchantment of the world." The Romantics in Europe and the Transcendentalists in North America shared the concern that human freedom would be constrained, stifled, and suffer greatly if nature, humanity and even certain abstract concepts could not be successfully re-enchanted and revitalized. In the minds of the European Romantics and the American Transcendentalists, unless strong precautions were taken, the life of the spirit would be snuffed out by Enlightenment rationalism. In the broadest sense, then, the re-enchantment of the world was Thoreau and Steiner's common task.

In terms of this broad goal of the re-enchantment—and hence, revitalization—of self and culture, where do Thoreau and Steiner come together and where do they part ways? This is a question to which I will return several times throughout this essay, first in terms of elaborating further on their theories of human nature and of knowledge acquisition, second, in terms of their views of what constitutes true education, and last, in terms of how Thoreau and Steiner constructed their lives in relationship to their firmly held convictions. Needless to say, for purposes of analysis, I am artificially separating categories that, in reality, constantly overlap and influence one another.

The Art of Seeing: Self-Cultivation and Clairvoyance

Before we dig into these three categories, however, it is important to take one more step back to consider Thoreau and Steiner not so much in terms of intellectual and cultural history, but in terms of what I understand to be the personal, psychospiritual "essence" of each. While both of these dynamic, original thinkers were able to "see" spirit in people and places where others ordinarily did not, Steiner called himself (and was called by others) a "clairvoyant" with special powers to see right into the heart of a person, a flower, or even the ambient emotional atmosphere in a room. Thoreau, on the other hand, followed Emerson's conviction that "Seeing" is a kind of skill that one cultivates out of desire and practice, not a "gift" that is acquired at birth. It is for this reason that both Emerson and Thoreau—much to my dismay when I first discovered this!—rejected coffee and wine as artificial stimulants that clouded one's otherwise keen powers of perception.[16]

Thoreau and Steiner's different views of "right perception" demonstrate how these two forceful critics of materialism and Enlightenment rationalism expressed the perceived needs of the times. In certain ways, although a self-described "born" clairvoyant, Steiner adopted something of a "democratic" view of the intermingling powers of body, soul and spirit. It was his belief that the many people who were not born with his mental and spiritual faculties could still learn to grasp the tripartite body/soul/spirit relationship through proper training and exercise of the will. Emerson and Thoreau, by contrast, both express a somewhat ironic, elitist point of view. While they understand their own capabilities as cultivated, rather than inborn, they also doubt that those who are not intellectual—and are more greedy and "market-driven" than they are—could overcome their earthly desires sufficiently to make themselves into "poet-seers."[17]

---

16. Apparently, Steiner held a different view and considered drinking coffee or wine to be a means of dulling his natural clairvoyance so that the process of *developing* clairvoyance would become more apparent to him and would help him effectively to teach the development of clairvoyance in others. While neither of us has unearthed written evidence for Steiner's views in this regard, I am indebted to Robert McDermott for sharing this insight through the stories he has heard. We might also chock up these opposing views to the long-standing cultural differences between Europeans and the descendants of New England Puritans.

17. For instance, in *Walden*, Thoreau remarks "The work of the great poets have never yet been read by mankind, for only great poets can read them" (*Walden*, Cramer ed., p. 102). Presumably, Thoreau considers himself to be one of these great poets.

Thoreau captures this elitist sentiment well when he speaks of the eponymous "John Farmer," who at the end of the work day sits at his door and feels a shift in his mood that is brought on by the sound of someone (quite likely Thoreau himself) playing the flute. Thoreau then recounts: "A voice said to him—'Why do you stay here and live this mean, moiling life, when a glorious existence is possible for you? Those same stars twinkle over other fields than these. But how to come out of this condition and actually migrate thither?'"[18] Thoreau holds out a trifle of hope for John Farmer's future, but mostly he draws a line of distinction: most farmers, he claims, are of the kind where "everything has its price, who would carry the landscape, who would carry his God to market, if he could get anything for him."[19] Compared to the market-driven farmers, Thoreau champions his own contrasting methods: keep your material "needs" few and your freedom will grow correspondingly rich; and with this ability to live against the social norms, comes a practice of disciplined self-cultivation that enables Thoreau to become a poet-seer in a way that he assumes most John Farmers cannot.[20] Given this slight, but important, distinction in their attitudes toward "the mass of men," it is no wonder, then, that Steiner founded and grew multiple generative institutions for arts, education, and learning, while Thoreau's most significant educational experiences were those that he created exclusively for himself.

In examining Steiner in Thoreauvian terms—and vice-versa—it is worth paying attention to an even greater, if less "nameable" distinction between them. In a broad and *gestalt* sense, Thoreau

---

18. *Walden*, 213.
19. Ibid., p. 190.
20. Many readers of *Walden* are eager to point out that Thoreau's material needs frequently were subsidized by the contributions of others. What is less often noted, however, is the extent to which Thoreau himself tips his hand in this regard. For instance, in Thoreau's reckoning of his accounts in the Economy chapter of *Walden*, he mentions that "washing and mending...were done out of the house and their bills have not yet been received," by which he meant—by way of an inside joke—that the female members of his family took care of these tasks. See *Walden*, 57 and Jeffrey Cramer's accompanying annotation (no. 310), p. 57.

and Steiner operate in fundamentally different modes coming out of what I take to be essential differences in character, temperament, and life work. Steiner's energy is essentially *centrifugal*. His interests multiply with every year, spinning outward in a profusion of expressions and projects. Thoreau, by contrast, conveys a more *centripetal* way of being. His task is to focus, "to confront the essential facts of life...to drive life into a corner," to keep his attention fixed on his personal writing projects and his hunger to know the history, culture and natural history of very particular locales.

Thoreau's famous (or infamous) comment, "I travel a great deal in Concord," should be understood in this interpretive light.[21] To my reader's ear, it serves as a clever rejoinder to an imagined question about Thoreau's recent travels posed by a hypothetical Concord gentleman who has just recounted, at length, the details of his European grand tour. "I travel a great deal," Thoreau replies—as if to agree, then pauses and finally adds, "in Concord." As is so often the case, Thoreau wins this imaginary contest of one-upmanship, not by out-classing his interlocutor in material terms, but by changing the rules of the game, such that simplicity and staying put wins the day.

It is worth noting that Thoreau did extoll a certain kind of free-spirited travel in his essay, "Walking." In describing himself as a "Saunterer" he attributes the term to a possible English transmutation of the French "Sans Terre," meaning "without land or a home" or, more broadly, without an attachment to a particular place, which Thoreau interprets as meaning "having no particular home, but equally at home everywhere."[22] But, in truth, Thoreau's sense of freedom was anything but *"sans terre"*; rather, it came from staying rooted to a particular place and a

---

21. *Walden*, p. 2.
22. Thoreau, "Walking" in *Nature/Walking* (John Elder, ed.), pp. 71-72. "Walking" was based on lectures Thoreau gave in 1851 and continued to refine, putting off publication so as not to undo his own lecturing success. In March 1862, sensing he was but a few months away from death (he died on May 6, 1862), Thoreau sent "Walking" and "The Wild" to the *Atlantic Monthly* as back-to-back essays, which were published in the magazine as "Walking, or the Wild" in June 1862.

particular town. In contrast to occasional expressions of restlessness in "Walking," Thoreau more often echoes Emerson's remark in "Self-Reliance" that "the soul is no traveler; the wise man stays at home," advice that Thoreau took to heart even more than Emerson did.[23] Indeed, we know from numerous accounts and letters that the few times that Thoreau actually did leave Concord, he was often unbearably homesick. [24]

In my view, Thoreau's self-described identity as a saunterer had less to do with being *sans terre* than with being *sans emploi* (without a traditional job).[25] It was Thoreau's refusal to be constrained by the demands of early industrialism and "the market" that ultimately fueled and defined his sense of freedom. Thoreau's understanding of freedom, which rests strongly on unconventional notions of time and work, is a theme to which I will return. For the moment, suffice it to say that were we to hold a list of Thoreau's central projects alongside those of Steiner, we would see that Steiner's "to do list" of worthy undertakings (lectures to give, plays to stage, music to perform, spiritual consultations to offer, organizational structures and politics to manage, essays to prepare for publication and so on) is prolific, perhaps even profligate. Thoreau, by contrast, would publically shun the idea of a to-do list altogether, even while privately attending to those writing projects most dear to him, ones that he continued to refine until the day before he died.

Even allowing for Thoreau's tragically early death, we see clearly an inward directionality of Thoreau's energy, with the exception, perhaps, of his philosophical commitment to abolitionism and civil disobedience, and his actual work for the Underground Railroad in Massachusetts. Steiner, on the other hand, seems to ricochet from contemplative practice to

---

23. Emerson, "Self-Reliance," *Essays: First and Second Series*, Library of America Series, p. 47.
24. Thoreau also confesses to reading "travel literature" as a shallow pursuit in which he only indulged when he was so busy building and setting up his cabin that he could read little else.
25. Many thanks to the patrons and owners of the Vergennes Laundry (the local French bakery in Vergennes, Vermont) for reassuring me that my high school French is still largely intact!

hyper-productivity to nourishing collegiality at the dinner table and back to meditation, all in rapid succession.[26]

Thoreau's centripetal energy and orientation, in contrast to Steiner's centrifugal way of being in the world, are matters not only of character and temperament, but also of biography. We often forget that when Thoreau speaks of his desire to live deliberately, to "drive life into a corner" and not to discover that "when I came to die, I had not lived" he is being starkly literal. Thoreau suffered his first severe bout of tuberculosis—the disease that would kill him at age forty-four—when he was a Harvard undergraduate. In 1836, he was forced to leave the college and return to his family home until he regained his strength. As with so many of his young friends and colleagues, Thoreau lived with the very real prospect of early death and while his journals are remarkably free of his direct comments on the subject, his life choices certainly reflect this profound awareness.[27]

---

26. Andre Belyi, one of Steiner's Russian colleagues, remembers how Steiner was duly cautious of those "followers" who could not follow his lead in terms of productivity and service, whose spiritual quests could lead them to be self-focused and self-satisfied. Belyi writes: "In [Steiner's] opinion, some anthroposophists 'had not been thinking' if they believed that through Anthroposophy everything would become clear and readily surveyable in Dornach: 'It just won't do—to have you running about constantly with such blissful faces and "meditating, meditating, meditating!" You could at least organize a group to further your education! Or simply sit down together and laugh a little and parody each other!'" See Andrei Belyi, Aasya Turgenieff, and Marfarita Voloschin, *Reminiscences of Rudolph Steiner*, Christy Barnes, ed., p. 31.

27. While Thoreau knew that his life would be cut short—and his tuberculosis was kept at bay for some time because of how much time he spent outdoors—he neither struggled with death when it was near, nor reclaimed a Christian view of the afterlife as others did in similar situations. Of his final days, his sister, Sophia wrote: "Henry was never affected, never reached [by his illness]. I never before saw such a manifestation of spirit over matter. The thought of death, he said, could not begin to trouble him.... One friend, as if by consolation, said to him, 'Well, Mr. Thoreau, we must all go.' Henry replied, 'When I was a very little boy I learned that I must die, and I set that down, so of course I am not disappointed now. Death is as near to you as it is to me'" (Sophia Thoreau, letter to Daniel Ricketson, in Walter Harding, *The Days of Henry Thoreau*, 464).

In addition, Thoreau's project at Walden included not only completing his first book, *A Week on the Concord and Merrimack Rivers*, but also creating the space and time he needed to grieve his older brother's sudden, premature death from a minor shaving accident that resulted in tetanus. *A Week on the Concord and Merrimack Rivers*, in fact, primarily serves the function of being a poignant elegy for his brother, John, who was Thoreau's co-teacher, sometime muse, and dearest friend.[28]

With the guiding metaphors of centrifugal and centripetal energy in mind, let us return to the three areas of investigation that I mentioned above: theories of knowledge, views of education, and approaches to constructing an authentic life, grounded in freedom. In his first published essay on Goethe, we first come in contact with Steiner's tripartite understanding of human nature, one that directly pertains to different kinds of knowledge and how they are obtained. Steiner's rendering of human nature recognizes *body*, *soul*, and *spirit* as ongoing, equally significant and interdependent aspects of human life. It is this tripartite structure that, in turn, forms the underlying principle of most of Steiner's later work.

Thoreau's understanding of the nature of reality is not as structured—nor as precise and consistent—as Steiner's. Nevertheless, Thoreau shares with Steiner the clear conviction that the natural world is not simply material, but contains spiritual information that, when accessed, both incites and nurtures spiritual growth. In this sense, we can see how both Thoreau and Steiner owe intellectual and spiritual debts to Goethe's view of Nature. For all three, the natural world always has significance beyond its strictly biophysical aspects and the spiritual lessons (or general wisdom) that can be found in nature is discernible to those who accept and attune themselves to this

---

28. Thoreau dedicated *A Week* to John with these four lines: "Where'er thou sail'st who sailed with me,/Though now thou climbest loftier mounts,/And fairer rivers dost ascend,/Be thou my Muse, my Brother John." This verse is discussed in chap. 7 of Franklin B. Sanborn's biography of Thoreau that includes personal remembrances of Thoreau, Emerson and others in Concord literary circles. See *Henry D. Thoreau: American Men of Letters*, 175.

ontological principle. Furthermore, by moving through life in accordance with this underlying principle, individuals—and, with luck, larger social groups—are able to counteract the most egregious aspects of a burgeoning industrial, scientific, and market-driven society. Finally, it is both the privilege and the duty of the artist-writer who accurately perceives the spiritual dimensions of the natural world to use art, writing, and speech to convey these insights to the broader world, with the intention of reforming that world.

As I mentioned above, there are some distinctions between Thoreau's and Steiner's visions of nature that are particularly worth noting. Steiner's worldview is not only built upon a tripartite understanding of human nature (body, soul, and spirit), but also consists of a kind of "nested" set of qualities wherein humans consist of a full array of physical, etheric, and astral forces, while animals, plants and minerals contain correspondingly fewer of these. Regardless of the particular subject at hand—whether Steiner holds forth on agriculture, education or the fine arts—I find myself imagining Russian dolls where each wooden doll opens up to reveal another, smaller doll and yet another and another until several individual dolls are finally revealed.

By contrast, Thoreau's view of nature is more "two dimensional" in structure, which is not meant to suggest that it is somehow of lesser value, only that its morphology, if you will, is twofold rather than threefold. For Thoreau, nature is sometimes simply "itself," full of particular genii and species that are knowable through science and history; but more frequently, at least until the last few years of his life, nature is a phenomenon "behind which" lie particular spiritual lessons or truths. Throughout *A Week on the Concord and Merrimack Rivers* and then more precisely conveyed in *Walden*, Thoreau gives his own rendering of Emerson's dictum that "Nature is the symbol for Spirit."[29]

---

29. Although this twofold theory of nature never fully disappears, in the later years of his short life, Thoreau's naturalistic writing becomes increasingly characterized by more scientific observations and fewer

Educational "Theory" as a Theory of Practice

What we see from quite early in Steiner's work is a systematic understanding of humanity which, while sometimes difficult to discern in Steiner's more esoteric writings, serves as the underlying scaffolding for his various ventures into literature, eurythmy, drama, fine arts, architecture, theories of social reform, theology, and agriculture. This structure is most visible, however, in Steiner's vision of education which explicitly builds on his notions of child development: the particular roles played by body, soul, and spirit at different ages and children's needs and capacities for learning which correspond to age, experience, and temperament.

Thoreau's views of education are more implicit and less systematized than those of Steiner. Nevertheless, it is clear from the language that Thoreau uses to describe his sojourn at Walden ("Here is life, an experiment to a great extent untried by me....; I learned this, at least, by *my experiment*...") that Thoreau understood his two years of "life in the woods" as a practical engagement in self-defined education: with books, writing and physical/spiritual experience in the natural world as his primary teachers.[30] In what contemporary experiential educators now call "a classroom without walls," Thoreau designed his own syllabus and set out his favored subjects: real-life economics, natural history, "post-Christian" spirituality, and the philosophical and literary cultures of both West and East. Moreover, the thread running through this self-designed course—although he did not name it as such—was "psycho-spiritual growth" with Thoreau, himself, serving as the primary subject of study. For readers who know Thoreau mostly through *Walden*, my argument that the Walden experiment was primarily one of self-education is plausible, but also debateable. But if one looks at Thoreau's choice to

---

    distinctly Transcendentalist readings of nature. See, for example, Thoreau's essays that appear in *Faith in a Seed: The Dispersion of Seeds and Other Late Natural History Writings*, Ed. Bradley Dean, in which Thoreau sets out one of the first, scientifically accurate, discussions of the workings of seed dispersion.

30. *Walden*, 9; 313.

live at Walden in terms of the professional lives he had pursued prior to living there, the theme of self-education emerges with even greater strength.

Thoreau's tendency toward self-education already was apparent at Harvard where his academic performance was consistently strong, but his "unofficial" intellectual labors were even more remarkable. Professors and peers alike remarked on his obvious intelligence, but also on his impatience with established courses of study. Like many genuine intellectuals, Thoreau sometimes eschewed the subject matter that the professors and administrators thought a Harvard graduate ought to have mastered and spent much of his time raiding the library for his own self-made courses of study. He also spent his free time less on socializing than on continuing his amateur naturalist ventures, now in a new and newly fascinating watershed where, much to his surprise, he discovered an even greater diversity of species than he had observed and recorded in Concord.[31]

In his first years following his graduation from Harvard, Thoreau pursued public school teaching, one of four major career choices for Harvard graduates at the time, along with medicine, the clergy, or the law. Not unlike Emerson, who resigned his Unitarian pulpit because he no longer believed in Christian miracles and went on, instead, to become America's first "public intellectual," Thoreau also embraced ways to be what I would call a "post-Christian" theologian—a kind of minister without a church, save perhaps the Concord Lyceum.[32] Thoreau left behind the quite liberal (but, at the time, still Christian) Unitarian Church that his family attended and found

---

31. Thoreau's best known biographer, Walter Harding, drawing on Edward Emerson's collection of personal remembrances of Thoreau, tells us that Thoreau considered the library as the best gift that Harvard had to offer—a comment that would have dismayed his tutors, had they heard it, even if secretly they might be inclined to agree. Harding also tells his readers of the naturalistic discoveries Thoreau made while in Cambridge and includes a charming story of how for one entire winter Thoreau visited a weasel's nest daily to track the goings on in the weasel world. Walter Harding, *The Days of Henry Thoreau*, 38.
32. I owe my understanding of Emerson as an early "public intellectual," in part to the work of Lawrence Buell, *Emerson*.

in the woods and fields of Concord a yet more sacred spiritual home. But before his sojourn in Walden Woods, Thoreau was already well occupied with the task of self-cultivation through challenging social convention, resisting the market and studying nature for its scientific and spiritual lessons.[33] At the same time, he sought to spread his homegrown methods of self-cultivation and cultural reform through teaching children whom—in accordance with Romantic thinking—he valued highly as not yet "corrupted" by civilization (including traditional education) and so holding the promise for a much-needed cultural shift.

Did Thoreau go into teaching because he desperately needed a job and this was the only one he could do? The short answer is "Yes." Indeed, the years after Thoreau graduated from Harvard (August, 1837) were some of the most economically depressed years of the century, as evidenced by the fact that reference letters from Emerson, as well as the highly regarded town minister, Ezra Ripley, and the then President of Harvard, Josiah Quincy, did nothing to help secure him a job.[34] Although Thoreau was briefly appointed to teach in the Concord public school, he refused to flog his students and, instead (as recounted by his dear friend Ellery Channing) vowed to "talk morals as punishment." But when a member of the School Committee (a deacon)

---

33. Thoreau's concerns about "the market" and the priority his New England neighbors gave to financial gain were on public display as early as his graduation from Harvard in 1837. As a reward for his academic achievement, Thoreau was invited to participate in a Commencement panel discussion along with his peers, Charles Wyatt Rice and Henry Vose entitled, "The Commercial Spirit of Modern Times, Considered in Its Influence on the Political Moral and Literary Character of the Nation." When Thoreau's turn to speak came, he remarked: "We are to look chiefly for the origins of the commercial spirit, and the power that still cherishes and sustains it in a blind and unmanly love of wealth." Thoreau, "The Commercial Spirit of Modern Times," as quoted in Harding, *The Days of Henry Thoreau*, pp. 49–50.
34. In his 1837 letter to Orestes Brownson, for whom he had worked before, Thoreau's wit only slightly masks his urgent need for work: "My apology for this letter is to ask your assistance in obtaining employment. For, say what you will, this frostbitten 'forked-carrot' of a body must be fed and clothed after all." Thoreau to Orestes Brownson, December, 1837, in Milton Meltzer and Walter Harding, *A Thoreau Profile*, p. 36.

burst into Thoreau's class and insisted that he use the "ferule" on his less disciplined students, Thoreau did as he was told, flogged six students and promptly resigned his post as a matter of conscience, national financial panic notwithstanding.[35]

Thoreau's resignation, however, ultimately led to a felicitous result, for he began to teach individual students in his home and later—together with his brother, John—reopened the Concord Academy building as a new, coeducational school where students would be taught solely according to the principles held by the two Thoreau brothers.

Thoreau's philosophy of education, while considerably less hyper-structured than the Waldorf approach developed by Steiner, is grounded in a similar understanding that the body, the intellect, and the life of the spirit are intimately connected and require equal cultivation and nourishment. In one of his many job-seeking letters of inquiry, Thoreau spells out this philosophy which, in several respects, snubs the rigidity of the very institution from which he has just graduated: "I would make education a pleasant thing, both to the teacher and the scholar," he writes:

> This discipline [education] which we allow to be the end of life, should not be one thing in the schoolroom and another in the street. We should seek to be fellow students with the pupil, and we should learn of, as well as with him, if we would be most helpful to him.[36]

Steiner would likely delight in Thoreau's comments, even if Thoreau's view is more fluid and comes from something of an instinctive sense of what education ought to be, based especially on what has worked for him. Here then, in a similar vein, is Steiner's perspective: "The worldview at the foundation of Waldorf education...consists equally of the knowledge of the human body, the human soul and the human spirit, being

---

35. As Thoreau puts it in his letter to Brownson (above) flogging "may teach a truth in physics, but never a truth in morals."
36. Thoreau to Orestes Brownson, in Meltzer and Harding, *A Thoreau Profile*, pp. 36–37.

careful to avoid any imbalance."[37] Steiner shares with Thoreau an understanding of education as being far more than a strictly intellectual process because, ontologically speaking, we are much more than strictly intellectual beings. Moreover, Steiner also insists (in considerable detail) that teaching and learning is a dialectical process for both student and teacher and that getting to know "of" the student—her nature, her style of learning, her particular stage of development—is perhaps the most crucial task of the educator. Steiner speaks directly to this matter in his 1924 series of lectures on education, published as *The Essentials of Education*:

> This relationship to the teacher—the activity of the hidden forces between the child's heart and that of the teacher—is the most important aspect of the teaching method; the conditions for life in education are contained in this.[38]

In Steiner's view, the on-going dialectic between student and teacher—understood as the unfolding of mutual spiritual growth—is a process that proceeds in something of a step-wise fashion, as does the process of learning to read and write. At the same time, however, the "heart connection" between student and teacher is also the result of "the activity of hidden forces" which, presumably are always unique to every student-teacher relationship. More so than in many of his other lectures and writing, Steiner describes education in terms that are necessarily fluid. He tells his audience:

> Knowledge of the human being...is a knowledge with "soft edges." It lacks sharp contours to the extent that it is not directed to any one person. Rather, over the course of the educational relationship it glides, as it were, weaving here and there between what happens in the teacher's soul and in the child's soul. In certain ways, it is difficult to be very sure of what is happening, since it is all very subtle. When we teach, something is present that flows like a stream, constantly changing. It is necessary to develop a vision

---

37. Steiner, *The Essentials of Education*, p. 3.
38. *The Essentials of Education*, lecture 5, "Living Education," p. 71.

that allows us to seize anything that is developing between human beings in this intimate way.[39]

Because, for Steiner, the relationship between the student and the teacher is much more significant than the particular content of what is being taught, it is not surprising that he speaks here of "knowledge with soft edges." At the same time, throughout his lectures on education, Steiner offers clear guidelines for what most students are capable of learning, in what way and at what point in the maturation process.

Thoreau, by contrast, does not lay out his philosophy of education as explicitly, or as comprehensively as Steiner does, but he clearly operates from similar principles.[40] Because of the exigencies of nineteenth-century travel and the modest size of the Concord school that Thoreau and John founded, students from more distant towns often boarded in the Thoreau family home and other nearby households. While Thoreau might have sought some time away from his students once the classroom hours were done, reminiscences from students and neighbors alike suggest the opposite. While in small towns it was common for students and teachers to know one another personally, Thoreau stood out as taking a special interest in all dimensions of his students' lives—literary, scientific, moral, and spiritual. His insistence on frequent classroom excursions into the woods, streams and fields of Concord was a particular expression of this commitment, for these excursions were meant to teach students that learning is often best done outside of the classroom.

The effect of this kind of experiential instruction was memorable for many of Thoreau's students who recalled their childhood experiences in any number of letters, reminiscences and

---

39. Steiner, *Essentials of Education*, p. 5.
40. Thoreau's letter to Orestes Brownson (above) was one of his more direct statements of pedagogical philosophy. This is not surprising given that he was looking for a job! Of the members of the Transcendentalist circle in New England, it was Bronson Alcott (more than Thoreau, Emerson or Margaret Fuller) who was the leader in innovative pedagogy and educational reform. Alcott's daughter, the writer Louisa May Alcott, was a student in the Thoreau brothers' school.

autobiographies. George Hoar, in his *Autobiography of Seventy Years* offers a typical window into one of these regular outings:

> We went to Goose Pond where we heard a tremendous chirping of frogs. It has been disputed whether the noise was caused by frogs, so we were very curious to know what it was. Mr. Thoreau, however, caught three very small frogs, two of them in the act of chirping. While bringing them home one of them chirped in his hat. He carried them to Mr. Emerson in a tumbler of water. They chirped there also.... I saw one of them chirping. He had swelled out the loose skin of his throat like a little bladder.[41]

Hoar's memories, recounted in a boyhood tone that suggests that the excursion had just taken place, demonstrates the effects of Thoreau's pedagogical certainty that scientific understanding comes from the study of flora and fauna in their natural contexts and that nature—more than church and theology—has spiritual lessons to teach.

The Fine Art of Living

In her book *Composing a Life*, Mary Catherine Bateson (daughter of Margaret Mead and Gregory Bateson) argues that the most creative, artistic act is dedicating oneself completely to be the author of one's own life (something the daughter of this famous couple no doubt had to work hard to achieve). When we bring Thoreau and Steiner into conversation with one another, perhaps the first, most basic realization we have about what binds them together is that they were both quintessential authors of their own lives, charging up against the assumptions and conventions of their times with vigor, conviction and an awkward kind of grace.

It is easy to envision that Thoreau and Steiner simultaneously would admire one another and take issue with the choices the other had made to compose an authentic life. Steiner might quote Emerson to Thoreau's face: "My dear Henry, a frog was made to

---

41. George Hoar, *Autobiography of Seventy Years*, vol. 1, p. 57; as cited by Harding, 85.

live in a swamp, but a man was not made to live in a swamp. Yours ever, R."⁴² Thoreau, in turn, might question Steiner's unflagging conviction that esoteric knowledge, at least in its Western forms, necessitates embracing the mystery of the sacrificed and resurrected Christ. Nor, I imagine, would Thoreau be as interested in the broad range of Steiner's esoteric wisdom as he would be in Steiner's more focused assertion that there are multiple spiritual lessons to be gained through paying attention to the natural world and employing the full range of our human faculties that most of us do not even know we have. Thoreau would also agree with Steiner that in order to grasp these lessons, one must engage in practices of self-cultivation including, especially, the sharpening of spiritual perception—without which "natural facts" would remain solely material and would be explored primarily for utilitarian purposes.

In terms of these important distinctions, however, it would be unfair to suggest that there is more that divides Thoreau and Steiner, than binds them. Indeed, as the initiator and "host" of this conversation, I would argue that the opposite is true. Both Thoreau and Steiner share a fundamental passion for the pursuit of freedom for the individual and, correspondingly, a reformation of the cultural assumptions and conventions that restrict these freedoms. Both also share an unflagging belief in the power of the mind to create reality, not, of course, *ex nihilo*, but through expanding the range of possibilities by which nature, people, and communities are perceived, encountered, and understood. For Steiner, these kinds of expanded encounters rest on an exquisitely conceived epistemology, whereby human ways of knowing rely on our ability to harness innate powers at the body, soul, and spirit levels. As Steiner states in one of his earlier writings, "Man is free insofar as he is able to obey himself in every moment of his life."⁴³ This condensed rendering of his complex understanding of human nature is, in its simplicity, as Thoreauvian as any moment in *Walden*, par-

---

42. Ralph Waldo Emerson, *Journal*, May 11, 1858.
43. Robert McDermott, ed., *The Essential Steiner*, pp. 72–73; for a different translation see Steiner, *Intuitive Thinking as a Spiritual Path*, p. 154.

ticularly when Thoreau speaks of the "quiet desperation" of the "mass of men" who do not know how—or dare not try—to obey their truest selves.

Thoreau and Steiner also belong together in a much more *gestalt* sense, in that—in each case—the impression they made on most people was unforgettable. Each was *sui generis*. Each occupied no categories except for the ones of their own making. As I have shown earlier in this essay, we learn much from a "history of ideas" perspective by understanding Thoreau and Steiner in the context of the broad intellectual and spiritual movements of Romanticism, German Idealism and Transcendentalism. Nevertheless, we would be remiss if we did not also keep in mind the extent to which Thoreau and Steiner remained utterly committed to the distinct paths each person must take in his or her own spiritual growth. We know that since the publication of *Walden*, Thoreau's experiment in the woods has been sometimes honored, sometimes mocked, and sometimes, unfortunately, unintentionally insulted by an endless stream of imitation *Walden*s. While the ever-growing phenomenon of Thoreauvian "knockoffs" illuminates our cultural hunger for contact with nature and for practicing a "simple," meaning-filled life, imitation was not something Thoreau ever wanted. As he tells his readers clearly in "Economy":

> I would not have anyone adopt my mode of living on any account, for beside that before he has fairly learned it, I may have found out another for myself; I desire that there may be as many different persons in the world as possible; but I would have each one be very careful to find out and pursue his own way and not his father's or his mother's or his neighbors instead.[44]

How can we "obey ourselves," both Thoreau and Steiner ask, if we seek only to imitate our mentors, rather than to learn from how they actually composed their own lives.

In closing, then, I want to return to where I began, considering the experiences of my students, as well as my own experience

---

44. *Walden*, p. 59.

as a scholar of Thoreau and as a considerably more recent interpreter of Steiner. My first image of Steiner comes from the initial personal remembrances of him that I read: that of Andrei Belyi a Russian follower of Steiner who was active in the community involved in building the Goetheanum. In ways both precise and enchanting, Belyi describes "the Doctor" as artist, sculptor, community leader, theater director, teacher, and visionary, but the most moving representations of Steiner are the ones that speak of "his expressions of kindness and love." "The wisdom that retains in itself duty and love was great," Belyi reflects, "but the force of love sometimes even surpassed the wisdom. If one went to Steiner's...there was a long line of waiting people; when one left him—the same line, the car parked in front of the house, suitcases packed; but Steiner sat and listened, and *how* he listened!" Belyi then goes on to describe his last meeting with Steiner:

> He turned his over-tired face with the good-natured eagle-nose in my direction and said with a smile difficult to describe, "We do not have much time, try to say briefly everything you have on your mind." This conversation of twenty minutes lives within me as if it had lasted many hours, not because I would have been capable of saying *everything* but because he replied to everything beyond any words. The answer grew out of the facts of the following years of my life.[45]

One of Steiner's greatest gifts was his capacity to respond. He answered with compassion and vigor to calls for lectures on the cosmic forces in compost (which, from my perspective as a gardener, I would be unwise to refute), to the requests of workers at a cigarette factory to find ways to educate their children (which resulted in the founding of the first Waldorf School), and—as Belyi describes here—to meeting the almost impossible challenge of being fully present to every searching person who wished to consult with him.

Providing this kind of total accessibility and tireless response to all who asked something of him would have crushed Thoreau. As I discussed earlier, the essential energetic dynamic of

---

45. Belyi et al., *Reminiscences of Rudolph Steiner*, pp. 8–9.

Thoreau's life was much more centripetal than it was centrifugal. But Thoreau's relationship with those who desired his wisdom was also deeply therapeutic, for Thoreau himself and for the students, friends and colleagues who sought him out. Moreover, while Thoreau did not attend to endless lines of seekers in the course of his own short life, his gift to those hoping to live an authentic life came through in another way, through having authored a book—so carefully and lovingly woven—that it has continued to speak with vitality to every generation.[46]

Would Thoreau have ever come to Steiner for a consultation on his spiritual life? And would Steiner ever have trekked out to Thoreau's cabin (which, we know, was not really that far from town), hoping that Thoreau would offer him a boat ride? Would they each be too independent-minded to want to learn from the other, or would they each be too intellectually and spiritually hungry to be able to resist? It is both fun and enlightening to entertain the multiple possibilities of such encounters and after dwelling in conversation with both Thoreau and Steiner, I find myself a bit wistful that these two never met, neither at Walden nor at Dornach. But then again, Steiner might insist that, on the cosmic plane at least, they actually did.

---

46. Thoreau completed eight substantive rewrites of *Walden* between 1847 when he left Walden and 1854 when *Walden* was published. My thanks to Cynthia S. Smith for her suggestion that Thoreau's contributions were also "therapeutic" by virtue of the wide-ranging impact of *Walden* through the ages. For help in the writing of this essay, I would like to acknowledge the ongoing influence of two of my mentors from Harvard, David D. Hall and Lawrence Buell. Cynthia S. Smith listened to my musings and discoveries with interest and affection. The first-year students in my Thoreau seminar inspired me with their enthusiasm and searching questions. Finally, I wish to thank Robert McDermott for the invitation to write this essay and for the wisdom, humor, patience and friendship he has graciously extended during the time I have taken to write it!

William James

4.

WILLIAM JAMES AND RUDOLF STEINER

Robert McDermott

This chapter discusses the philosophical method of William James (1842–1910) in relation to the Spiritual Science of Rudolf Steiner (1861–1925). James's religious thought is most explicitly developed in his *Varieties of Religious Experience* ([1902]1985); Steiner's Spiritual Science includes his spiritual epistemology and his presentation of the evolution of consciousness.

Steiner's Spiritual Science is developed in his first two philosophical works, *Truth and Knowledge* (1892) and *The Philosophy of Freedom*, or *Intuitive Thinking as a Spiritual Path*(1894) and his three foundational works: *How to Know Higher Worlds* (1904), *Theosophy* (1904), and *An Outline of Esoteric Science* (1909). James and Steiner lived barely a generation apart and wrote their major philosophical works during the same two decades before and after the turn of the century. It is almost certain that James was unfamiliar with Steiner's writings, and Steiner's only reference to James shows that he knew only James's *Pragmatism and the Meaning of Truth* ([1907)1975) and *The Will to Believe* ([1897]1979). It falls to us to arrange this dialogue on their behalf.

Consequently, this chapter offers a comparison of the account of religious experiences and religious knowledge that James presents in his *Varieties of Religious Experience* with the account of spiritual scientific discipline that Steiner presents throughout his writings and lectures and most systematically in three of his essential works, The *Philosophy of Freedom, How to Know Higher Worlds*, and *An Outline of Esoteric Science*. Religious experience and religious knowledge were central concerns for both James and Steiner, and the differences between their approaches provide a revealing perspective on the possible role of spiritual and esoteric discipline in relation not only to James's thought but to American culture.

Perhaps the most immediately obvious difference between James and Steiner is that James is "one of us"—he, too, is looking through a glass darkly, desperately trying to get a glimpse of something, anything, that will suggest "something more," some connection to a Source, to Reality, or even a reality. James wrestled with his nominalism, from which he never fully escaped—and, in this defining fact, we experience him again as one of us. To read James is to swim in the American psyche and to experience its characteristic split between the richness of its religious life and the limitations of its interpretive frame. James enables us to confront the variety and power of religious "experts"—examples of conversion, saintliness, and mysticism—and their collective ability to break the hold of dogmatism and skepticism. James shows us how to widen the research, sharpen the eye, and speculate on the source(s) of such rich transformative fare.

Whereas James emphasizes the surprising and idiosyncratic character of religious experience, Steiner focuses on many additional ways by which religious and spiritual experience can be rendered more intelligible. For an astonishingly broad array of individual and cultural experiences, or modes of consciousness, Steiner develops elaborate interpretive frameworks, including the biographical-karmic, bodily, planetary, linguistic, and historical-cultural. Steiner also offers a detailed discipline by which others can better understand and actually attain the kinds of transformative experience that James so prized. In works such as *How to Know Higher Worlds,* which has no analogy in James's writings, Steiner insists that every individual can develop a spiritual, transformed, consciousness:

> There slumber in every human being faculties by means of which one can acquire for oneself a knowledge of higher worlds. Mystics, gnostics, theosophists—all speak of a world of soul and spirit which for them is just as real as the world we

see with our physical eyes and touch with our physical hands. At every moment the listener may say to himself: that of which they speak I, too, can learn if I develop within myself certain powers which today still slumber within me. (p. 1)

In this respect, Steiner's approach to spiritual and transformative experience has something of a democratic quality that might be understood as closer to yoga or to a Roman Catholic emphasis on effort, all of which stands in contrast to James's attitude, which shows the influence of the Protestant experience of grace.

If we survey the contents of his thirty books and more than three hundred volumes of lectures, we will find that, in effect, Steiner wrote James's *The Varieties of Religious Experience* many times over, but Steiner's vantage point differs sharply from James's in three important respects: (I) James wrote typically as an observer, whereas Steiner wrote as one who regards his experience as authoritative, although Steiner did not intend the results of his spiritual scientific research to be considered infallible; (2) the evolution of consciousness informs all of Steiner's philosophic and esoteric descriptions, whereas James, despite his acceptance of Darwinian evolution, paid little attention to the evolution of consciousness as an interpretive category; and (3) both James and Steiner are thoroughgoing empiricists with an eye to the consequences of experience, but Steiner's empiricism is better described as transformational than as pragmatic.

James's Pragmatic Approach to Religious and Psychic Experience

One of the surest introductions to a philosopher is a glance at his or her opponents. James's opponents can be gathered into two groups: dogmatically skeptical scientific empiricists (the mentality that expressed itself subsequently as logical positivism and logical empiricism); and two forms of antiempiricists—orthodox believers and philosophical idealists.

Against these three opponents on two sides, James argued for a pragmatic, experiential empiricism, one that would faithfully observe and interpret the fullest imaginable range of human experience. It was this commitment that led James to serve as the first president of the Society for Psychical Research and to support the cause of parapsychological research throughout the entire three decades of his philosophical career.

In the conclusion of *A Pluralistic Universe* ([1909]1977) (his last work, and his only systematic philosophic work), James expressed his hope for his distinctive brand of empiricism: "Let empiricism once become associated with religion, as hitherto, through some strange misunderstanding, it has been associated with irreligion, and I believe that a new era of religion as well as of philosophy will be ready to begin" (p. 142). This version of empiricism seemed to James not only the most fruitful approach to religion and to psychical phenomena, but the proper philosophical corrective to the science-inspired narrowing of the model of knowledge or what in recent terminology is referred to as scientism.

Against all extreme, or overconfident, claims to truth, James insisted that truth and meaning are personal, provisional, processive—that is, in the stream or flow of consciousness. In *Pragmatism and the Meaning of Truth,* he gives a classic account of this perspective and philosophical method:

> Pragmatism represents a perfectly familiar attitude in philosophy, the empiricist attitude, but it represents it, as it seems to me, both in a more radical and in a less objectionable form than it has ever yet assumed. A pragmatist turns his back resolutely and once and for all upon a lot of inveterate habits dear to professional philosophers. He turns away from abstraction and insufficiency, from verbal solutions, from bad a priori reasons, from fixed principles, closed systems, and pretended absolutes and origins. He turns toward concreteness and adequacy, towards facts, towards action and towards power. That means the empiricist temper regnant and the rationalist temper sincerely given up. It means the open air and possibilities of nature, as against dogma, artificiality, and the pretense of finality in truth. (p. 31)

He continues:

> No particular results then, so far, but only an attitude of orientation, is what the pragmatic method means. The attitude of

looking away from first things, principles, "categories," supposed necessities; and of looking towards last things, fruits, consequences, facts. (p.32)

Nowhere is the effect of his opponents on his philosophy more apparent than in his pragmatic method: against the dogmatism and skepticism concerning the varieties of human experience that had limited the empiricist temper, and against a dogmatic religious and idealist position, James proposed a method that aims to study the outer reaches of consciousness in his research concerning both psychic phenomena and religious experience.

James sought to show facts and consequences to be more diverse—and more remarkably revealing—than scientific, philosophic, and conventional religious investigators seemed capable of imagining. Although the work of so productive, complex, and original a thinker as William James cannot easily or confidently be identified with one characteristic or culminating insight, his double affirmation of "Something More" and a "wider self" as discussed in *The Varieties of Religious Experience* seems to represent the furthest reaches of his philosophic imagination: "The conscious person is continuous with a wider self through which saving experiences come" (p. 405). James refers to this "wider self" as "a Something More." The case can be made that James's thought, in the end, is more accurately characterized by pluralism, or by pragmatism, or by process, or by the will to believe, but I think it can be shown that this concept of "Something More" is not only characteristic and defining. It is the end point of James's philosophical striving, what we ought to consider his ultimate, and most life sustaining, philosophical achievement.

This "wider self" or "Something More" is an insight that carries the imprint of James's philosophical attitude, hopes, and method. As a philosophical empiricist, James was a sympathetic observer, a patient and probing inquirer, a tough-minded data-collector ("data" here being the varied experiences of all possible subjects) and, as such, was on the lookout for news from the farthest, and most revealing, outposts. He sought out those whom he regarded as experts in the hope that they would confirm the reality of the "Something More."

In search of living evidence on behalf of this "Something More," or of what we might call a "Something More kind of knowledge," William James spent more than thirty years as a psychical researcher. He longed to find "one white crow" that would prove, finally, that not all human beings are forever separated from spiritual or psychic knowledge, such as knowledge of the afterlife. James remained committed throughout his philosophical career to "potential forms of consciousness" that are "discontinuous with ordinary consciousness." In a line often quoted from *Varieties of Religious Experience,* James reminds us that these exceptional states of consciousness "forbid a premature closing of our accounts with reality" (p. 308).

We can only imagine how James would have assessed the clairvoyant capacity of Rudolf Steiner. We know that on secondhand information he was not impressed by H. P. Blavatsky (James, 1986: 96). After a thirty-year search for a subject who convincingly exhibited the kind of special consciousness that produced reliable knowledge of the suprasensory, James settled on one candidate, Mrs. Piper, as his "white crow," and, in *Essays in Psychical Research* (1986), concluded undramatically:

> I find myself believing that there is "some thing in" these never ending reports of physical phenomena, although I haven't yet the least positive notion of the something. It becomes to my mind simply a very worthy problem for investigation. Either I or the scientist is of course a fool, with our opposite views of probability here; and I only wish he might feel the ability, as cordially as I do, to pertain to both of us. (pp. 271–72)

Mrs. Piper's disclosures might appear at first glance to be more dramatic than Steiner's, but as they dealt with trivial matters, none were as significant for knowledge of spiritual or psychic realms. Steiner was disinterested in displaying his occult powers and instead concentrated on knowledge of spiritual beings and guidance of humankind. Particularly, he sought to develop an epistemology by which others could attain such knowledge.

Steiner's Spiritual Science

Steiner's most significant insight in philosophy (Steiner made original contributions in many other areas) would seem to be the epistemological method, which stands at the base of all of his extraordinary research. This method can be referred to as imaginal thinking and, in the form that would enable us to experience and evaluate it, can be understood as a method for generating spiritual (including philosophical and moral) insights that can be known to be simultaneously individual and universal. Steiner's insight, then, issues from, calls for, and confirms a new capacity, namely the ability to establish a cognitive link between the spiritual dimension of the moral self and the spiritual dimension of the universe—in this case, the moral-spiritual universe. Steiner exemplifies and recommends the same capacity for the sciences, the arts, and other areas of inquiry.

It is easy to miss the significance of Steiner's philosophic work because the body of his writings that can properly be classified as philosophical—approximately three to five volumes—constitutes a minute portion of his entire corpus, consisting as it does of approximately three hundred volumes, forty books and two hundred and sixty volumes of lectures. Further, the same sociology of the field that hides the philosophy in the writings of medieval Christian thinkers such as Aquinas or classical Indian philosophers such as Sankara would similarly lead philosophical inquirers (assuming they looked in Steiner's direction) to fold the philosophical into the spiritual.

Given the probability of this predisposition, it might be useful to look at Steiner's spiritual position before turning to his philosophical position per se, though it is important to note that Steiner's first two books, his doctoral dissertation and his major philosophical treatise, are technical, carefully argued epistemological treatises that he intended to be evaluated by philosophical (albeit highly introspective) criteria.

Steiner's massive body of writings, his entire teaching, evidences spiritual and esoteric development yet is definitely a unified whole: there is no early/late dichotomy. His *Philosophy of Freedom* predates the spiritual experience of 1899 that resulted in his viewing the deeds of Christ as the central transformative event in human history. After 1900, Steiner's writings typically contained esoteric and spiritual-scientific disclosures. Whether we approach *The Philosophy of Freedom* from the perspective of subsequent writings or entirely on its own, it is clear that at its core this work is a spiritual epistemology. Using a teleological principle characteristic of Steiner's worldview, we might say that the following definition of his teaching, referred to alternately as Spiritual Science and Anthroposophy, is the end toward which his early epistemological writings were aiming—and toward which he was intending to lead his reader.

In the first of a series of letters to members of the Anthroposophical Society (in *Anthroposophical Leading Thoughts*), written in the last year of his life, Steiner defined Anthroposophy (or Spiritual Science) as follows (McDermott 1984):

> Anthroposophy is a path of knowledge leading the spiritual in the individual to the spiritual in the universe. It arises as a need of the heart, and justifies itself to the extent that it answers that need. (p. 415)

From the perspective of philosophy (temporarily ignoring Steiner's role at the end of his life as the founder of a spiritual-esoteric school and the author of an incomparable body of occult revelations), this statement would seem to occupy a place in Steiner's thought comparable to James's "Something More." It is the end point, or the full expression, of that life-defining insight that was striving to come forth in his earliest writings. It is also—as it is the purpose of this article to show—a call to a thoroughgoing empiricism, a method of philosophy that can significantly advance the American philosophical and cultural agenda.

Philosophy, in this teaching, comes to mean a heart-filled, warm and willful, imaginative reflection on, and by, the deepest level of the self in relation to the entire universe—from stars to soil, including gender, the economy, history, language, ethics, education, and myriad other areas of inquiry—far more, in fact, than any American philosopher, including Dewey, attempted to illumine. Even when Steiner is at his most explicitly spiritual—as in his description of Anthroposophy quoted in the passage above—he is calling for a mode of thinking that, while spiritual, is not based on belief. In these words written for the Anthroposophical Society, members of a new mystery center and a community of spiritual seekers, he advocates the path of spiritual thinking.

Steiner's emphasis on the feeling dimension of thinking should not be mistaken for softness and sentimentality: whether expressed in spiritual terms (as in the passage quoted above) or in terms of concepts and precepts (the terminology of *The Philosophy of Freedom*), Steiner consistently strives to show, by example and precept, that the thinking "I" can be the source and instrument of a self-generated, perfectly adequate and essentially true grasp of reality—including the concept and reality of the self as a moral agent.

Steiner's basic philosophic text, *The Philosophy of Freedom*, offers an epistemology and a moral philosophy as a way of solving the most fundamental problems of modern life. With James, Steiner was intrigued by and sought to provide a way out of the impasse of philosophical disputes. But whereas James sought primarily to remove the sting from philosophical conflicts by removing their pretense of adequacy or finality and, secondarily, to establish the attitude and value of philosophic pluralism, Steiner offers an epistemological discipline to be developed in order to move past conflicts to a pluralism of ideally adequate perspectives. More important, and more radically, Steiner chronicled the history of philosophy as a series of appropriate, or symptomatic, expressions of the evolution of consciousness.

Whereas James rests in a pluralism of partial versions of the truth, Steiner affirms a pluralism of positions that are simultaneously harmonious and individual. This process seems perfectly plausible to Steiner because he is convinced that true ideas live harmoniously in a spiritual realm and can be accessed through one's highly disciplined, individual spiritual effort. To a degree quite foreign to James, Steiner depicts all such individual efforts in historical, or evolutionary, contexts. For Steiner, it makes all the difference when Socrates, Plato and Aristotle—or St. Paul, or

Descartes—impressed their vision of reality on the consciousness of subsequent centuries.

Concluding Comparisons and Contrasts

In addition to the contrasts just developed between the religious thought of James and Steiner, it is worth noting some commonalities. Specifically, they share determination to establish their positions between scientific rationalism on one side and traditional religious belief on the other. Of the first of these two excesses, both James and Steiner forcefully opposed the negative implications of nineteenth-century scientific thought. They both struggled with the realization that their immediate scientific and philosophical predecessors precluded an easy affirmation of what James refers to as "the religious hypothesis." Yet in quite different but entirely compatible ways, James and Steiner begin with the recognition that Humean skepticism (or its later version—positivism) and Kant's critical philosophy fail to account for the depth and varieties of religious experience.

James and Steiner also shared a critique of belief as a way to overcome the limits on religious knowledge set by science and naturalistic philosophy. Their case, again in different terms, rested on privileged, and highly transformative, experience, not on a belief system oblivious to the demands for validation and discernible positive effects. James sought evidence for the source of religious experience, for the "Something More" to which large segments of the human community—some quite demonstrably—have access, and Steiner looked to the tradition of mystics, gnostics, and theosophists as evidence on behalf of the case for knowledge of the spiritual world.

Almost all of the contrasts that could be explored between James and Steiner fall under three general headings: (1) individual experience, (2) evolution of consciousness, and (3) spiritual discipline.

The first point of comparison concerns the role of individual experience. In the two years during which James delivered the Gifford Lectures, published in 1902 as *The Varieties of Religious Experience,* Steiner wrote several chapters on nineteenth-century

William James and Rudolf Steiner

thought (published as part of *The Riddles of Philosophy* ([1914]2009), lectured on Goethe and Nietzsche, and delivered two series of lectures published as *Mystics after Modernism: Discovering the Seeds of a New Science in the Renaissance* ([1901]2000) and *Christianity as Mystical Fact: And the Mysteries of Antiquity* ([1902]2006). All of these lectures and publications presage the distinctively twentieth-century fascination with religious experience(s) of paradigmatic individuals. Both James and Steiner point to the transformative experience of figures such as Buddha, Augustine, Eckhart, and Luther, as evidence for a spiritual reality as the source of the kinds of religious experience that James refers to as conversion, saintliness, and mysticism.

Although James himself had little to report in the way of personal experience—the lone exception being the autobiographical passage that he inserted in *The Varieties of Religious Experience*, with attribution to a "French Correspondent" (pp. 134–35), he did recognize the primacy of personal, and particularly autobiographical, perspectives for the fashioning of an adequate worldview. But because his own experience seems to have been undeveloped, or at least lacking confidence relative to those whom he referred to as "experts" and on whom he relied for religious insight, he remained an observer and interpreter.

While his reach toward the psychic and spiritual may be more adventuresome than any major American philosopher, there is scant original or autobiographical religious reflection in James's writings, considerably less so than in the writings of Josiah Royce, his primary philosophical and religious foil. James's "circumspection of the topic" of religion in *The Varieties of Religious Experience*, in terms of individual experience without regard to what he acknowledges as the institutional (and historical) half of the topic, must be seen as a limiting device entirely characteristic of his psychology, philosophy, and view of religion. Steiner similarly did not focus on the institutional dimension of religion, but he invariably emphasized the historical and cultural context of all individuals, including those with highly idiosyncratic experience. More to the point, for Steiner, all experience, and particularly transformative spiritual experience, must be understood in the double context of individual and cultural evolution.

For Steiner, a transformative experience—whether conversion, enlightenment, or salvation—has its place in the destiny of individuals who, in turn, have their places in the destiny of cultures. In this respect, Steiner's view is closer to Royce, who offers a profound account of individual ideals in relation to one's community; it was against Royce's view—and, indirectly, Steiner's—that James delivered and published his *Varieties*. In his emphasis on the evolution of consciousness, Steiner goes against James and beyond Royce: he insists that in pre-Christian times an experience such as mysticism was nearly ordinary and is considered extraordinary in the modern West because of the radical transformation wrought by modern Western rational and scientific consciousness. Or rather, the rarity of mysticism is due to the transformation of consciousness that produced both rational scientific consciousness and the gap between the experiential self and the spiritual world.

This leads to the second major difference between James and Steiner, namely, Steiner's comprehensive use of the evolution of consciousness. Steiner emphasizes the historical and cultural context of individual biographies, as well as their cultures, in the light of the evolution of consciousness. Although James was committed to an evolutionary and radically processive view of human experience, his view of religious experience is not as evolutionary as Steiner's. References to religious personalities throughout *Varieties of Religious Experience* pay little or no attention to the century or culture that provided the distinctive character of the religious qualities for which James provides such shrewd and memorable phenomenological analyses.

For Steiner, the exact place of every religious experience in the evolution of consciousness—including the particular language, folk soul (or psyche of the people), religious beliefs and practices, and many other influential factors—accounts for the essential meaning of each experience. In Steiner's grid, the individual and the culture of the original experience are interdependent.

The third general contrast between James's view and Steiner's centers on the significance for Steiner of spiritual discipline. In his *Varieties,* James explains two types of conversion—volitional and self-surrender—but nevertheless allows the impression that life-transforming experiences, saintliness, and mysticism just happen. Throughout *The Varieties of Religious Experience* and his thirty years devoted to psychical research, James generally ignored the preparation, particularly deliberate and disciplined preparation, for religious transformation and focused instead on the fruits of exceptional experiences:

> If the grace of God operates miraculously, it probably operates through the subliminal door, then. But just how anything operates in this region is still unexplained, and we shall do well now to say good-bye to the process of transformation altogether—leaving it, if you like, a good deal of a psychological and theological mystery—and to turn our attention to the fruits of the religious condition, no matter in what way they have been produced. (p. 218)

Steiner acknowledges the limits of his knowledge concerning the process of transformation in individual cases, but the intent of his spiritual scientific method is to penetrate such mysteries, beginning with one's own experience. Such knowledge, of course, requires disciplined effort, or spiritual practice.

What would seem to be missing in James's work is precisely such a practice that might have enabled him to see deeper into the subjects who so intrigued him and on whose transformative experiences he tried to build a genuinely radical empiricism, that is, a philosophy that grants primacy to individual experience. It might be time to supplement, and perhaps transform, James's philosophical and religious insights by means of the kind of spiritual discipline that Steiner exemplified and explained.

Charles Sanders Peirce

3.

CHARLES SANDERS PEIRCE AND RUDOLF STEINER

PROPHETIC PHILOSOPHERS

Robert McDermott

C. S. PEIRCE: LIFE AND WORK

Peirce needs to be included in this volume even though his worldview is dissimilar to Steiner's. Their biographies, as well as their philosophical methods and some of their philosophical assertions, are clearly at odds. They do have some of the same sources among the major figures in the history of Western philosophy (particularly Goethe, Kant, and Schelling), but unlike Peirce, Steiner is steeped in spiritual texts and esoteric traditions. Whereas Peirce was a logician and philosopher throughout his entire life, Steiner was a lifelong esotericist who wrote philosophy only in his early years. Rather, Peirce is included because he is an essential component of classical American philosophy, the focus of half this book. Peirce is foundational for the core methods and ideas shared by Emerson, James, Royce, Dewey, and Whitehead. It is a given that Peirce and Steiner are philosophically more different than they are similar; the purpose of this chapter is to explore some of their similarities, or at least comparabilities, without attempting to dissolve their fundamental differences.

In the double issue of *ReVision: A Quarterly Journal for Consciousness and Transformation* entitled *Rudolf Steiner and American Thought* in which five of the chapters in this volume were initially published, there was nothing on Charles Sanders Peirce. On rereading the chapter in this volume on Royce by Frank Oppenheim, S.J., I was led to his *Royce's Mature Ethics* and to his magnum opus, *Reverence for the Relations of Life*. In these works Oppenheim makes a compelling case for the brilliant, tragic, inspiring, and rather inaccessible Peirce. As a result of Oppenheim's treatment, I began reading Peirce (whom I had read intermittently and indifferently in the 1970s and 1980s) and decided to hold back the publication of this volume in order to add this essay on Peirce and Steiner.

Oppenheim shows very clearly Royce's deep philosophical debt to Peirce as well as his deep reverence for Peirce's loyalty to his mission as a philosopher despite his inability to secure an academic appointment. In a dramatic passage Oppenheim reveals the religious dimension of Peirce's vocation. On March 24, 1892, when he was fifty-two, and visiting New York City, Peirce felt a compulsion to attend church. Here is the report that he wrote later that day to the pastor of St. Thomas Episcopal Church on 5th Avenue concerning his experience that morning. This experience followed several sleepless nights reflecting on the conflict between his attraction to church and his rejection of some core Christian teachings.

> I felt I had to go to church anyway.... No sooner had I got into the church that I seemed to receive the direct permission of the Master to come [to partake]. Still, I said to myself, I must not go to communion without further reflection! I must go home and duly prepare myself before I venture. But, when the instant came, I found myself carried up to the altar rail, almost without my own volition. I am perfectly sure that it was right. Anyway I could not help it....
>
> That which seemed to call to me today seemed to promise me that I should bear a cross like death for the Master's sake, and that he would give me strength to bear it. I am sure that

will happen. My part is to wait. I have never before been mystical; but now I am. After giving myself time to reflect upon the situation, I will call to see you....

Oppenheim reports that three weeks later, on May 17, Peirce wrote to Francis Russell:

I now feel that if a way is shown to me to teach logic [at Chicago], it is my sacred duty to pursue it.... If I am to be put into a position to do the work I was brought into the world to do, I desire to lay aside all other ambitions and vanities and give myself up to that work exclusively.[1]

Peirce did indeed "bear a cross" for his vocation. In painful contrast to the successful careers of his father, Benjamin, a professor at Harvard and the most famous American mathematician of his generation, and his brother who was also professor of astronomy at Harvard, and his friends James and Royce, Peirce was unable to secure a professorial appointment. Because of lifelong fibromyalgia, he used pain killers, including opium and cocaine; because of poverty he nearly starved to death more than once. Peirce had strong narcissistic traits. He could be very selfish and occasionally violent. Some of these traits suggest that he might have been bipolar. He was raised to consider himself extremely special—which he clearly was intellectually, though of course not at all socially.

In 1897 William James dedicated his *Will to Believe and Other Essays in Popular Philosophy* to Peirce:

To whose philosophic comradeship in old times and to whose writings in more recent years I owe more incitement and help than I can express or repay.

Not even the celebrated William James, however, was able to arrange for Peirce's appointment at Harvard.[2] As a result,

---

1. *Reverence for the Relations of Life*, pp. 54–56.
2. In 1895 William James tried unsuccessfully to arrange for Peirce to teach a course on philosophy of nature while James was busy teaching psychology. Here is an exception of that exchange: "He is the best man by far in America for such a course, and one of the best men living....

Peirce had a spectacularly difficult life. At one time he lived on the street for three years. He wrote 80,000 pages (or 200 volumes at 400 pages per volume), most of them unpublished and without remuneration in his lifetime. *The Collected Papers of Charles Sanders Peirce*, edited by Charles Hartshorne and Paul Weiss in the 1930s, twenty years after his death, include technical essays on mathematics, logic, epistemology, philosophy of science, semiotics, ethics, philosophy of religion, and contemporary social analysis. Peirce dedicated his life, not easy in any respect (except for his genius) to the advancement of science and philosophy. He served his conviction that his philosophy would lead to a profoundly positive transformation for anyone who would devotedly follow his method.

Certainly Peirce himself, despite the lifelong negative effect of his unusual childhood, his poor health, and his vocational impasse, did experience transformation in service to logic and philosophy. His devotion to pragmaticism, or will-filled consequential thinking, leads Frank Oppenheim to refer to Peirce, along with Royce, as "prophetic pragmatists."[3] Peirce lacked, and more accurately did not want, James's amazing facility of expression. His writings are extremely technical, highly specialized essays in logic and philosophy and hampered by neologisms. To learn from Peirce one has to read deep, precise, technical thinking and writing (or read one of the many excellent secondary sources[4]).

Peirce was born in 1839, three years before William James, six before Royce, and twenty two years before Steiner who was born in 1861, the same year as Whitehead. He died in 1914, four years

---

and it would be a recognition of C. S. Peirce's strength, which I am sure is but justice to the poor fellow." Eliot's reply: "All that you say of C. S. Peirce's remarkable capacities and acquisitions is true, and I heartily wish that it seemed to me possible for the University to make use of them." Ralph Barton Perry, ed., *The Thought and Character of William James*, II. 417.

3. Ibid., pp. 43–60.
4. See especially Joseph Brent, *Charles Sanders Peirce: A Life*; Elizabeth Flower and Murray G. Murphey, *A History of Philosophy in America*; Cheryl Misak, ed., *The Cambridge Companion to Peirce*; Eugene Freeman, ed., *The Relevance of Charles Peirce*.

after James, two years before Royce, and eleven years before Steiner. Whitehead died in 1947 and Dewey in 1951, thereby ending this fabulous period of classical American philosophy just before half century.

From a karmic perspective it is painful to contemplate and difficult to understand the relationship between Peirce's intellectual genius and his dysfunctional, tragic personal life. Where were his angels? Or was "carrying the cross" of his intellectually brilliant but socially lonely, physically painful life karmically intended? Steiner considered it to be one of his, and ideally everyone's, task to research the intent of the full arc (and accompanying details) of one's life. More than most lives, Peirce's life invites the observer to wonder whether his extreme difficulties juxtaposed with his extreme brilliance were karmically appropriate and to some extent determined, or might have been otherwise.

Rudolf Steiner: Life and Work

Unlike Peirce who lived at the margins, Steiner was always front and center, the object of intense widespread support, though also the object of serious opposition. As Steiner was in some important respects amazingly successful during his lifetime and after, it might appear that his life was in sharp contrast to Peirce's lonely suffering. Each suffered in his own way. Steiner's suffering was internal and seems to have been from a spiritual source: socially and visibly he was kind, generous, admired, and followed. During his lifetime many hundreds of thousands of people heard him lecture, read his books, and sought his advice. Yet, like Peirce, he suffered for his mission. He spent ten years overseeing the Goetheanum, the building that he designed, only to have it burned by arson the year it was completed. He almost died from poisoning. He was profoundly disappointed that many, and perhaps most, of his followers were unable to advance his esoteric research, and instead quarreled with one another. Although he saw many positive trends in Western society (greater freedom, individuality, tolerance) he also saw clear indications of a downward spiral of Western civilization. He saw contemporary civilization as a great battle between freedom and unconscious indolence.

Whereas Peirce was primarily a logician and a philosopher throughout his entire life (from his teen years to his death at age seventy-five), Steiner wrote philosophy from age twenty-one only to his mid-thirties on the way to his primary life task as a spiritual and esoteric teacher. Like Peirce's lifelong task, it was Steiner's task to create and establish a healthy, transformative way of thinking. After writing philosophy of science, or natural philosophy, based on Goethe and philosophy based on the German Idealists (especially Kant, Fichte, and Hegel), Steiner began his career, or rather his mission, as an esoteric researcher and teacher, first as a leading teacher in the Theosophical Society (1902–12), and then as the teacher of the Anthroposophical Society (1912–1925). His philosophical writings served as a foundation for his work as head of a community of spiritual seekers who would use his esoteric method to advance the research that he initiated.[5]

Steiner considered that his major work in philosophy, *The Philosophy of Freedom*, would outlast all of his other writings. Like Peirce, Steiner lacked, and apparently did not want, James's amazing facility of expression: he deliberately wrote philosophy in a style intended to encourage his readers to think his sentences meditatively. One reads Peirce exclusively for philosophy but there are many reasons to read Steiner: in addition to his philosophical writings, one can also read literally hundreds of volumes of lectures dealing with science, arts, religion, education, economy, psychology, and spiritual development. In a way that is similar to Frank Oppenheim's characterization of Peirce and Royce, Steiner wrote philosophy as an expression of his vocation, in service to what he understood to be a spiritual and karmic obligation.

Rudolf Steiner's life was marked as very special from childhood but definitely not because of a brilliant and learned father. His father was a stationmaster on the Austrian railroad. The

---

5. For Steiner's life and thought see Robert McDermott, ed., intro., notes, *The New Essential Steiner*.

Steiner family lived very simply, surrounded on the one side by trains and on the other by mountains. At about age seven he was visited by a ghostly figure who asked him for help; he learned the next day that his father's cousin, whom the young Steiner had not met, had committed suicide. In his teen years he was enchanted by geometry. With his own meager pocket money he purchased and studied Kant's *Critique of Pure Reason*. At eighteen he met an herb gatherer who introduced him to the secrets of herbology and homeopathy. This shamanic healer also sent Steiner, at age 18, to meet one whom Steiner referred to as his Master (whom he did not identify, not even to say whether his Master was living on Earth or discarnate). According to the autobiography that Steiner wrote in 1924,[6] the last full year of his life, this Master gave him the double task of exposing the deadly effects of materialistic thinking and teaching a way of thinking by which the West might reconnect with its interior life as well as with Earth and with spiritual beings.

From age twenty-one to twenty-eight, Steiner served as the editor of a national edition of Goethe's scientific writings. His introductions to these volumes were subsequently published as separate volumes.[7] In 1891, at age thirty, Steiner published his doctoral dissertation, *Truth and Knowledge*, and in 1894 he published his major work in philosophy, *The Philosophy of Freedom*. In addition to his work on Goethe's natural science, Steiner's early philosophical writings include *Nietzsche: Fighter for Freedom* (1895), and *The World and Life Conception of the Nineteenth Century*, first published in 1900, and republished as the second half of *Riddles of Philosophy* (1914).

In his *Autobiography* Steiner reported that in 1899 (following a profound religious struggle that sounds rather like Peirce's sleepless nights before his experience in St. Thomas Episcopal Church in New York City), he experienced the presence

---

6. Rudolf Steiner, *Autobiography: Chapters in the Course of My Life, 1861-1907.*
7. See Rudolf Steiner, *Goethean Science*; *The Theory of Knowledge Implicit in Goethe's World*; *The Science of Knowing: Outline of an Epistemology Implicit in the Goethean World View*, all published by Mercury Press, Spring Valley, NY.

of Christ in the evolution of the cosmos, Earth, and humanity. After this experience Steiner continued to think, write, and lecture on philosophy but his focus had clearly shifted to his more fundamental commitment to researching and teaching esoterically. Of course, the Steiner who wrote *The Philosophy of Freedom* at age thirty-three, and who experienced the Cosmic Christ at age thirty-nine, was the same esoteric person who had been initiated by his Master at age eighteen. Beginning at age thirty-nine, he began to lecture, mostly to audiences of Theosophists, on the results of his esoteric research concerning the evolution of Earth, ancient civilizations, the destinies of souls (both on Earth and between death and rebirth), as well as on Krishna, Buddha, and Christ. The point of Steiner's philosophical writings during his twenties and thirties was to provide theoretical support for his esoteric research—specifically an epistemology that sought to establish the possibility of knowing spiritual beings and the spiritual reality of all parts of Earth and the material world.

Steiner wrote his first important work, *The Philosophy of Freedom*, as a contribution to mainstream philosophy, particularly epistemology and ethics. In this respect this book for which he had high expectations clearly failed: it has been completely ignored by mainstream philosophers, and appears to be studied only by anthroposophists. Assuming that his philosophy ought to be discussed, it is possible to regard this neglect at least partly as a positive case of prophecy: like the prophets of the Hebrew scriptures, Steiner's writings are neglected because they call the reader to a higher mission, precisely the message to which the reader would rather not be called. As the Hebrew prophets called the would-be faithful, the Chosen People, to attend to the terms of their covenant with Yahweh, Steiner calls the reader to what he considers the proper (though not the usual) requirements of philosophical thinking in will-filled opposition to the lethargy characteristic of contemporary thinking. According to his *Philosophy of Freedom*, philosophy requires free, original, spirit-based thinking, unrestricted by prosaic convention.

Peirce's Philosophical Sources

Both Peirce and Steiner were steeped in Kant (whom they both drew from and criticized) and Schelling. Steiner drew from Thomas Aquinas (1225–1274) and Peirce drew from Duns Scotus (1266–1308), two Dominican monks. Peirce and Steiner differed completely in their colleagues: Peirce learned profoundly from and influenced William James and John Dewey, and especially Josiah Royce. Unfortunately, Steiner had no such collaborators. Further, he stopped writing his own philosophy at age forty; he spent the last twenty-five years of his life as an esoteric researcher.

Kant: Like Martin Buber (a Jewish existentialist philosopher who was born on the Polish–Russian border) and C. G. Jung (a Swiss gnostic Christian psychologist), Steiner (in Austria) and Peirce (in Massachusetts) began reading Kant in their teen years. There are many versions, or uses, of Kant. Almost all philosophers after Kant feel obliged to take a position for or against parts of his philosophy. It is often said that all European philosophy after Kant is either "Kantian" (explaining, justifying, and extending Kant's method and ideas) or "post-Kantian" (revising some or all of Kant's ideas). But Kant's philosophy evolved so that his critiques—*Pure Reason* (1781), *Practical Reason* (1788), and *Judgment* (1790)—make quite different claims. The most famous part of Kant's philosophy, *The Critique of Pure Reason,* is the one that changed modern philosophy decisively, and is usually intended when one refers to Kant, or Kantianism. This critique set the limits to pure or theoretical knowledge.

By arguing that because reason could equally well prove and disprove three fundamental philosophical concepts—the existence of God, the order of the universe, and the immortality of the soul, or God, Cosmos, and Self—reason is clearly limited. This argument by antinomy—the proof (or disproof) of opposite claims—established a ceiling on knowledge, the affirmation or denial of which is one of the major divides among philosophers and religious thinkers from Kant's time to the present. It is often stated, for example, that Jung accepted the Kantian restriction on knowledge "above the line" even though his own insightful experience of the archetypes of the collective unconscious should have led him to break with Kant's restrictive epistemology.

Kant's *Critique of Practical Reason,* along with his *Foundations of the Metaphysics of Morals,* developed an important revision of his *Critique of Pure Reason:* it established the possibility of practical, or moral, knowledge, not certain but with a lawfulness made possible by the participation of the moral agent in a transcendent reality called the noumenal realm. By virtue of being noumenal beings (in addition to being a determined physical being in space–time) moral agents, i.e., anyone choosing between a more and a less moral action (accompanied by a more or less universalizable maxim of one choice or the other), can activate their capacity for noumenal lawful action. This is not pure theoretical reason (which is still disallowed by the first *Critique*) but the reasonableness of the moral life. It is a short step from here to Peirce's pragmatism and to Steiner's case for the intuition of freedom and moral action.

Kant's *Religion within the Limits of Reason Alone* argued that religion, which he assigned to the realm of belief, cannot be established, or refuted, by reason. Because it has been so influential among subsequent generations of philosophers and theologians, this separation between belief and reason might seem merely sensible, but it essentially denied knowledge to religion. This exclusion of pure or certain knowledge from religion and spirituality is exactly the position that Steiner set out to replace by Spiritual Science. Peirce's case for religious knowledge is more complicated, and at the same time more fully developed: it is his pragmaticism, the method that Peirce articulated as a way of reconciling scientific and religious knowledge. However, prior to that discussion we should review other sources of Peirce's and Steiner's philosophies.

Realism of Thomas Aquinas and Duns Scotus[8]: The question of the limits of knowledge, as already discussed, is one of the major choices in modern philosophy. There are two

---

8. See John Boler, "Peirce, Ockham and Scholastic Realism," in Freeman, pp. 93–106.

other equally foundational positions to develop or deny—the complex opposition of realism and nominalism, and the more straightforward opposition of idealism and materialism. By ordinary language one might expect that the opposition to idealism would be realism but this is clearly not so as both Peirce and Steiner are idealists and realists, and opposed to nominalism and materialism. Essentially, at the beginning of one's epistemology and metaphysics, which typically begins in the womb of an earlier philosopher, very often Plato or Aristotle, one needs to establish knowledge of objects and concepts, specifically whether one is more knowable, or more real, and why. Answering these questions at the foundation of one's philosophy sets the parameters for almost every other philosophical decision. (A perfect example of this process is Descartes's division of reality into *res cogitans* and *res extensa*—there is a thinking thing and an extended thing.)

The development of these decisions in philosophical terms and arguments couldn't be more complicated—certainly more so than is needed in a brief essay on Peirce in a book of essays on American philosophy and Steiner. But core or base epistemological and metaphysical choices have a way of making a fundamental difference further along, e.g., with respect to ethics, aesthetics, and philosophy of religion. Not the least of the obstacles, as noted above, concerns terminology; Idealism, including the Idealism of Peirce and Steiner, refers to the conviction that all reality is ultimately mental. The opposing position to idealism, then, is materialism; all reality is ultimately material, whether objects or sensations. The other core choice is between Realism, which affirms the reality of ideas, and nominalism, which claims that ideas are essentially names. Realism can refer to the reality of universal concepts, e.g., Plato's transcendental ideals—Truth, Beauty, and Justice (properly with initial upper case).

Peirce built his epistemology and metaphysics on Duns Scotus, whom he considered to be a thoroughgoing realist. He frequently invoked Scotist realism against the nominalism of John Stuart Mill and William James. It is also true, but not important for our purposes, that the realism of Scotus is more qualified than that of Aquinas. One wonders why he did not base his realism on Aquinas. More than Peirce acknowledged, Scotus's realism is halfway between that of Aquinas and the thorough nominalism of William of Ockham, another Dominican priest, whose version of nominalism gained prominence from his time to the present. According to Ockham, universals do not exist outside the human mind; they are the creation of language. This is the position of William James, Ludwig Wittgenstein, and to some degree and in various modes of expression, most twentieth century philosophy—Whitehead being a prominent exception. Peirce and Royce opposed all forms of nominalism in favor of an affirmation, which they expressed differently, of universals made possible by a universal mind.

Schelling. Additionally, Peirce drew from Friedrich Schelling's philosophy of nature. Peirce wrote to James in response to James's question as to whether anyone but Peirce "treated the inorganic as a sort of product of the living?" Peirce responded: "Your papa [Henry James, Sr.[9]], for one, believed in creation, and so did the authors of all the religions." And then he adds:

> My views were probably influenced by Schelling,—by all stages of Schelling, but especially *Philosophie der Natur*. I consider Schelling as enormous; and one thing I admire about him is his freedom from the trammels of system, and his holding himself uncommitted to any previous utterance. In that, he is like a scientific man. If you were to call my philosophy Schellingism transformed in the light of modern physics, I should not take it hard.[10]

Peirce's realism is best understood in terms of two other sources, the British scientist and logician, William Whewell (1794–1866) and the Scottish philosopher and psychologist, Alexander Bain (1818–1903), both of whom Peirce saw as the sources of his pragmatic understanding of belief and action. Whewell and

---

9. Henry James, Sr., was a wealthy intellectual, a friend of Ralph Waldo Emerson and a prominent Swedenborgian.
10. Perry, *Thought and Character*, II. pp. 415–16.

Bain were vigorously opposed by John Stuart Mill, a nominalist. On the other side of the realist/nominalist argument, it was to Mill that James dedicated his book, *Pragmatism*:

> To the memory of John Stuart Mill from whom I first learned the pragmatic openness of mind and whom my fancy likes to picture as our leader were he alive today.

As our focus in this essay is on Peirce and Steiner, not Peirce and James, let it suffice to say that an essential feature of Peirce's pragmatism is realism, and not at all the nominalism of Mill and James. As we will see, he shares this commitment to realism not only with Josiah Royce but also with Steiner.

Peirce held the world to be in a loop with the will of a thinking person. It is important for a person to think volitionally, to know the object or idea in its effort to express its goal. All ideas, all components of the world, are striving, are teleological. *Telos* is the essential characteristic of the world, and therefore of thinking. This fact is also at the core of Peirce's pragmatism: the meaning of an idea or object is the consequence that it holds for the knower. Here is Peirce's definition of what he called pragmaticism (to distinguish it from James's popularized pragmatism which Peirce, like Royce, considered to be increasingly superficial and nominalist):

> Consider what effects that might conceivably have practical bearing you conceive the object of your conception to have. Then your conception of those effects is the WHOLE of your conception of the object.[11]

It makes sense to ask, pragmatically, what "practical bearing" does this conception of pragmatism have on deep philosophical questions such as knowledge, truth, beauty, and love? An attempt to answer this question will follow an account of the sources which helped Steiner create his philosophy.

---

11. C. S. Peirce, "The Essential of Pragmatism," in Justus Buchler, ed., *Philosophical Writings of Peirce*, p. 269; CPCSP, vol. 5, p. 402.

Rudolf Steiner's Philosophical Sources

Steiner's philosophy has three sources:

- his own philosophically informed spiritual and esoteric experience of the spiritual world, including thinking as a spiritual activity and a direct knowledge of spiritual beings;
- his work on Goethe in his twenties, and thereafter an extension of Goethe's imaginative experience of nature, including plants, animals, and light;
- and his deep study of German idealism, and an idealist understanding of the Self in the context of an absolute mind as developed by Kant, Fichte, and Hegel.

All three of these philosophical sources, and commitments, are implicitely served in *The Philosophy of Freedom*, and explicitely served in all of his writings beginning 1899, as in esoteric works such as *Theosophy* and *How to Know Higher World*, both published in 1904.

Steiner sought to establish both the reality and the possibility of intuiting universal ideals such as Truth, Love, and Beauty. He extended this claim, and practice, in service of the hierarchies (Seraphim down to angels) and the deeper levels of the human being (etheric or life principle, soul or psyche, and spirit or "I"). For Steiner, these are real, not names or fictions; they are non-physical entities that perform important deeds. They inspire as well as love the evolution of the Cosmos, Earth, and human beings. This is where, and how, the subtleties of epistemology and metaphysics support an individual worldview and way of life. According to Steiner's idealist-realism (and of course denied by nominalists), the soul (both living and so-called dead), angels, bodhisattvas, and ideals such as Love are active and influential realities that are confirmed but not generated by individuals and communities. If nominalism were true, there would be no point in practicing intuition or praying in an attempt to communicate with, or receive communication from, the spiritual world: It is not there, it is not real, it is a fiction in which people mistakenly believe. Would-be revelation is news from nowhere. A throughgoing nominalist would agree with the quotable statement of George Santayana, the skeptical colleague of James and Royce: "religion is poetry in which people believe."[12]

At the far end of this important epistemological and metaphysical conflict between realism and nominalism, Steiner holds to a consistent and we might say urgent realist position; and at the other end stands the nominalism of Ockham (1285–1349), Kant, William James, and John Dewey—and according to Peirce, the entire tradition of modern science. Steiner's realism, which is also idealist, is rooted in Plato (in whose early and middle dialogues the human soul and transcendent forms are real), and especially in Aristotle (for whom universals are dependent on the human mind but are nevertheless real). Steiner was steeped in the idealist-realist philosophy of Thomas Aquinas (1225–1274), the foremost philosopher of the late middle ages who reintroduced Aristotle to Christian thought. Aquinas is always referred to as an Aristotelian, which of course he was, but as a medieval Roman Catholic theologian as well as an Aristotelian philosopher, he was also a Platonist. The same is true of Steiner, except that he was of the twentieth century and broadly Christian rather than specifically Catholic. With Aquinas, Steiner argued for the reality of both spiritual beings such as souls, angels, and bodhisattvas, and certain Platonic ideals such as Truth, Beauty, and Love.

PEIRCE'S EPISTEMOLOGY, METAPHYSICS, AND COSMOLOGY

It would be wonderfully helpful to know how, or why, one philosopher begins as a formist/Platonist, another as a mechanist/Cartesian, another as a contextualist/Deweyite, and another as an organicist/Roycean or Whiteheadian. It is sometimes possible to track a philosopher whose position evolves from one root metaphor to another, but even in such cases it is not clear why such a philosopher was open to arguments against his or

---

12. George Santayana, *Interpretations of Poetry and Religion*, p. 27.

her current position and in favor of another. James offered the start of such an analysis by his tough- and tender-minded distinction by which Peirce and Steiner, as well as James and Royce, all seem to me a rich combination of these two defining temperaments. All four of these thinkers seem to combine a tough-minded empiricism, and particularly "scientific loyalty to facts," with a tender-minded idealism, particularly a "confidence in human values and the resultant spontaneity, whether of the religious or romantic type."[13]

Peirce set out to provide a comprehensive philosophy comparable to Aristotle's.[14] He developed a new logic, a new way of thinking, and foundational insights in every field he studied. He certainly thought carefully about almost every important problem in epistemology and metaphysics, as well as, of course in logic in which field he made major contributions. Like the philosophies of Plato and Aristotle,[15] Peirce's philosophy evolved. His early writings show him to be a nominalist, appropriate for a pragmatist (and in fact the primary creator of pragmatism), but by 1905 Peirce announced in *The Monist* that his philosophy is a thoroughgoing realism as well as idealist.[16] This is one of the decisive, foundational assumptions that must be made, implicitly or explicitly, for every epistemology and metaphysics. An emphatic and exclusive commitment can assist the articulation of a metaphysics but at a cost: nuanced and inclusive epistemological and metaphysical commitments, such as Aris-

---

13. William James, *Pragmatism: A New Name for Some Old Ways of Thinking;* complete editions in John J. McDermott, ed., *The Writings of William James,* and *William James: Writings 1902–1910.*
14. He wrote that he intended his system of relations to be a "theory so comprehensive that, for a long time to come, the entire work of human reason...shall appear as the filling up of details." Quoted with reference in Brent, *Charles Sanders Peirce,* p. 347.
15. The evolution of Plato's philosophy from the early to middle to late dialogues is obvious throughout Plato scholarship; for the evolution of Aristotle's philosophy, see Werner Jeager, *Aristotle: Fundamentals of the History of His Development.*
16. See Eugene Freeman, "Peirce and Objectivity in Philosophy," in *The Relevance of Charles Peirce,* p. 76, and Max Fisch, "Peirce's Progress from Nominalism toward Realism," *The Monist,* 51, No. 2 (April 1967), pp. 159–78.

totle's and Peirce's, can lead to complexities and tensions, and perhaps minor contradictions (providing excellent material for subsequent philosophers and doctoral students), but they also avoid easy attack and unfortunate lacunae. Peirce's philosophy is as complicated as it is subtle and nuanced, one essay at a time, amounting to 80,000 pages written over five decades.

Steven Pepper's *World Hypotheses*—an old book on metaphysics, and still very helpful—suggests four root metaphors: formism, mechanism, contextualism, and organicism.[17] It seems to me revealing that Peirce must be one of the very few philosophers, perhaps along with Aristotle, who affirms parts of at least three of these root metaphors. Peirce's basic metaphysical assumption explicitly and emphatically opposes mechanism, the core assumption following from and reinforcing Newtonian science. This is a revealing opposition in that Peirce is one of the rare philosophers who is at core a scientist. Peirce opposes Descartes, who with Newton is the source of the mechanistic worldview, because of the Cartesian division of reality into mind and matter. He also opposes mechanism because it cannot account for organic nature—a very important argument for Steiner.

Peirce would appear to be anti-formism (which is essentially anti-Platonism) because he opposes all forms of dualism (e.g., Plato's division of Form and physical object in his central work *The Republic*), but he holds to the reality of certain transcendent ideas, or Ideals, that are real and influential even while only possible and dependent on human thinking (Peirce's idealism). By virtue of his commitment to the community of inquiry and evidence, his starting point can be seen as contextualism; but by virtue of his emphasis on continuity, and on an evolving universe guided by a divine mind, he can be classified as an organicist. In short, Peirce's philosophy has the range to serve well the future evolution of philosophy.

Peirce's philosophy would seem an ideal combination of devotion to empirical science as well as to such metaphysical commitments as agapism, the claim that love drives the

---

17. Steven Pepper, *World Hypotheses*.

universe. To be a Peircean in philosophy would require one to think purposively and to experience the purposive character of one's ideas. All intellectual activity, like the universe itself, is teleological. Such volitional work is at the foundation of Peirce's pragmaticism, the way of thinking that William James popularized. As we have seen, however, Peirce was not entirely satisfied with James's rendering, not only because of his popularization (with inevitable loss of precision) but because James introduced a subjective dimension at odds with Peirce's commitment to scientific objectivity. (Whereas Peirce was a working scientist—he was a research scientist in the Coast and Geodetic Survey, 1861–1891—James was a psychologist turned philosopher.) What follows is a very brief sketch, or characterization of Peirce's metaphysics—i.e, his attempt to provide a general description of reality, with its major categories. This summation of Peirce is too brief to show the kind of verification that he considered essential in order to show his metaphysics to be scientific.

If we can grasp Peirce's understanding of the three categories of being, along with his idealism-realism and his vision of the evolving universe that is guided by love, we will have enough to see why James, Royce, Dewey, and Whitehead were all, in various ways, influenced by Peirce and why Peirce deserves to be included in any treatment, however brief, of classical American philosophy. Furthermore, Peirce's categories brought the Hegelian triad—thesis, antithesis, synthesis—to American philosophy in a way that advanced the synthesis of pragmatism, evolution, and early-twentieth-century science.

Three categories of being. A close look at Peirce's metaphysics requires the introduction of his three categories of being, which he calls Firstness, Secondness, and Thirdness (or: quality, fact, thought; or: quality, relation, synthesis). As he explains in his essay, "The Principles of Phenomenology,"

> My view is that there are three modes of being. I hold that we can directly observe them in elements of whatever is at any time before the mind in any way. They are the being of positive

qualitative possibility, the being of actual fact, and the being of law that will govern facts in the future.[18]

Peirce's descriptions are vivid but in accumulation, perhaps not so obvious as he claims:

Firstness is the realm of possibility—red before anything in the universe is red. "The idea of first is predominant in the ideas of freshness, life, freedom.... The first is predominant in feeling, as distinct from objective perception, will, and thought." Firstness is a mere maybe. "A quality of feeling can be imagined to be without any occurrence, as it seems to me. Its mere may-being gets along without any realization at all." Firstness is "the quality of what we are immediately conscious of, which is no fiction."

Secondness can be thought of as brute factuality—your shoulder pushing against a door. "The idea of second is predominant in the ideas of causation and of statistical force." "The second category...is the element of struggle." It has the character of "what has been done."

Thirdness is the mode of being which consists in the fact that future facts of Secondness will take on a determinate general character. "By the third, I mean the medium or connecting bond between the absolute first and last. The beginning is first, the end second, the middle third. The end is second, the means third. The threat of life is a third; the fate that snaps it, is second."

As with almost all of Peirce's philosophical contributions, it has taken, and will undoubtedly continue to take subsequent generations of philosophers to interpret and improve Peirce's positions. Charles Hartshorne, for example, one of the editors of the *Collected Papers of Charles Sanders Peirce* (1931–35) and an original philosopher in the tradition of Peirce and Whitehead, introduced his essay on "A Revision of Peirce's Categories," as follows: "I have tried, through most of my long career, to revise Peirce's categories."[19]

It would not be inaccurate to offer as a broad characterization of Peirce to say that he excelled at Thirdness. Like

---

18. Buchler, p. 75.
19. In *The Relevance of Charles Peirce*, p. 80.

Whitehead, he had a genius for synthesis, and also like Whitehead he combined mathematics, logic, metaphysics, and evolutionary cosmology. More dramatically, in a way that Whitehead later developed,[20] he included in his metaphysics, and particularly into his philosophy of evolution, distinctly Platonic concepts, such as Truth, Beauty, and Love. Like Peirce, Whitehead introduced many neologisms, though none as infelicitous as Peirce's Tychism (chance), Synechism (continuity), as well as Agapism and Agapasticism (evolutionary love). John Smith offers a clear summation of Peirce's conception of evolution through creative love:

> The theory of evolutionary love is an attempt to make the Christian virtue the basis of a cosmology and an interpretation of the course of history. It is a doctrine of God at the same time. Peirce saw that love cannot be the logical opposite of hatred, for in that case Satan would become a coordinate of hatred.[21]

In 1905, Peirce wrote:

> Thus the love that God is, is not a love of which hatred is the contrary; otherwise Satan would be a coordinate power; but it is a love which embraces hatred as an imperfect stage of it, and Anteros—yea, even needs hatred and hatefulness as its object. For self-love is no love; so if God's self is love, that which he loves must be defect of love; just as a luminary can light up only that which otherwise would be dark.[22]

It is difficult not to imagine Peirce trying to serve as that luminary in a dark world. Here is Peirce in 1887 writing to William James (with Royce the most loyal if frequently frustrated and perplexed friend of the brilliant and tragic Peirce):

> I have learned a great deal about philosophy in the last few years, because they have been very miserable and unsuccessful years—terrible beyond anything that the man of ordinary

---

20. For Whitehead on Truth, Beauty, Adventure, Art, and Peace, see his *Adventures of Ideas*.
21. John Smith, *Spirit of American Philosophy*, p. 34.
22. Quoted in Brent, p. 338.

experience can possibly understand or conceive. Much have I learned of life and the world, throwing strong lights upon philosophy in these years. Undoubtedly its tendency is to make one value the spiritual more, but not an abstract spirituality.... [It has] led me to rate higher than ever the individual deed as the only real meaning there is [in] the Concept, and yet at the same time to see more sharply than ever that it is not the mere arbitrary force in the deed but the life it gives to the Idea that is valuable.[23]

Steiner's Epistemology, Metaphysics, and Cosmology

With Peirce, Steiner considered his philosophy to be scientific—though they held different understandings of scientific method and verification. It was one of Steiner's core tasks to join science—which he and Peirce identified with verification—to spiritual and esoteric research. Steiner's claims in all areas of philosophy, and in all of the disciplines that he tried to advance by Spiritual Science, extend far beyond what Peirce would consider evidential, or, perhaps even plausible. Yet Steiner's own research, the methods he taught to others, and research continuing to be conducted by his many thousands of followers in endeavors such as the Waldorf approach to education, biodynamic agriculture, classification of homeopathic remedies (produced by WALA and Weleda), understanding of money, and insights concerning religions—all provide some, and in some cases dramatic, verification of his claims and methods.

Steiner wrote epistemology, both precisely and at length, particularly with the intent of teaching his readers and followers how to intuit spiritual beings; he modeled and taught clairvoyance. Clearly his commitment to such beings involves metaphysical affirmations built into his epistemological claim that such beings as the hierarchies are real in being and action. Steiner was primarily devoted to observations and reports—what are spiritual beings doing, how can others access them and feel their effects, how can souls of the dead be contacted?

---

23. Quoted in Brent, p. 341.

Perhaps it is most accurate to describe Steiner, as well as Peirce, as phenomenologists. By phenomenology with respect to Peirce and Steiner (and not necessarily as a description of Edmund Husserl or Maurice Mearleau-Ponty) we mean the attempt to grasp and describe being (in its generality and particulars) at its most fundamental core, with the least possible assumptions. Steiner, of course, would reply that he was not assuming anything: he is directly experiencing what he is reporting. Whereas for Peirce, all phenomena and all being can be classified by three categories—First, Second, and Third—Steiner's description of core reality would seem to be the relationship between percept and concept. In his view, the percept would seem to be Firstness, i.e., a potentiality awaiting its concept; concepts would seem to be Secondness; the joining of percept and concept, first and second, would be an idea made real by a thinking person, or Thirdness. "Philosophy of Freedom" thinking (whether by Steiner or anyone else) would seem to be an ideal example of Thirdness—joining potential (percept) and actual (concept) in knowledge by the agency of a thinking individual (Thirdness).

Steiner did not seem particularly focused on creating a systematic metaphysics *per se*—his task was to heighten or deepen, and more importantly liberate, thinking from passivity and alienation. Yet, it does seem that he makes important metaphysical assertions about the ontologically given (being per se or the ground of being) awaiting human participation; this is presumably Firstness. Like Peirce, Steiner's metaphysics (to the extent that it was developed) is a Third: it joins the potential (the possibility of knowing) with its negation (the blunt fact of alienation, of not knowing, the characteristic epistemological situation of contemporary humanity). For Steiner, Peirce's Thirdness, though universal as a logical relation, is nevertheless difficult to attain while remaining in dualism, or Secondness, which is more characteristic of modern Western thinking. Yet it is precisely Thirdness that is essential for humanity at the present time.

Steiner knew of pragmatism only from James's *Pragmatism*. Steiner is a pluralist in that he considers it usual for there to be many valid ways of knowing an object, event, or idea, but his pluralism was not as radical as James's in that he was convinced that all true perspectives and ideals are compatible. In his *Philosophy of Freedom* he supports this claim by affirming a spiritual realm.[24] In his later writings and lectures he names these guarantors in terms very similar to Peirce's Divine Mind or Royce's Logos Spirit. To the extent that Peirce's and Royce's pragmatism claims that ideas are purposive and that their truth and meaning are to be judged by the quality of the action to which they lead, Steiner would probably agree. He clearly would disagree, however, with James's claim that the practical result, the action following an idea, is what is meant by that idea, and is the sole determinent of its truth. Steiner's treatment of percept and concept in his *Philosophy of Freedom* did not lead him to pragmatism but to his claims on behalf of free, intuitive thinking in contact with higher beings and true, universalizable ideals. One of Steiner's core universal ideas, love, is close to Peirce's:

> One must not say that the world is imperfect because it contains evil. Far rather is it perfect precisely on that account. The creators of the world needed evil in order to bring the good to unfoldment. A good must first be broken on the rock of evil. The All-Love can only be brought to its highest blossoming through self-love.[25]

Again in agreement with Peirce, Steiner holds that the ultimate battle between love, both human and divine, and evil (also both human and divine, though at a level below God) is the meaning of evolution. All human thought and behavior—by creativity, by participation in the designs and sacrifices of spiritual beings, by love, pain, suffering, and sacrifice—contribute to this evolutionary battle. In Steiner's understanding of the cosmos and human experience, his and Peirce's suffering have been gathered up by the evolutionary process, a process that is both tragic and ultimately redeemed. This is what Royce calls atonement.

---

24. See *Intuitive Thinking as a Spiritual Path*, ch. 9: "The Idea of Freedom."
25. Steiner (1906). "The Origin of Evil," lecture in Berlin, Nov. 22, 1906.

Josiah Royce

5.

JOSIAH ROYCE AND RUDOLF STEINER
A COMPARISON AND CONTRAST
Frank M. Oppenheim

Josiah Royce (1855–1916), a classic American philosopher of community, was a polymath deeply interested in Goethe and Eckhart, Eastern mysticism and Western science, logic and romanticism, and many other points of seeming concurrence with the tradition of Rudolph Steiner (1861–1925).

Good reasons exist for exploring the possible connections between the thought of Royce and Steiner. The mature Royce taught that a process of universal pedagogy was guiding the human race and the entire evolving universe toward a universal community under the direction of the Logos–Spirit. This Spirit, described in John's Fourth Gospel, is both pedagogue and guide during this universal pilgrimage occurring through the ages. Royce also taught that, through its "doctrine of signs" and its "Christian doctrine of life," this Logos–Spirit teaches minded beings. This may remind us of Steiner's theory of revelation because Steiner felt that "the knowledge and realization of the intentions of the living Christ" constitute "the essential meaning of the Earth."[1]

Then, too, Royce developed his early epistemological distinction between descriptive and appreciative knowing into his mature period's distinction between perceptive-conceptual knowing and interpretive knowing. He held that the latter was indispensable

---

1. *The Essential Steiner: The Basic Writings of Rudolf Steiner* (ed. Robert A. McDermott), p.22 [hereafter *TES*].

for philosophy, religion, art, and ethical life. Did Steiner resonate with Royce through his emphasis on esoteric knowing?

Again, the challenge of understanding the problem of evil is a neuralgic point both in Royce and in Steiner. The mature Royce taught the need of undergoing both moral and amoral evils—broken loves and lost causes, mischances and natural calamities—to reach a purification of values and a freedom from over-concentration upon the material aspect of the universe. Does not a somewhat similar purification process mark the thought of Rudolf Steiner?

Finally, throughout Royce's thought, Ekhart's doctrine of the "divine spark" (or *Funkelin)* is the basis of the human self's belonging to the divine. This "internal meaning" of the finite human self derives from the Spirit's self-constitution through Its diversification into finite selves representative of Itself. Viewed teleologically, this "internal meaning" of the human self seeks the Spirit and Its universal community through loyal commitment to its own uniqueness and to a particular community. Did Steiner paint a similar canvas?

Such first scoutings, then, may whet our appetite to explore similarities and differences between Royce and Steiner. Toward this comparison-contrast, I first present the mature Royce, focusing especially on his late ethical thought.

I need, however, to demarcate from the start the range included by the term, "the mature Royce." Using his "religious insight" of early 1883 as a first major benchmark, I divide his intellectual development into his "pre-formed" (1855–1882) and "formed" (1883–1916) periods.[2] This insight provided Royce with the basic religious orientation from which thereafter he never changed fundamentally. Later his mental striving achieved two other maximal insights: into the individual (1896) and into the community and its Spirit (1912).[3] Relying on these three maximal insights, I subdivide the Harvard years of Royce's "formed" thought growth into three sub-periods: the early Royce of 1883

---

2. See Frank Oppenheim, "Josiah Royce's Intellectual Development: An Hypothesis," *Idealistic Studies* 6 (Jan. 1976): 85–104; and F. Oppenheim, *Royce's Voyage Down Under: A Journey of the Mind*, pp. viii–x.
3. Because occasioned by his rereading of C. S. Peirce, this third maximal insight (of 1912) is often called Royce's "Peircean insight."

to 1895; the middle Royce of 1896 to 1911; and the mature Royce of 1912 to 1916.

In his mature period, Royce employed a Peirce-inspired epistemology of interpretation to develop his ethics of loyalty. Before entering this mature period, however, a brief look at the ethics of his early and middle periods seems needed.

Royce's 1883 "religious insight" lay in detecting that some of our judgments could not even be erroneous unless judged so by a superhuman mind. As Royce later rephrased it:

> This view which I set forth about the nature and conditions of error is true or false. Whether it is true or false, we have here a teleological situation which brings the thought of the moment into contact with a type of consciousness which is not the merely human type.[4]

This religious insight into the truth that a superhuman mind is a reality brought Royce out of his preformed period of being "a decidedly skeptical critical empiricist"[5] and into his formed period of thereafter being an experiential and critical religious thinker. Royce's early "moral insight" was also reciprocally involved in this religious insight and supportive of it. That is, he grasped through performative contradiction that he could not sincerely want the total ultimate disharmony of minded beings. Put positively, he identified that the human self inexpugnably and most deeply desires the harmony of minded beings, a harmony to be approached, at least in the end, as an ultimate community.

This early emphasis on a superhuman Knower and a desire for ultimate harmony of selves needed a counterbalance in unique individuality. In 1896, Royce broke through to his novel American definition of an individual as "the object of exclusive interest." That is, one is constituted an individual by some Other who chooses this one in exclusion of other possible beloveds. Royce's insight into individuality initiated his middle period and showed itself in his Gifford Lectures, *The World and the Individual*

---

4. Royce, *Royce's Last Lectures on Metaphysics*, lecture of Jan. 11, 1916, p. 135 (quoted with permission) [hereafter *LLM*].
5. Ibid. (p. 130).

(1899–1901). During his years in the twentieth century, Royce concentrated more on symbolic logic and ethics. These intensified interests showed themselves first in a significant logical study of 1905[6] and in his most popular work, *The Philosophy of Loyalty* in 1908.[7] These researches finally flowered in his *Principles of Logic* (written in 1910) and in *The Sources of Religious Insight*, his Bross lectures, delivered in 1911.[8]

The physical price for these labors, however, was an attack of apoplexy on February 1, 1912. This event caused Royce to leave the classroom for three semesters and gave him time to reread carefully the early and later published writings of Charles S. Peirce. Thus Royce's "Peircean insight" of 1912 gradually dawned—his insight, he said, was as transformative of his mind as was his religious insight of 1883[9]—and one that gave his philosophy a new method, a new manner, and a new message. This was the start of his mature period (1912–1916). Having surveyed his early and middle periods most briefly, we can now focus more carefully upon Royce's philosophical ethics during his mature period.

General Survey of Royce's Mature Ethics: 1912–1916

What happened, then, to Royce's view of loyalty once he had created his "Principles of Logic" (1910), pioneered his general philosophy of religion in the *Sources of Religious Insight* (1912), and then underwent his "Peircean insight" (1912)?[10] In *The Problem of Christianity*, (1913),[11] Royce's mature grasp of loyalty "came

---

6. Royce, "The Relation of the Principles of Logic to the Foundations of Geometry," *Transactions of the American Mathematical Society* 24 (1905): pp. 353–415; reprinted in *Royce's Logical Essays,* ed. Daniel S. Robinson, pp. 379–441 [hereafter *RLE*].
7. Royce, *The Philosophy of Loyalty* [hereafter *PL*].
8. Royce, *The Sources of Religious Insight*, [hereafter *SRI*].
9. See Clendenning, *The Letters of Josiah Royce,* p. 645 [hereafter *Letters*].
10. Royce estimated that this gradual insight, which began in 1912, had by itself produced as radical a transformation of his thought as had his original "religious insight" in 1883. See *Letters,* p. 645.
11. Royce, *The Problem of Christianity,* 2 vols.; republished as a single-volume edition by the University of Chicago Press in 1968, to which our citations in parenthesis in the text refer [hereafter *PC*].

of age." He asserted that "the depth and vitality of the ideal of loyalty have become better known to me as I have gone on with my work."[12] But this "ideal of loyalty" resembled no abstract Platonic form. Rather it was concretized within the directed life streams of communal religious experience (40). In the *Problem*, he clearly saw and formulated how genuine loyalty depends upon a *specific fundamental orientation*. The genuinely loyal self must adopt a psychic stance that is primarily neither self-assertive nor self-effacing, but self-dedicative to the whole universe. One must commit oneself to the entire processing world by loving it with wholehearted loyalty (270). This chosen radical orientation was Royce's "third attitude of will" (355–357).

In the *Problem*, the term *transformation* became even more central for Royce (218).[13] He claimed that a transformation of ethical ideas results if one simply recognizes and adequately considers the experiences of the Pauline–Christian churches. They experienced a concretized dynamic form of social religious experience that first generated a full articulation of the "Christian doctrine of life." In this experience and articulation, a gift "as from above" (that he called "grace") unified the three most essential Christian ideas: Community, lost state, and atonement. Now the "highest good of man"—both as individual and as community—lay in his ethical transformation from a merely natural form of existence, that is, one "morally detached" from community, to a genuinely united mode of life in touch with the Universal Community (218). Neither individual nor community can effect this moral conversion unless aided by the Spirit of the Universal Community that usually operates through one of its human representatives, such as an honest banker or a sufferer for unity, like Abraham Lincoln. That *atonement* became central to the *Problem's* doctrine of loyalty constituted one of its most striking developments. Royce described atonement as "the function in which the life of the community culminates" (42, 208). His fifth plan for the

---

12. *PC*, pp. 38, 41–42. In this section, subsequent references to *PC* will be included in parentheses within the text.
13. See also *PC*, pp. 128, 130, 190, 207, 224; cf. with *PL*, pp. 294, 388.

Problem revealed that he had broken through to "a rationalized form of the Atonement doctrine."[14] This defensible view could fittingly replace both the merely moral and the substitutionary (scapegoat) versions of that doctrine. Royce's emphasis on the need for a highly intelligent design of the strategy that guides the deed(s) of the suffering atoner became far clearer in 1912. Far clearer, too, became the atoning role of the whole genuine community, as well as that of any of its particular suffering servants. In this way, Royce penetrated near the heart of Christianity—the sacrificial side of its Paschal Mystery.

Moreover, in the *Problem*, "the Will to Interpret" functioned as an immanent and fruitful way of viewing the Logos–Spirit of the community. This Will is committed to seeking the unity of two minded beings who perhaps merely differ or even stand opposed. It embodies itself sometimes in ordinary leaders like honest business agents and trustworthy bankers. The Will to Interpret is also the name of the Spirit of the universal community. As pedagogue sign-sender, this Logos–Spirit guides the historical development of both individuals and nations—a development that has its ups and downs and ups—and usually unifies only slowly. In his maturity, Royce also installed the Will to Interpret at the heart of his new method of philosophizing by "interpretive musement."[15] Within human limits, this method participates concretely in the Interpreter Spirit's synoptic vision that integrates the processing experiences both of human selves, taken individually and communally, and of the world.

Finally, Royce's 1912 doctrine of loyalty radiated a striking balance of temporal process and mysticism. The ever-accelerating rate of change will gnaw away many of Christianity's formulas, institutions, and outdated practices. Meanwhile, the Spirit of loyalty will lead human selves to focus with increasing intensity upon that "Christian doctrine of life," which is the living "sword of the spirit" (215). This is the only central nerve of doctrine required for

---

14. See "Essence of the previous [fifth] plan," in the Harvard University Archives Royce Papers, Symbolic Logic Box 4, no. 4, p. 1 (according to the 1967 listing of box contents) [hereafter *HARP*].
15. See Oppenheim, *Royce's Mature Philosophy of Religion*, pp. 68–69 [hereafter *RMPOR*].

the perduring life and growth of Christianity and of humanity. In this nerve, there operates that mystic touch with the divine that had characterized Royce's thought since his 1883 religious insight.

In *The World and the Individual* of 1899[16] he had refined from impurities what was genuine in his "mystical" (or "second") conception of being and transformed it into his "fourth" and final conception of being—that of the unique individual as the object of exclusive interest. Thus he retained, critically purified, and emphasized his mystical touch with the divine.

How this touch perdured through the quantum leap of his 1912 insight appeared in the *Problem's* teleological unity with the Spirit of the universal community.[17] This bondedness *(epsilon* relation) provides the constancy needed amid the universe's otherwise chancy, ever-evolving process.

In sum, then, we find that in the *Problem* Royce markedly transformed and developed his doctrine of loyalty from his first edition of it in 1908. During his four final years of 1912 to 1916, might Royce's loyalty doctrine have undergone an equally vast development? I think so, because, as I see it, Royce's doctrine of loyalty developed and matured as much after the *Problem* as it had done between 1908 and 1912.

Already in 1914 at Berkeley, he created a new synthesis of his philosophy of loyalty by integrating three theses: 1) that, under certain conditions, communities are genuine selves; 2) "that the salvation of every individual man depends upon his voluntary devotion to some such living and lovable community"; and 3) that in and through and above his commitment to such a community, one "comes into some genuine touch with...one and the same live spiritual reality"—a union that constitutes loyalty.[18] This integrated vision is more significant than any of its parts. Yet Royce's insight into his third thesis lifted him into a paean

---

16. Royce, *The World and the Individual* [hereafter *WI*].
17. Royce's late interest in mysticism found expression in his "George Fox as a Mystic," *Harvard Theological Review* 6 (Jan. 1913): 31–59—even before his two months of lecturing on mysticism in spring 1916; see *LLM*, pp. 288–355.
18. First Berkeley Lecture, 1914, "Illustrations of the Philosophy of Loyalty," *HARP* 84, no. 3, pp. 31–33 [hereafter *"Illustrations"*].

about loyalty that could remind one of Plato's poetic and mystical expression when he described his noetic vision of the Forms. But unlike Plato's vision, Royce's insight came through the light experienced through one's loving union with and deed-doing service of community—that is, through Royce's voluntary "absolute pragmatism." Of his final thesis on loyalty, then, Royce wrote in a periodic crescendo:

> Thirdly, that, in and through and above all the countless social forms in which we are accustomed to interpret to ourselves our relation to the community which we learn to love—in and through and above a man's love for his country, in and through and above a devout man's love for his church universal,—in and through and above our love of the ideal community of all mankind, as we hope that mankind is yet to be realized in the future,—in and through and above all these special forms which the loyal spirit takes, we all, precisely in so far as we are loyal, come into some genuine touch with one and the same reality, with one and the same cause, with one and the same live spiritual reality. To this one cause all the loyal are, according to their lights, faithful. One undivided soul of many a soul, whose life constitutes the divine life, one genuine and universal community there is. To be united in and with this community, to love it as our father and our mother, as our goal and as our fulfillment,—this is loyalty.[19]

For an even better detection of how much Royce's final theory of ethics grew, we focus mainly on the Extension Course in Ethics that Royce conducted during his final year, 1915/1916.[20]

When studying Royce's plans and few extant written lectures of this course, I am impressed by how much Royce's ethics grew after the *Problem*. To arrange the data of this course, I classify these further developments as concerned chiefly with the basic problems, method, and content of ethics.

Concerning problems, Royce clearly identified at the start (of this course) several questions that must be both raised and

---

19. Ibid. (pp. 31-32).
20. The only extant written lectures from this course seem to be lectures 2-5 and "Comments on the Mid-Year Examination," preserved in *HARP* 94, no. 1, pp. 1-4, 95 [hereafter *ECE* and "Comments"].

answered positively *before* philosophical ethics can begin. He found that the ordinary experience of any even slightly reflective human person will inevitably generate such questions as "What's going on here (in this world I find myself in)?" "Is life worth living?" "Can my life have meaning?" "If so, under what conditions?" "And if so, then, in general at least, what is that meaning?"

Ethics cannot begin if human life ultimately makes no sense, if at bottom it is simply "a tale told by an idiot." But for Royce in 1915, since *"a common reasonable human nature"* characterizes each human self, its human life must make sense.[21] This nature, however, is neither some pincushion (like Locke's "substrate") nor "beingness" (like Aristotle's *ousia*). Rather it is a *processing-minded being* whose inmost identity lies in its progressive interpretation of the mystery of itself within a mysterious universe.[22] In 1915, Royce agreed with Schopenhauer that we have to start ethics by facing up to the mysteries experienced in the "Who am I?" question.[23] Progressively we can gain familiarity with the mystery of the individual self even if we can never comprehend it definitively (V, 12).

His mature method rested on the conviction that the individual self and the community were equally ultimate realities in process. That is, the "Who am I" question is inseparable from the question "Who are we?" These two questions initiated Royce's individual and social approaches to ethics in 1915.[24]

After emphasizing the need to win some self-identification before beginning ethics, Royce immediately added, "So I hold; and thereon I shall found a large part of our later ethical thesis." Through its efforts at self-identification, then, each human self

---

21. ECE, lecture 2, "The Idea of Duty," HARP 94, no. 1, pp. 3–4. In this section, subsequent references to this course will be inserted in parentheses within the text; e.g., for the above, (II, pp. 3–4), and with "C" designating his final "Comments" lecture.
22. See Royce's article "Mind," published in Hastings' *Encyclopaedia of Religion and Ethics*, 8: 655–56; reprinted in *RLE*, p. 175.
23. Royce had been putting this "Who Am I?" question to himself personally since his youth; see *The Life and Thought of Josiah Royce*, ed. John Clendenning, p. 42 [hereafter *Life*].
24. See *ECE*, III, pp. 3–8, 10.

finds that it possesses a "reasonable human nature" and yet does not exist alone because it cannot escape being aware that other human selves also exist. For each self encounters ideas not its own that disclose the reality of other minded beings. This disclosure cannot occur unless all of them share some unity of reasonable life, that is, the concretely shared life of a community of minded beings. The experience of a community of human selves—diverse yet communicating with basic success—evidences, then, the common reasonable nature they share. Such, then, are the experiential bases for the conviction guiding Royce's method and doctrine that the individual self and the community are equally ultimate realities in process.

An ethical philosopher cannot recognize this membership in community, however, unless he adopts a new mode of knowing. Going beyond the traditional modes of knowing—by concepts or percepts or combinations of these two—he must shift into that deepest mode of knowing: *interpretation*. Royce had been saying this since his 1912 Peircean insight, but his latest writings insisted on this shift even more pointedly and clearly.[25] Unless ethicians turn themselves into interpreters, they will be incompetent to handle those basic ethical questions of significance and value—such as, Does my life have meaning? And if so, what is that meaning?

Furthermore, by 1915, Royce saw that his interpretive method in ethics had to work in what we would today call an interdisciplinary manner. In his Extension Course in Ethics of 1915/1916, he had his students read Graham Wallas's *The Great Society*, along with Royce's own *Philosophy of Loyalty* and *War and Insurance*.[26] By having them read socioeconomics and philosophy, Royce wanted his students to find contrasting effects and added concreteness to enrich the method of interpretation propelling his course. He told his students, "Let us learn, then, to drive the social and the ethical problems as a team. Therein will consist the principal undertaking of this course" (III, 17).

---

25. See *First Berkeley Conferences of 1914*, and *ECE*, "Comments" lecture, pp. 8–15.
26. Royce, *War and Insurance* [hereafter *War*].

Josiah Royce and Rudolf Steiner

In order to study and develop ethics most concretely, then, the maturest Royce committed himself more than ever to a method of interpretation and interdisciplinary contrast.

Not any kind of interpreter, however, can create such an ethics. To respond rightly to the basic questions of ethics requires that no interpreter attempt philosophical ethics other than *he who has adopted the only fitting attitude towards the universe*. If a human self is to use its freedom wisely, it must, according to Royce, adopt that "third attitude of will," which he had identified in the *Problem*.[27] One must avoid both the self-assertive will to life and the self-denying will that withdraws from universal life. Instead, one must "fall in love with the universe"[28] and commit oneself to contribute to the overall direction of the ongoing universal community. This requires one to admit that there is something greater in the world than oneself and to give oneself freely to this something greater.

Exemplifying this choice of needed, initial, methodological attitude, Royce opted for Peirce's model of nonconflictive mediation (based simply on the "will to promote union") rather than for Hegel's conflict-based dialectic. Referring to Peirce's theory of mediation, Royce had already written in 1914, "I believe that we are only beginning to realize what type of mediation promises most for the future both of philosophy and of the social order."[29]

In summary, then, of Royce's most mature developments in ethical problems and method, I find that Royce became even more sensitive to how profoundly William James had asked, "Is life worth living?" If this question is left in doubt, ethics cannot begin. For answering it correctly, Royce's requisites were 1) prioritize this question; 2) insist on interpretation as the only mode of knowing that can answer it—and this it cannot do unless it arises from Peirce's simple "will to promote union" rather than from a Hegelian dialectic of conflict; and 3) show

---

27. *PC*, pp. 355–357.
28. Ibid., p. 270.
29. "The Spirit of the Community," *HARP* 91, no. 3, p. 11; see also "Comments," *HARP* 95, no. 1, pp. 5, 15.

that for this type of interpretive method, one's fundamental orientation toward life and the world has to be a loving loyalty toward the whole universe. This initial attitude had to replace both an individualistic self-assertion (as if others did not count as much as oneself) and a self-withdrawal into an individualistic mysticism that avoided the "bumps and bruises" of real human life.

We have seen the mature Royce's new and integrated way of using interpretation to create ethical thought and solve ethical questions. I turn now to the content of his 1915/1916 ethics. It consists, according to my survey of his final work, in three insights of the second magnitude and four insights of the first magnitude. His insights of the second magnitude were

1. his increased indication of family as a starting point and symbolic sign of ethical life in community;
2. his use of solidarity to emphasize the concreteness of community; and
3. his Peirce-inspired purification of the key idea of mediation—which included significant applications to the theology of redemption and to the economics of investment.

His insights of the first magnitude were:

1. his identification and synthesis of the "three leading ethical ideas;"
2. his consequent discovery within humankind's three basic interpersonal relationships of three species of genuine loyalty that are distinct yet complementary within family-like communities;
3. his pioneer creation of an "ethics of the fitting"—a cathecontic ethics; and
4. his explication of genuine hope as an indispensable dynamic within true loyalty.

This list of seven developments in the content of Royce's maturest ethics outlines the remainder of this section even as it calls for some elaboration of these insights within the present overall survey of how Royce's ethics developed during the final decade of his life.

Three Insights of the Second Magnitude

Family

I begin by focusing on the mature Royce's intensification of interest in and concern for family, the first of the three meaningful, if seemingly less significant, developments of content in Royce's most mature ethics as listed above. In one of his "John Fiske" manuscripts of 1901, Royce had carved a cameo-sketch of a mother and child encircled by various levels of society.[30] Through evolution, these latter had arisen in order to support and develop that central community of mother and child. Later, in his 1907 Urbana Lectures, Royce had directed attention to the family as the natural seedbed of loyalty, even as he pointed out the many deformed shapes family loyalty too frequently takes.[31] By 1914, although he often focused on communities of agents, bankers, and counselors to illustrate loyalty, he then recurred far more frequently than in his early writings to the natural community of the family as a primordial social reality and as a "symbolic sign." Noticing that the family arises largely in a natural and unconscious way, Royce found it more basic and enduring than those communities of interpretation that are formed more artificially and deliberately. For instance, in his *Last Lectures in Metaphysics* (1915–1916), he pointed out that the family "exists on a purely natural basis without the conscious intent of anybody that it should become a community at the outset."[32]

It was in *War and Insurance*, however, that the mature Royce's concern for family came most to the fore.[33] Here he portrayed the family as the "natural unity of society in all its stages of evolution" (36–37). The Royce of 1914 saw the family as the seedbed of more stable love. Animated at first by a natural, less than ideal, loyalty, this love may become charged with a "more ideal loyalty." The family community creates a norm of stabil-

---

30. See *HARP* 72, no. 1, pp. 35–38, 42.
31. See *HARP* 76, no. 3, pp. 16–17, 33.
32. *LLM*, pp. 41–42.
33. See *War*, pp. 36, 37, 42–43, 49, 56, 71. Subsequent references to *War* in this paragraph are set within parentheses in the text.

ity and fruitfulness, and this usually provides a basis for family peace and loyalty. Because of these traits, the family lies at the root of many vast social organizations (42–43). To the family, Royce compared any Community of Interpretation because the latter was a "sort of artificially created but marvelously fruitful family" (49). Even if the four kinds of Communities of Interpretation that Royce cherished—the judicial, banking, insurance, and federal/state communities—were removed from the world, "the family triads aforesaid would indeed remain as the principal basis for the loyal life of mankind" (56, 86–93). Moreover, if the nations of the world became bonded together by mutual international insurance against calamities both natural and manufactured (like war), their unity would make the "family of nations" become "visibly represented." In all of this, Royce pointed toward that training in loyalty that family life promotes. This schooling in a community's ethical life occurs even when family life is simply natural (or self-preferential), but it occurs far more strongly when it is genuinely loyal through its openness to wider communities, including the Universal Community. For the family naturally and powerfully trains selves in loyalty, through its diversity of selves, its calls for mutual help, and its will to promote union and future life.

How did Royce reach this view of the family? The troubles and tragedies touching his own family during his final decade account in large part for this noticeable change of emphasis. Christopher, his brilliant and so promising firstborn son, grew mentally ill, had to be committed to an institution, and was cut off by death in 1910. Ned, his musically gifted second son, had such marital and employment difficulties that he entrusted Randolph, his mentally retarded son, to Josiah and Katherine for safe keeping from 1912 onward.[34] Stephen, his last son, had a child, Marion, who died in early 1915 as an infant, thus

---

34. See *Letters* (p. 574), and *Life* (p. 360), where one finds the "hopelessly retarded" Randolph living in Josiah's home during the last four years of the professor's life and thereafter cared for magnanimously by the widowed Katherine for over two decades until he had to be committed to an institution in 1940.

robbing Royce of his granddaughter "Petsy."[35] Thus, enough "lost causes" had cumulated within Royce's hopes for his family to convince him how precious and meaningful is genuinely loyal family life.[36]

Besides the family trials just mentioned, Royce sensed that after 1907 many Americans were increasingly bypassing his philosophical work and rushing into a popularized pragmatism. The outbreak of World War I with its spreading conflagration, horrors, and tragic breakup of the community of nations seemed to mock all his endeavors to build the Great Community of humankind in peace. This progressive immersion into the acid bath of adversity had already led Royce in 1911 to create in his *Sources* that stirring chapter, "The Religious Mission of Sorrow." Next, it led him in the *Problem* to find Christian life culminating in deeds of atonement. This led him in his final year to see Americans' widespread problems of estrangement from themselves, their spouses, families, friends, institutions, nation, and family of nations as that sickness that loyal suffering servants were called to remedy. In this way, Royce approached nearer and nearer to that central Christian mystery of "dying and rising" in company with the Christ-Spirit who continues his life in his members.

If he found increasing tragedy and diminishing physical strength marking his final decade,[37] still his hope grew ever stronger. Founded on the Spirit of the universal community, Royce's hope suffused these tragedies and transcended them. It led him to direct the practical portions of the *Problem* "for the strengthening of hearts."[38] He voiced confidence at the close of his late 1915

---

35. This child is buried in the Royce plot in Mt. Auburn Cemetery, Cambridge, Mass.
36. This conviction of Royce is manifest in the recently recovered Royce Family Papers, in the Crystal Falls Collection of the Harvard Archives Royce Papers, A and D. For a description of this 1989 recovery, see John Clendenning and Frank Oppenheim, "New Documents on Josiah Royce," Transactions of the Charles S. Peirce Society 26 (winter 1990): pp. 131–45.
37. For this increasing tone of the tragic, especially in Royce's final years, see *Life*, pp. 340–44, 357–61, 376–77, 382–90.
38. *PC*, p. 40.

autobiographical sketch when he quoted Swinburne's hope-filled "Watchman, What of the Night." He counterbalanced his grief over the war with his *Hope of the Great Community*.[39] These "raisings up of the spirit" reveal how, in the mature Royce's life and doctrine, hope functioned as the dynamic animator of genuine ethical life.

Solidarity

Another significant, if less-noticed, development in Royce's late thought is his increasing substitution of the term and idea of solidarity for that of community, among his late leading ideas. This fitted in with a trend he acknowledged in his late ethical thought: to think much more concretely. His mature stress on solidarity may have been born out of that inner conflict that the late Royce experienced between the growing intensity of World War I—that concrete abomination of his hoped-for ideal—and his Great Community of an undivided human family of nations. Whatever its source, the term "solidarity" appeared most frequently in Royce's *War and Insurance*.[40] As this work made clear, Royce was convinced that genuine communities, which comprise his "second level" of reality, are even more concrete than individual human selves. Each of these genuine communities is "a genuine beloved,—a living soul,—a quickening spirit."[41] Each genuine community resembles the consolidated reality of the family that concretizes the basic triadic relation between father, mother, and child and not that dangerous dyadic relation between pairs of human selves.

Two years before he died, Royce identified the root of this solidarizing trend: people's interest in groups that comprise more than mere pairs.

> In such interests in groups which are larger and richer than pairs consists men's very desire for human solidarity. For human unions can become stable and fruitful only through the

---

39. Royce, *The Hope of the Great Community* [hereafter *HGC*].
40. See *War*, pp. 7, 9, 39, 51, 92, with cognates at 32 and 92. See also "Illustrations," in *HARP* 84, no. 3, p. 24.
41. "Illustrations," *HARP* 84, no. 3, p. 24.

establishment of relations which are very different from the dangerous dyadic relations of lovers, of rivals, and of warriors.[42]

This "desire for human solidarity" pressed in upon Royce and some of his contemporaries during World War I. For the root of the mature Royce's passionate hope for the coming of humankind's "Great Community" lay in human solidarity—both extant and still to be fostered.

At the close of the twentieth century, however, this desire for solidarity seems needed even more urgently than at the start of the century. For such "dangerous dyadic relations" as richpoor, theist–atheist, East–West, North–South dominate much current thinking. Caught in this conflictive net, global villagers can gain psychic freedom if they attend to, experience, and commit themselves to human solidarity at its various levels. The human family's deep solidarity lies in that "common reasonable human nature" in which every human person shares. Solidarity next shows itself in the *nationes*,[43] each of whose distinctive ethnic and cultural identity calls for mutually helpful exchanges among these diverse interdependent groupings. As community members of the one human family, these *nationes* have a solidarity more profound than they do through their subsequent status as political nation-states or as members of the United Nations. Their intersolidarity, then, promotes, even as it contrasts with, that frailer, largely fabricated solidarity of political states and of the United Nations. In brief, the mature Royce's passionate concern for solidarity offers a healing model for current "dangerous dyadic relations."

Mediation

A third little-noticed, yet significant, development in Royce's late interpretation-based ethics is his refinement of the idea of mediation. If grasped and implemented, this purified idea will create large dividends in many areas—including ordinary human

---

42. *War*, p. 39.
43. A *natio* is a natural human grouping formed through the centuries by a distinctive common stock, history, language, culture, and politico-economic tradition.

interactions, people's relation to the Holy Mysterious One, and revisions both of a theology of redemption and of an economics of investment. From Peirce, Royce derived the central idea of a "Community of Interpretation," even as he developed and applied it in his own original ways. He found that a Community of Interpretation was naturally a peace-loving community inasmuch as by its nature it furthers good will, unity, and loyalty.[44] Very adaptable to highly diversified social tasks, the life of a Community of Interpretation "essentially tends to enrich both the power and the unity of mankind."[45] This means that such a community's interpreter or mediator functions primarily as a unifier of wills that are simply different but not necessarily conflictive. True enough, Royce noticed that at the dawn of recorded history people recurred to mediators and institutions of mediation only when conflicts had arisen and a judge and judicial system were needed to settle disputes. Unfortunately, this led people to view mediation within the context of a prior dispute, within an ambiance of hostility. As a result, mediation became identified with only one of its forms: forensic mediation.

What Royce detected in his 1914 address, "The Spirit of the Community," was that the idea of mediation has only an accidental bond with a preceding conflict.[46] Such a bond made mediation forensic, but the simpler form of mediation is nonforensic. One can mediate without having to settle a quarrel. Nonforensic mediators, like bankers and counsels, simply aim to maintain and promote unity, even though forensic mediators, like judges and lawyers, must deal with conflict situations and aim to adjudicate between alienated contestants.

Among other applications of this key notion, Royce used it to revise redemptive theology and investment economics—to which I now turn. Unfortunately, when theologians borrowed this notion of mediation to explain redemption, they too frequently also borrowed its familiar baggage of conflict and hostility. Was this not, after all, the natural background for understanding the

---

44. *War*, pp. 46–47.
45. Ibid., p. 49.
46. *HARP* 91, no. 3, pp. 3, 7.

key scriptural phrase, "Mediator between God and man"?[47] So following St. Anselm, they tended to present God as irritated and angered by our human disobedience and thus in need of being appeased.[48] Many theologians assumed, then, that, to think about the mystery of redemption, they had to view God as needing to be placated, as, in short, the "Hostile One." Even when such thinking avoided the bizarre popular extremes of turning the mediating Christ into a "substitute victim (of a punitive King)" or a "sin-ladened scapegoat," the more restrained theologies of redemption frequently still employed a notion of forensic mediation that forced them to perceive God as the "Hostile One."[49]

Royce saw the current pressing need, then, to use a non-forensic version of mediation to explicate redemption. He said the "best forms of mediation in the practical world are not forensic...[but rather those processes that] prevent disputes from arising."[50] To start talk about redemption by saying sin had made people into "God's enemies" only too easily makes people think of God as offended or even hostile toward sinful human selves. Upon reflection, one can detect how anthropomorphism oppresses this view of God. Not many people, however, take time enough to reflect accurately that, from their sense of guilt as sinners, they are projecting upon God a hostile attitude toward themselves. Nothing is more human, nothing more misleading regarding God. Thus the warped image of a hostile God damages their relation with the Holy Mysterious One.

On the other hand, if the Interpreter-Spirit of the universal community is really a Logos–Spirit of loving loyalty toward human selves, He can never be other than understanding, patient, and ever-merciful toward human sinners. All throughout human history, He can only be inviting sinners to convert into ways more open to further union or reunion. From His side, no adversarial

---

47. See I Tim. 2:5, and Heb. 8:6, 9:15, 12:24.
48. Anselm of Canterbury (1033–1109) started this tradition by his *Cur Deus Homo*.
49. *HARP* 91, no. 3, pp. 3, 7.
50. Ibid., p. 9.

relation can exist. Thus, from the human side, there really is no war, only a misperception of the Holy Spirit as the "Hostile One."[51] From this tragic misperception, the Royce of 1914 tried to free people through his idea of nonforensic mediation.

Royce also applied the idea of a Community of Interpretation to economic investment.[52] It resulted in what he called a "new moral idea." The moral calling of the banker is to create and inspire his threefold community (of investor, borrower, and himself as mediating interpreter) with this interest.

> That neither the borrower nor the lender shall, when the day of reckoning comes, regret the loan, but that both of them shall desire to continue, through the banker's aid and under his advice, similar transactions.... In this community the greed that deceives or despoils may indeed continue to exist, but it will have no necessary place. It will at least tend to disappear.[53]

Whether these final words reveal a Royce more economically naive than the Adam Smith who depended on generally reliable businesspeople to respond to "market forces" is a question the reader may wish to examine. In any case, the late Royce chose to develop the modern man's economic insight a step further. He knew that modern capitalists had reached the economically fecund insight that it is morally just, and no longer usurious, to invest money by loaning it at interest.

First, Royce detected that, by attending to the common interests of the parties involved, capitalists intend to invest money with risk and thus create a functional union of the investor, borrower, and banker. Our "modern spirit" is marked by this kind of union. Expressing "the Will to Interpret," the intent to invest aims, then, to continue these parties' common interests so long as their union proves fruitful. In this way, Royce first developed the moral idea within capitalism by setting it into the operating context of a "community of interpretation."

---

51. Richard H. Niebuhr, a close reader of Royce, skillfully elaborated this theme in *The Responsible Self*, pp. 117, 138–43.
52. See his "The Spirit of the Community," 1914 address, *HARP* 91, no. 3, pp. 29–32.
53. Ibid., p. 32 (emphasis added).

Second, since such a community cannot be well ordered unless it belongs to and responds to the universal community, Royce inserted a criterion for judging whether any investment community of interpretation is morally open or closed. If such a community is genuinely open, then, through its disciplined process of cumulative investments, it will tend to make greed disappear and to increase the economic standard of living for all peoples throughout the world. By being in solidarity with humankind's entire Great Community, each investment community of interpretation would have to make its primary cause the greater union of all the Earth's peoples through their greater economic development. Thus all nations, rather than just a few more powerfully positioned ones, would effectively benefit from increasing the wealth of the Earth. In sum, then, Royce added this new criterion for ethical profitmaking to the intent that he required of investors: to continue the common interests of all participants as long as it is fruitful for them all.

Of all the "classical American philosophers," Royce seems to have been most convinced of the depth and power of sin and of "communities of hate." Recent scandals have revealed this depth and power in top-level chief executive officers and even more so in the too frequently shortsighted, self-advancing middle managers who operate in First-, Second-, and Third-world businesses. The question remains, then, whether Royce, even with his immersion into the problem of evil, adequately appraised the morally corrosive power of greed.

Four Insights of the First Magnitude

Having surveyed the second magnitude insights of Royce's final years, I turn to his even more significant advances in ethical content made in 1915/1916, for he then identified and synthesized the three principal ethical ideas. He discovered three distinct species of genuine loyalty. He pioneered in creating an "ethics of the fitting"—a *cathecontic* ethics. He focused on hope as an indispensable dynamic within genuine loyalty. In our present survey of his most mature ethics, we merely take a brief look at these four insights of the first magnitude, leaving their more careful exposition to a work in progress.

Three Leading Ethical Ideas

Genuine loyalty always remained Royce's way of viewing the interpretive process of ethical life. By 1916, however, he had advanced to interpret ethics as an effort to integrate "the three leading ethical ideas" into an integrated communal life:

> Loyalty, as you remember, is an effort to bring into union, into a sort of synthesis and cooperation the three leading ethical ideas, the idea of independence, the idea of the good, and the idea of duty.[54]

Familiar with the history of ethical thought systems, Royce recognized those that had emphasized primarily either the good, or the right, or the fitting. So, he chose to integrate ethical life—and accordingly to organize his 1915/1916 ethics—around the following "three leading ideas." *Independence* meant that one's ethical choices arose primarily from one's own unique personhood through one's free autonomous initiation. *The good* meant one's generally successful quest for becoming humanly happier. *Duty* meant that one so accepted the mix of equality and diversity within the human community that one also felt obliged to respond to the consequent requirements for mutuality, justice, and benevolence that fitted such a diversified community and its members. By 1916, then, Royce's ethical quest had become an endeavor to use his interpretive process to create and sustain a cooperative union of these leading ideas of personal freedom, happiness, and responsibility. By integrating these ideas into a real community of signs, which formed the focus of one's synoptic ethical vision and directed one's sound moral choices, Royce created a more balanced and nuanced philosophy and art of loyalty in his final year.

Royce's will to interpret this triad of leading ethical ideas into a life-giving unity seems closely linked to his desire to

---

54. "Comments," *HARP* 95, no. 1, p. 20.

unify humankind's three ideas of God.⁵⁵ In many pre-1916 writings, Royce had already exposed the need to unite the Greek, Hebrew, and Indic traditions about God as, respectively, the Good, the Righteous, and the Only Really Real. In his last year, when he wrote that "the threefold contrast [of our ideas of God]...will help us to make clearer the philosophical issues of monotheism," he could truthfully have added "and of ethics,"⁵⁶ for he found in this triadic contrast that the Hellenic religious idea of an order-producing Goodness suggests the ethical idea of a "blessed goodness"—the goodness of a loving loyalty "as from above."⁵⁷ The Hebraic religious idea of a righteous, redeeming Ruler suggests the ethical idea of holy duty; and the Indic idea of the only fully Real One suggests the ethical idea of independent autonomy. But just as genuine religion calls for a delicate balancing of these three ideas of God, so the mature Royce saw that the life of genuine loyalty requires a process that integrates the energy and thrust of his three leading ethical ideas. Accordingly, Royce's 1915/1916 integration of the three leading ethical ideas of autonomy, the good, and duty constituted a new and highly significant development in the content of his final ethics.

THREE SPECIES OF LOYALTY

Another insight of the first magnitude occurred when Royce's continuing studies of loyalty led him in 1916 to speak of three fundamental species of genuine loyalty.⁵⁸ His attention to the leading ideas of freedom, goodness, and duty guided him in finding three forms of estrangement. These endanger the family, humankind's foundational community,⁵⁹ in its three most basic interpersonal relationships: those between spouses (lovers and

---

55. See Royce's 1916 "Monotheism," in *ERE* 8: 817–21 or in *The Basic Writings of Josiah Royce*, 1:403–17 [hereafter *BWJR*].
56. See *BWJR* 1:408.
57. See *PC*, p. 269.
58. See "Comments," *HARP* 95, no. 1, pp. 18–32, with pp. 11–17 (the source for this and the next three paragraphs).
59. *War*, pp. 42–43.

friends), between parent and child, and between siblings. When estrangement infects these relationships, Royce discerned how needed it is both to identify the particular missing element and to give primacy to that leading ethical idea that will restore the peculiar kind of genuine loyalty proper to that kind of basic family relationship.

Through these different estrangements, Royce came to see the need to recognize the three distinctive species of genuine loyalty. If within Royce's triad of ethical ideas a different idea plays the leading role in each of these basic family relationships, then the different resulting syntheses will create three species of loyalty. Lacking its unique kind of loyalty, each of these three relationships will slip back into the estrangement and conflict that only too frequently turn pair relationships into tragedies. Royce's insight holds valid both for family relationships and derivatively for all similar interpersonal relationships within human societies. In 1916, then, Royce insightfully discovered the basis for the difference between spousal, parental, and sibling loyalties. His art lay in identifying which ethical idea needed to be most emphasized in each of these relations, without losing the synthesis of this idea with the other two that also always play an indispensable, if less central, role in each species of loyalty distinctive of the spousal, or parental, or sibling relationship.

Siblings: Independence. Thus with siblings, each is called to emphasize the other's equal freedom and autonomy, the first leading ethical idea (independence). If each sibling does so, increased union, perhaps even reconciliation and healing of past alienation, will arise. If a brother or sister principally respects the independence of the other, both will enjoy physical and psychological "free space." Both need this if each one's self-development is not to be interfered with or diminished by a fellow sibling. Sibling-loyalty, then, respectfully creates "free space" for the other.

Spouses: Goodness. Royce saw that the interpersonal bond between spouses (friends or lovers) was based on goodness, the second leading ethical idea. This goodness is found when friends' primary need for shared happiness is fulfilled. This occurs, however, only if they continue to avoid radical estrangement.

Royce pointed out that if their love is to endure, it must be "born a triplet." That is, to win happiness, spouses, friends, and lovers must tend in some way to generate their own kind of loving loyalty. Now the goodness distinctive of spouses, friends, and lovers tends to be fruitful, to give birth to a "third"—be it a child, a joint project, play, joy or some other extra good.

Parent-Child: Duty. Finally, in the parent-child kind of loyalty, Royce saw the need to tie successive generations together fittingly. This required, however, that the fullness of life be transmitted unharmed and, if possible, enhanced to the next generation. Only a sense of mutual duty can keep this channel fully open for effective transmission of physical, sociocultural, affective, intellectual, moral, and religious life, along with the fullest purified wisdom of the past generations. Clearly, for the mutual loyalty distinctive of the parent-child relationship, the idea of duty is the primary and indispensable preservative. By 1916, then, Royce had significantly developed his doctrine and art of loyalty. He had synthesized his three leading ethical ideas. He had also found that each of them was more suited than the other two for the role of principal interpreter in some one of humankind's three basic interpersonal relationships.

Ethics of the Fitting

The third of Royce's first-magnitude insights gave birth to his mature "ethics of the fitting." When Royce used such terms as *reasonable, right, worthy,* and *saving* in War and Insurance (1915), he brought his norm of the fitting to an almost explicit formulation. For instance, facing his current context of World War I, Royce stated:

> If anywhere we are to find a reasonable guide towards a solution [to our current issues of war and peace], then, my greatest question is not: "Do I love my neighbor or do I hate him?" but "Have I, or have I not the right, the worthy, the saving

relation to my community, to my family, to my country, to mankind?"[60]

In this text, the norm of the fitting guides the discerning interpreter between various forms of unreasonableness to a reasonable solution. It detects the correct rather than errant paths. It seeks the worthy and honorable solution rather than the many inhumane and dishonorable ones. It creates the relation that will heal and develop ("save") all one's communities rather than permit any of those other relations to arise that will mainly manipulate or weaken or even corrupt any or all of those communities. A good interpreter must keep asking, "What is fitting?" At the heart of loyalty, then, Royce's interpretive process required the discovery of "the fitting."

For instance, in 1915, Royce insisted, as we saw, that the fitting integration of his "three leading ethical ideas" was required for genuine ethical life. This kind of fittingness was far more important than that merely pragmatic fittingness of results for which the utilitarians settled.[61] But Royce employed this norm of the fitting well beyond the apt union of ethical ideas and proper proportioning of practical consequences; in his address, "The Spirit of the Community," he portrayed a triadic Community of Interpretation that consisted of a principal, the principal's agent, and the one to whom the agent represents the principal. Summarizing the work of its agent-interpreter, Royce had already said in 1914:

> In brief, it is the work of the agent to make this community of three act, in certain respects, as if it were one man. It is therefore not merely his principal whom the agent serves. He serves the threefold personality of his community. For only through such services can he hold this community together. And unless

---

60. *War*, p. 26.
61. Royce regarded as "wholly inadequate" Bentham's suggestion that we calculate the sum of pleasures and pains to find the "good for us"; see *ECE*, lect. 4, p. 14. However indispensable the calculation of consequences is for ethical life, Royce could not tolerate such calculation as the full sum of one's ethical reasoning. Rather, he thought that such calculation was "always required but never enough."

he hold this community of three together, he cannot accomplish the purpose of his principal, not yet succeed as an agent. He does not merely live in his community of three. He is the inspirer and creator of its own life, and of its unity.[62]

If the agent is to create and inspire life into his community and hold it in unity, he must fittingly serve the community's major interest and that of his principal and recipient. Hence, whether the agent be banker, insurer, counselor, judge, salesperson, or some other intermediary, his central role is to discover the fitting. This includes listening discerningly enough both to his principal to fit into his intent and to the needy client to fit this latter's mentality. Especially does it include a twofold discovery or invention. He must first find that "fitting third idea" that effectively indicates to principal and client the common interest that bonds them. Further, he must continue to find or invent those "fitting third ideas" that will inspire and create his agent-community's life and unity for as long a time as is mutually "profitable" for all its members.

This search for the fitting is also found within the individual ethical agent. She has her past self (A) with her choice of some life-plan, her present interpretation (B) of her life-plan, and her future self (C), which is partly shaped by her present reading and decision. Within her interpretive process, then, B's present ethical act needs to find or create that "third sign," which fits both A's choice of life-plan and C's hoped-for self. In his 1914 Berkeley Lecture, "The Triadic Theory of Knowledge," Royce made this clear:

> I am a life more or less coherently fulfilling purposes. I can define myself only in terms of my memory of what I have intended to do and of my expectations with regard to what I hope yet to do.[63]

Any further self-definition depends upon finding the fitting link between one's remembered intentions and one's expectations.

---

62. "Spirit of the Community," *HARP* 91, no. 3, pp. 22–23.
63. *HARP* 84, no. 1, pp. 30–31.

Likewise, to build and maintain an ethical relation between a human self (X) and the other human self (selves) (Y) within their unifying community of interpretation (Z) requires the discovery of the "fitting." In this paradigmatic situation for ethics, X lives with his partly shared and partly unique memories, hopes, freedom, interests, and promises. So, too, do other selves (Y) live with their partly shared and partly unique memories, hopes, freedom, interests, and promises. The problem becomes how to unite these two without violating either. And the interpretive process operating in their community (Z), being reasonable in the long-run, tries through its mediating agent to discern a "fitting" way of either uniting them further or of healing an alienation existing between X and Y or between X and Z or between Y and Z. Thus only through the influence of the life of this Community of Interpretation and its agency of wisely reasoning (Z) will an individual human self (X) be led in the end to *prefer what is better* for the whole community, for himself, and for the other members (Y) who comprise the community(ies) involved—local, national, or global. It is this interpretive process operating in the community (through its language, customs, religion, discoveries, and hopes) that leads the community's mediating agent to find or invent that "third idea" that is now *more fitting* in its long-range consequences. As communicated to X and Y, it calls them to *this* mode of action rather than any other, leaving the personal decision making to the autonomy of X and Y.

Hope

Finally, if bold hope became an insight of the first magnitude for Royce, it did not come easily to him. More than four decades earlier, when confronted in his mid-teens with physical evolution's stern law of tooth and claw, his hope had withered and pessimism appealed to him as a wiser view of the real world.[64] His escape from pessimism had come less through philo-

---

64. On this point, see the young Royce's sharings to his close friend, George Buchanan Coale, in *Letters,* pp. 104–05, 62–63, 91–92.

sophical argument and more through his meetings with persons of sterling character.⁶⁵ In his final year, despite domestic, professional, and world tragedies, bold hope arose within his diminishing physical strength. It empowered him to draft "The Hope of the Great Community."⁶⁶ His title suggested the vision of a united humankind that called forth such hope. It was kindled by advances in science, industry, and the social arts—advances unexpected two centuries earlier but tending to unify the human family. Like the apostle Paul, Royce looked forward to "this triumph of humanity, this hope of all the faithful, this salvation of a community through an universally significant human transformation, without which no salvation of an individual man would be possible."⁶⁷ He knew such salvation required the ethico-religious transformation of humankind, but the hope of such an eventually united "Beloved Community" "became the most essential and characteristic idea of the Christian Church."⁶⁸ Ultimately this hope was rooted in that community's Logos–Spirit, whose pedagogy of teaching wisdom would gradually heal humankind of alienating forces. In Royce, this hope was suffused with his humor and slowly acquired humility along with his Peirce-like tentativity and fallibility. As far as human instruments for implementing this hope, Royce placed more trust in the social arts and the sciences than in political leaders and a political federation of nation states. This "reasonable hope," then became a central dynamism in Royce's mature loyalty.

Glancing backward to summarize, we have noticed the significant ethical creations of Royce in his developmental stages of 1883, 1896, and 1912. From 1912 to 1916, Royce's psyche was transformed by his ever-developing Peircean insight and

---

65. In Royce's recently discovered account of his early studies (1886?), he wrote, "For my part, the study of character saved me from pessimism and every day I grow more surprised at the large number of nice people in the world"; See HARP-CFC, Box 1, "Royce MSS," "Account of His Studies from 1866 to 1886(?)." p. 19.
66. See HGC, pp. 25–70.
67. Ibid., p. 35.
68. Ibid.

his courageous hope in the face of tragedy. Thus by 1916, he achieved an unprecedented depth in identifying ethics' starting problematic, he reached for the first time a fully viable method of doing ethics, and finally he enriched ethics with seven insights of great magnitude. All this should contribute toward weighing the ways in which his thought is like and unlike that of Rudolf Steiner.

COMPARISON AND CONTRAST OF ROYCE AND STEINER

Having studied Royce for decades and Steiner for less than a year, I feel somewhat unbalanced in attempting this comparison–contrast.[69] Steiner wrote more than two hundred books, of which I have read eight basic works—and these only once.[70] So, as a beginner with Steiner, I speak tentatively in what follows.

From Steiner's basic writings, I learned that his interests extended well beyond even those of Royce the polymath. Royce, a self-styled Christian metaphysician, was primarily a philosopher, skilled in logic, ethics, and psychology. Steiner, an especially Christian thinker, was an educator, artist, scientist, economist, agronomist, literary writer, philosopher, and the founder of Anthroposophy. For all this difference in range, both thinkers underwent three stages of intellectual development. They both showed startling distinctiveness in their final

---

69. After several revisions of this comparison–contrast, I detected a change in my overall perception of these two thinkers. In an early draft, I concluded that despite some striking similarities, Royce and Steiner were at bottom quite different. Yet after further reading and listening to Steiner more carefully, I found that the mental worlds of Royce and Steiner converged far more than I had at first thought, even though significant differences remained.

70. Beyond my own introduction to Rudolf Steiner through McDermott, *The Essential Steiner,* I gradually became familiar with Steiner's more foundational writings: *The Philosophy of Spiritual Activity* [hereafter *PSA*]; *An Outline of Occult Science* [hereafter *OOS*]; *Theosophy* [hereafter *Theos*]; *Knowledge of the Higher Worlds and Its Attainment* [hereafter *KHW*]; *The Gospel of St. John* [hereafter *GSJ*]; *Riddles of Philosophy* [hereafter *RP*]; *The Redemption of Thinking: A Study of the Philosophy of St. Thomas Aquinas* [hereafter *RT*]; and *The Course of My Life* [hereafter *CML*].

periods because by then each was undergoing a profound spiritual development.

Royce and Steiner were philosophers of *life* primarily, rather than philosophers of concepts, or of substance, or of methodology. These latter may have played indispensable secondary roles in life as experienced, yet these thinkers kept focused on life. In similar ways, both Royce and Steiner practiced strenuous inner efforts and called others to do the same.[71] Paradoxically, part of this involved for Steiner the use of one's freedom to become docilely open to reality and for Royce that kind of docility to experience that became central in his psychological dynamisms.[72]

Both Royce and Steiner engaged in scientific research and urged further scientific investigation of the human and natural realms. Yet both regarded the physical universe as a "world of illusion" and less important than the inner life of the spirit.[73]

Then, too, both experienced difficulties in lifting their audiences out of habitual modes of cognition and into deeper ones—into "suprasensory knowing" for Steiner and into "genuine interpretation" for Royce. Finally, both encountered and witnessed the Paschal Mystery—that hidden dynamism of the Christ Spirit continuing his dyings and risings in the present members of his body.[74]

These difficult doctrines and demands may explain, at least in part, why both Royce and Steiner were misunderstood so frequently, contradicted so fiercely, and rejected so generally by their peers during the decades just after their deaths. A closer look, then, at these parallels seems in order.

In 1899, Steiner underwent a profound religious experience that he called "the Mystery of Golgotha." Thereafter, he occasionally dropped hints of its profound impact on his subsequent thought.[75] As mentioned, after 1900, and especially after 1910,

---

71. See *Theos.*, pp. 155–58, 167; and *PL*, pp. 16–17, 357.
72. *OOS*, pp. 18–20; and *OP*, pp. vii, 197–298.
73. *RP*, pp. 443–48; *CML*, p. 193; and *RAP*, ch. 8, *WI*, II, chs. 4–5.
74. *Theos.*, pp. 184–85; *PC*, p. 38.
75. See *CML*, pp. 276, 300–301; *GSJ*, pp. 184–86. Prior to his Golgotha experience of 1899, Steiner had so stressed the freedom of the human individual that he rejected the idea of humans being called to cooperate

Royce increasingly encountered tragedy in his familial, intellectual, and professional life.[76] Hence, atonement found more place in his mature life and thought. He focused on atonement as the peak in which Christian life cumulates.[77] We need, then, to examine how the Paschal Mystery permeated the late lives and thought of Steiner and Royce.[78]

For Steiner, one contacts Golgotha when one observes the blood and water flowing from the crucified Jesus into the Earth. One truly enters the Mystery of Golgotha, however, only when one discovers through this image that the Christ-Spirit thus entered the Earth, transformed the entire Earth-body, and imparted a new upward direction to the whole of post-Atlantean history.

As Steiner saw it, this impulse of the Logos–Spirit freed (or redeemed) human thinking in particular, and not simply the natural and human worlds overall.[79] The human psyche lay burdened by biased thought patterns and distorted by self-centered sets of value. For instance, one might view the "scientific method" as the only valid way to knowledge and thus constrict his or her psyche. From such psychic constraints, a person could become freed, according to Steiner, only if the Spirit of the risen Christ healed such thinking in the person and led his or her thought beyond concepts and propositions into the genuine realm of the spirit.[80] In this way, the Mystery of Golgotha continues its work of liberating thought from a work that is merely intellectual. The Logos–Spirit integrates sense percepts and images, and especially spiritual affects and will, into human thinking. These render thought holistic enough to enter the world of the spirit.

---

with a co-suffering God in carrying their crosses to generate more life; (see *PSA*, pp. 164–65). Not so after 1900, In 1902, he wrote *Christianity as Mystical Fact* to elucidate the Mystery of Golgotha, and in 1917 he wrote *Building Stones for an Understanding of the Mystery of Golgotha*.

76. *Life*, pp. 307–17, 340–44, 359–65, 380–90.
77. *PC*, pp. 42, 165–86; *SRI*, p. 254.
78. A dissertation is clearly needed to explore Steiner's and Royce's near conjunction of insights into the Paschal Mystery.
79. See *RT*, pp. 114–15.
80. See ibid.

Josiah Royce and Rudolf Steiner

On Royce's side, even if he spoke of neither the Mystery of Golgotha nor the Paschal Mystery, he applied his doctrine of atonement mainly to the moral life. Occasioned by sin and treason, misunderstandings and alienations, the atoning deed is directed by the Beloved Community's Logos–Spirit who employs his own human suffering servants.[81] By their atoning deeds, these servants more than offset the evil inflicted by the above-mentioned tragic misinterpretations. They experience the Logos co-suffering with them and bring Christian life to its peak of fecundity for more life.

To my knowledge, Royce did not explicitly apply his teaching on atonement to deeds of thinking as such, the way Steiner did. Yet Steiner, even with his occasional references to the archangel Michael's spiritual combating against evil forces, was not so preoccupied with the problem of evil as was Royce throughout his works. Nevertheless, the way both Steiner and Royce insisted on strenuous efforts, especially in thinking and choosing, suggests that both knew experientially how indispensable it is to follow Christ in his current "way of the cross" if more spiritual life is to be generated. In this way, both touched the Mystery of Golgotha.

Both let the Paschal Mystery enter their Christian lives and their relations to the visible Christian Church. These Christians practiced strenuous psychic efforts in their thinking and decision making. Royce's characteristic dictum, "It is good to strive" reflects this, as does Steiner's, "Striving in itself creates joy."[82] As for the visible Christian Church, both experienced a love–hate relationship. The Bible-based life that the young Royce imbibed from his family struck lasting roots, but he was put off by the dogmatism of church ministers and later belonged to no denomination. The young Steiner interacted easily with friendly monks and priests,[83] but his father, a "free-thinker" and non-church attendant in Rudolf's youth, sowed in his son's soul a disaffection toward much in the official Roman church. As a result, both

---

81. PC, pp. 184–86, 233–35; Letters, pp. 645–47.
82. See Royce's Fugitive Essays, pp. 342–44; and Steiner's PSA, p. 178.
83. CCL, pp. 9–19.

Royce and Steiner showed signs of being spiritually malnourished for lack of frequent contact with the Eucharist.[84]

After these introductory remarks, I look more at the convergences of Royce and Steiner in the principal areas of philosophy—epistemology, its view of the human person, metaphysics, and ethics—before turning to some of their divergences and omissions.

Convergences in the Main Areas of Philosophy

In Theory of Knowledge

Epistemologically, Steiner and Royce agreed on some preconditions for a sound theory of knowledge as well as on much of their central doctrine about it. Both insisted on starting from experiences, especially interior experiences.[85] They were anti-nominalists—Steiner more strongly so than Royce.[86] As for the mind's intentional union with real beings—realism, in this sense—Steiner was more clearly a realist, yet after 1900 Royce approached this position more and more.[87]

Both thinkers employed a Logos epistemology. That is, for the mature Royce, human knowing is influenced "from above" by the Logos–Spirit who serves as pedagogue of the evolving human race by means of his "doctrine of signs" and "Christian doctrine of life."[88] On his side, Steiner held a much richer and more complex view of numerous spiritual influences coming upon the human self from higher realms led by the Logos to assist human knowings.[89]

---

84. Ibid. and *RMPOR*, pp. 17, 317.
85. *PSA*, p. 135; *OOS*, p. 35; and *PC*, p. 40.
86. For Steiner's anti-nominalism, see *RT*, pp. 87–89, 115. In Royce's earliest published book, *A Primer of Logical Analysis*, Royce acknowledged, "The author is at heart no Nominalist." Later he attacked the nominalist view that an idea might be unrelated to things (in *WI*, vol. 1, pp. 47–138). Yet in his final years, despite his deep drafts from Peirce, Royce did not manifest his anti-nominalism as strongly as did either Peirce or Steiner.
87. For Royce, see *LLM*, p. 462; *HARP* 91, no. 2, p. 13; and Fuss, *The Moral Philosophy of Josiah Royce*, pp. 259–63.
88. See *PC*, p. 58, esp., chs. 7 and 14.
89. *RP*, pp. 6, 10–11, 49; *OOC*, pp. 300–43.

For both, theoretical knowledge remained incomplete and reached the fullness it needed only when enriched by artful practice.[90] Steiner stressed the need of artistic experience as the vehicle through which the human spirit effected this holistic kind of knowledge. His Goethe-like artistic knowing required dispositions and energies supplied from the agent's imagination, affects, intellect, and morally creative will. Yet it also needed sense perceptions and images as its indispensable guides.[91]

Although usually unnoticed, the mature Royce held that knowledge came to its genuine fullness only if enriched by an artist's kind of experience. To create genuine moral knowing, Royce insisted on complementing his doctrine of loyalty with the art of loyalty.[92] His theory of interpretation was a mere pointer to that interpretive insight, which only a skilled mediator or "artist in interpretation" achieved.[93] Overall, however, while Royce emphasized the need of an artistlike discernment in moral knowing, it was the Goethe-led Steiner who stressed the need for esthetic experience in all genuine human knowing.

As mentioned earlier, both thinkers stressed the role that affects exert upon cognition. For instance, Steiner pointed out the need to balance inquiry and critique with a childlike awe, veneration, and openness if one's knowing is to enter into reality.[94] Royce not only made docility central to his psychology, as we saw, but often touched on the role that hope and fear, sorrow and joy, adoration and love, and other affects play in ethics.[95]

For both thinkers, *process* integrates human knowing, even if acts of insight mark moments in that process, much as milestones

---

90. That is, both wanted knowledge in the Hebraic sense (of "Adam knew Eve") and not merely in the Greek sense of *theoria*.
91. *CML*, pp. 35–36, 49, 67.
92. Royce stressed the need of knowing the art of balancing a rational individualism with genuine loyalty (*PL*, pp. 199–200, 211, 289–90). See also his second Pittsburgh lecture (1910?), first Berkeley lecture (1914), and 1915–16 Extension Course in Ethics—that is, respectively, *HARP* 82, no. 2; no. 3, pp. 84, 94–95, passim).
93. *PC*, pp. 295–304, 334.
94. *KHW*, pp. 10–17.
95. *OP*, pp. vii, 197–298; *PL*, pp. 18, 282–83; *SRI*, pp. 232–40; *RMPOR*, pp. 38, 93, 120.

do along a pilgrim's path. Both thinkers "saw" something eternal in these intuitive breakthroughs into the higher realm of the spiritual world.[96] Royce had spoken of moral and religious insights from his earliest years. Much later, he described insight as "a special sort and degree of knowledge" whose three marks are "breadth of range, coherence and unity of view, and closeness of personal touch."[97] If the Peirce-inspired mature Royce disallowed a nonmediated intuition, he still held that "interpretation seeks an object which is essentially spiritual"; "it is a conspectus...[that] discovers or invents a realm of conscious unity."[98]

Concerning intuitive knowing, Steiner taught that

> although *on the one* hand intuitively experienced thinking is an active process taking place within the human spirit, *on the other hand* it is at the same time a spiritual perception grasped without any physical organ.[99]

Quotations like these lead us well into Steiner's and Royce's mature theories of knowledge. As philosophers of life, both needed a mode of knowledge that entered life, especially the life of minded beings or spirits. For the mature Royce, such entry required interpretation, in contrast to perception or conception or their mere union. For Steiner, such entry required genuine spiritual knowledge, in contrast to merely intellectual cognition, or sense perception, or the mere combination of these two.

Steiner exhibited rigorous vitality in his endeavor to make spiritual knowledge scientific—that is, to extend the "scientific method," albeit with a psychic transformation, into the spiritual world. To do this, he approached the universe holistically. He disallowed starting, as most scientists did, from the abstract atomistic hypothesis that confined them to materialism. Instead, Steiner started concretely from the whole universe, which includes the Spirit who is the source of the physical world and makes it intelligible through our senses. He saw

---

96. Cf. *Theos.*, pp. 41, 172; with *PL*, pp. 357, 394–95; and *PC*, pp. 387.
97. *SRI*, pp. 5–6.
98. *PC*, pp. 285, 291, 306.
99. *PSA*, p. 244 (Steiner's emphases); see also *RP*, pp. 117–18; *PSA*, p. xiv.

this Spirit-rooted universe by direct intuition, starting from the way Goethe saw the "archetypal plant."[100] As his scientific studies of anatomy and physiology led Steiner to see, Goethe's archetypal plant "represented, in a sensory/suprasensory form, the plant as a whole, out of which leaf, blossom, and so forth, reproducing the whole in detail, take form."[101]

Steiner's "Spiritual Science," then, is distinct from,[102] yet grows out of, the rigorous method of the physical sciences, for it is verifiable through inner experiences that any suitably disposed person can have. The intelligent soul-consciousness of such a person must be liberated from the common biases and prejudices, be morally committed to respect every human person, and enjoy a freedom that only the Christ-Spirit can effect in persons.[103] Clearly, Steiner's method of "extending" physical science into Spiritual Science also had to avoid various extremes: on the one hand, a mere intellectualistic conceptualism devoid of human affect and volition; and on the other, fantastic thinking and sentimentalism.

For his part, the mature Royce spoke of moving from a perceptivo-conceptual mode of knowing into a more fundamental mode, called interpretation, which won union with being, life, and spirit.[104] Like Steiner, he required that true interpretation employ sensory or imaginal perceptions as well as such moral prerequisites as "falling in love with the universe" and his "third attitude of will."[105] In many ways, then, Royce and Steiner seem to converge on this higher mode of knowing.

But concerning the relation of faith and knowledge, there seems more divergence. For Steiner saw a deeper meaning in the medieval controversy about the "double truth" of philosophy

---

100. *CML*, pp. 35–36, 71–73.
101. *CML*, p. 72.
102. See *Theos.*, p. 182.
103. *RT*, pp. 114–15.
104. *PC*, pp. 281–82, 285. For a fuller view of interpretation, see *PC*, pp. 273–342; and *RMPOR*, pp. 264–79.
105. See *PC*, pp. 270, 286–89, 299–302, 355–57; and Royce's many sense-based illustrations of interpretation in his 1914 Berkeley lectures and in his 1915–1916 Extension Course in Ethics (*HARP* 84, pp. 94–95).

and faith-based theology. It lay in Aquinas's ultimate inability, despite his superb achievements, to answer the question: "How does Christ lead human thought up to that sphere where it finds itself in agreement with the spiritual content of faith?"[106] According to Steiner, although Aquinas held that original sin had not twisted human reason essentially, he failed to grasp just how Christ had redeemed this power. Thanks to his own experience of Golgotha's effects, as well as the spiritual evolution of intervening centuries, Steiner held that in every person human reason now includes "an inner clairvoyant power" whereby a person can intuit revealed truths even if he cannot comprehend them.[107] This can free human reason from dependence upon prophets and mediators, because "Spiritual Science has no desire to lead to belief, but to knowledge."[108]

About the faith–knowledge relationship, Royce also held that human reason could discover the most essential ideas of community, fallen state, and atonement even if never revealed.[109] But I find the mature Royce more explicit than Steiner about various human limitations in knowing, about mysteries "on the divine side" into which we cannot penetrate, and about human fallibility.

In Their View of the Human Person

Both thinkers set "freedom" (*Freiheit*) at the core of the unique human individual. Steiner seems to have derived this largely from Schelling, while Royce drew his emphasis on a radical human initiative at least partly from Eckhart's doctrine of the "divine spark" (*Funkelin*).[110] Moreover, both thinkers anchored the human spirit self in the Eternal.[111]

For Steiner, in the evolution of the seven-membered human person,[112] unique individuality with its "freedom" is the deepest

---

106. *RT*, pp. 81–83.
107. *GSJ*, p. 191; *CML*, p. 147.
108. *GSJ*, p. 191.
109. *PC*, pp. 42–43.
110. See *RP*, p. 28; and *OP*, pp. vii, 299–332, 364–79; and Royce, *Studies of Good and Evil*, pp. 288–92.
111. *OOS*, pp. 35, 37–38, 43; and *PL*, p. 348.
112. *Theos.*, p. 39. In this section, subsequent references set in parentheses

reality. This emerges in the person's becoming conscious of itself as an "I":

> In the "I" the spirit is alive. The spirit sends its rays into the "I" and lives in it as in a sheath or veil, just as the "I" lives in its sheaths, the body and soul. The spirit develops the "I" from within, outward; the mineral world develops it from without, inward. (pp. 29–30)

Human consciousness can intuit this "I" as the soul's enduring element, its kernel, when it "becomes aware that the soul has experiences not limited by its perishable factor" (p. 42).[113]

Moreover, Steiner's individual resembles that of the Stoic, centered in his "citadel of the soul," surrounded by many forces of illusion and decadence, and thus capable of moral development "only by a severe self-discipline," which eventually must even control and supervise one's dreams.[114] I do not find Royce's human self so defensive.

For Steiner, the free human "I" makes its choices serially because it lives within a cosmic evolutionary process. Each choice of the timeful "I" generates more of the person's destiny, his karma; the overall process in which the human person is situated requires the human self's previous existences, its reincarnations, and the gradual development of its physical, then etheric, and still later astral bodies. Paralleling these bodily developments, there arise the sentient soul, then the intellectual soul, and currently the consciousness soul.

Steiner observed, in reference to one's *choice* to act, "*Through the deed* it acquires permanence just as my impressions of yesterday have become permanent for my soul through memory" (p. 42).[115] One's deeds live on through their inescapable consequences in the world and thus arises the need for reincarnation. In subsequent lives, then, the reembodied human spirit appears as a repetition of itself with the fruits of its former experiences

---

  are to this same source.
113. See also *Theos.*, p. 172.
114. *KHW*, pp. 156, 191.
115. Emphasis added.

from previous lives (p. 59). Unlike Steiner, Royce did not speak of etheric and astral bodies, did not explicitly teach reincarnations and karma, and did not compose the human self of seven members, as Steiner did.[116]

In Metaphysics

Evolution and process became dominant dimensions in Steiner. He spoke of the "mobile, flowing character of the [spiritual] world" (p. xiv). His writings conveyed, almost overwhelmingly, the sense of cosmic memory and future hope. His mind grasped the evolutionary flow from Lemurian, through Atlantean, into post-Atlantean epochs and even into future epochs.[117] When Steiner's memory and sense of destiny grasped this evolutionary flow, he had that basis for a "community of memory" and a "community of hope" that Royce made explicit.[118]

For the mature Royce, the cosmos recorded its process both in legible bodily traces—as in the Grand Canyon—and in the spiritual signs or truths open to all minded beings.[119] Steiner had his Akashic Record.[120] Because of both thinkers' deep sense of timefulness, then, it is hard to say that Royce surpassed Steiner in his stress on the "irrevocability of past deeds," or that, because of his teachings about karma and reincarnation, Steiner surpassed Royce in the latter's sense of destiny and hope. And both thinkers, however permeated with evolution and process, also insisted on the eternal: that constant all-embracing knowledge of and in whatever is real. Moving from process to spirit, we have already seen how central the idea of spirit was to both Steiner and Royce, particularly the Logos–Spirit.[121] They both converged

---

116. *RP*, p. 14; *CML*, p. 100; *OOS*, pp. 21–46.
117. See *TES*, p. 173.
118. See *GSJ*, pp. 139, 166, and its concluding chapters.
119. *PC*, pp. 288–89.
120. See *TES*, pp. 174–76.
121. See the start of the present comparison-contrast. For Royce, see *PC*, pp. 234–35; *Letters*, pp. 645–46; for Steiner, *TES*, pp. 183–86, 39–43, 50–55. See also Oppenheim, "The Idea of Spirit in the Mature Royce," *Transactions of the Charles Sanders Peirce Society*, XIX (fall 1983), pp. 381–95.

on how central this idea is. And however differently they viewed individuality,[122] they grounded their notions of it on the idea of spirit.

In both thinkers' metaphysical universes, then, spirits or free-minded beings exercise influences even more centrally than do the forces of physical nature. Nevertheless, both Steiner and Royce refused to create an ontological realm lying beyond what humans experience. Instead, Steiner, countering Kant, held that

> knowing does not consist in a mirroring of something possessing essential being, but the soul's living entrance into this reality of being.... Thus, the sense world is a semblance (phenomenon) only so long as consciousness has not mastered it.
>
> In truth, therefore, the sense world is spiritual world, and the mind is in living union with this recognized spiritual world as it extends its consciousness over it. The goal of the process of knowledge is the conscious experience of the spiritual world, in the visible presence of which everything is resolved into spirit.[123]

Thus Steiner saw spirit within the sense world[124] and disallowed inferences to some "beyond." Royce, for his part, asking "Why double your trouble?" found it useless to project one's thinking into a realm beyond experience—that of ontological substances. Instead he searched within the process of interpretation for such "thirds" as Spirit and Universal Community.

The question thus arises how the individual is related to what Royce calls "the universal community" and to what Steiner calls the "unitary spirit world." Steiner uses a "spirit sheath" so that the individual is separated from yet can osmose with the universe: "The spiritual skin that separates the spirit man from the unitary spirit world makes him an independent being within it, living a life within himself and perceiving intuitively the spiritual content of the world."[125] By contrast, Royce uses a "relation of

---

122. Steiner's individual seems constituted by its own freedom. Royce's individual is constituted by the exclusive interest of some Other.
123. *CML,* p. 183 (Steiner's emphasis).
124. *CML,* pp. 79, 90.
125. *Theos.,* p. 33.

belonging" (*epsilon*) to bond the individual to the community.[126] These different images may suggest how profoundly they diverge on community. For Steiner, community derives from individuals. For Royce, community—not fabricated societies—is equally primary with individuals. When Steiner speaks of folk-souls and race-souls, he may approach the human desire for the Great Community of humankind.[127] But such a "community" forms no metaphysical "level" of reality, as it does in Royce.

Their divergence concerning community seems partly influenced by their different views of church. Both thought that Western Christianity had lost the spirit of the earliest Christian communities and currently needed radical reform.[128] The mature Royce studied Christian communities in depth and learned from Pauline churches many of his insights into the conditions for, and degrees of, community consciousness.[129] But Steiner, even with his work on *Christianity as Mystical Fact*, seems not to have allowed an ecclesiology to affect deeply his view of community.

In Ethics

Both Royce and Steiner derived much of their ethical approach from Fichte. With him, they focused on the moral constitution of the self by deeds of will whereby one creatively fulfills his vocation. With the Fichte who said, "In the beginning was the deed,"[130] Royce and Steiner chose a knowledge-based voluntarism as the living nerve of their ethics.

Earlier we saw how the mature Royce began his ethics from the question: "Who (and what) am I?" Like Royce, Steiner found Socrates' "Know thyself!" to be seminal for

---

126. See *Letters*, pp. 604–09, esp., 609.
127. *GSJ*, p. 166.
128. For Royce, see *PC*, p. 78–79, 222–23; and *RMPOR*, p. 11; for Steiner, see *Building Stones for an Understanding of the Mystery of Golgotha*, pp. 23–27.
129. *PC*, pp. 252–71.
130. Fichte's "*Im Anfang war die Tat*" is almost a motto for both Royce and Steiner.

philosophizing—particularly for the moral development of the truth seeker.[131] Propaedeutic to this, both thinkers examined which affective basis better suited a sound ethics—what underlies pessimism or optimism.[132] Both scorned a superficial optimism. If in the face of evil and struggle a person disregarded moral imagination, he or she sowed pessimism.[133] A properly human moral life, then, required a moderated optimism. It arises out of an individual's free *striving*—to create ideals, to appropriate a life plan, and to execute it.

Thus both thinkers located the psychological taproot of their ethics in individual freedom. Royce sketched this in his *Outlines of Psychology*, and Steiner made it his starting point in *The Philosophy of Spiritual Activity*.[134] Autonomy and the cultivation of spiritual freedom became the main thoroughfares of ethical life for both these thinkers. Freedom, the first of the mature Royce's central ethical ideas, produced his three basic and radically different "Attitudes of Will."[135] Steiner, for his part, stressed the creative initiative of the human individual.[136] Such initiative develops further freedom by thinking of spiritual realities.

Their convergences in ethics continued. Both thinkers required a manifestation of the eternal in moral deeds. Both required taking account of foreseeable consequences—including karmic destiny for Steiner—even though moral decision making also demanded authentic individual initiative and, at least for Royce, some open relationship to the universal community. Finally, both thinkers held that the service of humanity distinguished a mature ethical character.[137]

---

131. *RP*, pp. 3–4, 126.
132. See *PSA*, pp. 193–223; and Royce, *Religious Aspect of Philosophy*, pp. 107–70.
133. *PSA*, p. 220.
134. See *PSA*, pp. 152–53; and *OOS*, p. 35, along with *OP*, pp. vii, pp. 299–332, 364–79.
135. *PC*, pp. 351–57.
136. *PSA.*, pp. 141–142; *CML*, p. 104.
137. Cf. *KHW*, p. 94; with *PC*, pp. 269–71, on the requisite loyalty toward the Great Community of humankind.

As mentioned, the relation between the individual and community was their point of issue. For Steiner, the individual had no other purpose than his own because it could arise only from within the individual.[138] For Royce, the mutuality of the equally fundamental individual and the community called for interactive sharing. The community needed to communicate its cause to the individual. The individual needed to constitute itself freely by adopting some communally proffered cause and by generating his own life-plan from it. Steiner placed more emphasis on freedom, Royce on being loyal to everyone's loyalty.

I also find that Royce faced the problem of evil more persistently, directly, and profoundly than Steiner did. The mature Royce spoke of a process of salvation that began if one entered the life of a saving community.[139] I do not find that Steiner emphasized this theme nearly so much.

As for social ethics, Steiner emphasized that for social cooperation, the radical need is for trust.[140] Royce, however, went much further in designing the conditions and degrees needed for an effective consciousness of community.[141]

Finally, Royce and Steiner both encountered much opposition in their lives. After 1899, Steiner's experience was charged with the Mystery of Golgotha. Yet it was Royce who emphasized "the doctrine of the Atonement, [as] the most vital of all Christian teachings."[142] And it was Royce who built this doctrine into his ethics through his "religious mission of sorrow." He saw the role of an authentic mediator to be that of a suffering servant in any genuine community of interpretation.[143] More than Steiner, then, Royce seems to have stressed the act of "self donation for others" (the *se tradidit* theme) at the heart of any genuine Christian ethics.[144]

---

138. *PSA*, pp. 174, 187–88.
139. See *SRI*, pp. 5–17; *PC*, pp. 42, 121–42.
140. *CML*, p. 343.
141. *PC*, pp. 252–71.
142. *SRI*, p. 254.
143. *SRI*, pp. 215–54; *PC*, pp. 317–18.
144. Other themes affecting ethics that Steiner emphasized less than did Royce are faith, ecclesiology, witness-mission, and covenant.

In conclusion, given where the hearts of most people in the First World are currently, many will hardly hear the challenging calls of Josiah Royce and Rudolf Steiner to enter into the way of genuine loyalty or onto the path of Spiritual Science. Perhaps this explains why, in academe and elsewhere, both Royce and Steiner stand, as their Master, "a stone rejected by the builders that has become the keystone of the structure."[145]

---

145. Psalms 118:22; Mark 12:10; Acts 4:11.

Alfred North Whitehead

6.

STEINER'S ANTHROPOSOPHY AND WHITEHEAD'S PHILOSOPHY

David Ray Griffin

Alfred North Whitehead and Rudolf Steiner were born in the same year, 1861, with Whitehead being Steiner's elder by twelve days. Had Whitehead not outlived Steiner, however (which he did by twenty-two years), there would be little to compare, because the first book of Whitehead's American metaphysical period, *Science and the Modern World*, was published only in 1925, the year of Steiner's death.

Steiner and Whitehead had more in common than simply the year of their birth. In spite of their different cultural backgrounds (Whitehead was British, Steiner Germanic) and their very different approaches to constructing a worldview (Whitehead engaged in "speculative philosophy," thinking of metaphysical cosmology as an all-inclusive "hypothesis," whereas Steiner saw his work as "science" based on direct "perceptions"), their overall enterprises had much in common, both formally and substantively. They both challenged the reigning orthodoxy of the day, especially in scientific circles, namely, a materialistic view of reality and a sensationalist view of perception. Because of these challenges and because—a closely related point—attempts to present all-embracing interpretations of the universe have been out of fashion for most of this century, both philosophers have been outside the mainstream of intellectual thought. Steiner's thought, which has challenged modern thought in both ontology and epistemology even more explicitly and sweepingly than Whitehead's, has accordingly been even more thoroughly outside the mainstream. This presents the possibility—a rare one for a Whiteheadian—that Whitehead's philosophy, by supporting some of the more controversial features of a system of thought even less reputable than itself, might lend a touch of credibility to it.

This is not to say that Whitehead's philosophy could be used to support all aspects of Steiner's position. Besides the fact that most Whiteheadians would simply remain agnostic about many of Steiner's claims, there are other points, some fundamental, on which the two systems diverge. Whereas commonalities between two systems arising from different contexts are appreciated because they give us grounds for increased confidence in these views, differences are also important because they provide the basis for progress in thought: followers of each thinker may find things to appropriate from the other.

One central difference between the two systems that is simply a difference of emphasis involves their fundamental aims. The writings of Whitehead are most explicitly concerned with truth. He is not uninterested in transformation, whether individual or social, but references to the need for transformation and how to bring it about are not central in his writings. With Steiner, however, although he is interested in truth, he is clearly interested in truth primarily for the sake of transformation—of individuals primarily, and through them of the world as a whole. This difference of emphasis opens up the possibility that Steiner may have provided a method of personal transformation that would be appropriate for those who find Whiteheadian thought convincing.

In the first section of this article, in order to show that Whitehead's Process Philosophy and Steiner's Anthroposophy have enough in common to make a dialogue promising, I list a number of similarities. In the second section, I show that Whitehead's philosophy gives support to some of Steiner's "occult" notions. In the third section, I point out why some of Steiner's views are incompatible with the Whiteheadian worldview and how this worldview provides a basis for accepting some of Steiner's views without accepting all of them. In the

Steiner's Anthroposophy and Whitehead's Philosophy

fourth section, I suggest that Steiner has provided a method of spiritual discipline that is, at least in its basic approach, appropriate for Whiteheadians.

A word about point of view and slant: I write this article as a follower of Whitehead on most points, and I write it primarily for readers who know Steiner's thought better than Whitehead's.

I. Similarities between Steiner's and Whitehead's Positions

Because the purpose of this section is mainly to set a context for the following sections, and because space is limited, I simply, for the most part, list a number of points *ad seriatim* with little commentary. Because I am writing primarily for people who have minimal knowledge of Whitehead's thought, I give more quotations from him.

1. Both thinkers saw as central the task of reconciling science and religion. Whitehead, in fact, said that philosophy "attains its chief importance by fusing the two, namely, religion and science, into one rational scheme of thought" (1978, 15).
2. Both thinkers held that this reconciliation should be achieved not by belittling logical thinking, not by reducing the results of natural science to the status of mere appearance in a Kantian way, and not by bifurcating science and religion into two separate realms or "language games," but by developing a more inclusive scheme of thought in which one can see the harmony of both types of truths. "The tests of accuracy" of this inclusive worldview, says Whitehead, are "logical coherence, adequacy, and exemplification" (1960, 86). He elsewhere adds the pragmatic test (1978, 181). Steiner sometimes suggests that his system needs no verification beyond his claim that it rests on direct perception of realities that would be perceived by others who have gone through the path he prescribes (1972: 14, 63, 280; 1986, 40). But elsewhere he indicates that his system is verified by the fact that it makes life comprehensible (1972: 92, 106; 1971, xxi) and leads to successful applications (1983, 136). Self-consistency,

adequacy to all facts, illuminating power, and pragmatic effectiveness were thus regarded by both thinkers as the criteria with which to test their systems.

3. Both thinkers affirmed that the starting point for constructing a worldview should not be objects of experience, such as "this stone of grey," but immediate experience itself. Whitehead accepted the "subjectivist bias" introduced by Descartes, which is that "subjects enjoying conscious experiences provide the primary data for philosophy, namely, themselves as in the enjoyment of such experience" (1978, , 159). Steiner affirmed this Cartesian starting point (1968, 34–35) and said: "We consider ourselves, each one, justified in taking our starting point from our immediate experiences, from what we live through directly, and in ascending from there to knowledge of the whole universe" (1968, 257).

4. Closely related to the previous point, both thinkers affirmed the reality of genuine freedom. By genuine freedom, I mean what used to be called the "freedom of indifference," which means, in Steiner's words, the capacity for "choosing, wholly at will, one or the other of two possible actions" (1968, 4). Freedom in this sense is not compatible with our actions' being completely dominated by antecedent causes, so that our actions would in reality be as necessitated as the movements of a stone (1968, 6–7). This affirmation of genuine freedom follows, for both thinkers, from taking seriously one's immediate experience. In Whitehead's words (1978):

> [I]n the case of those actualities whose immediate experience is most completely open to us, namely, human beings, the [self-determination of the immediate occasion of experience] is the foundation of our experience of responsibility...of self-approval or of self-reproach, of freedom, of emphasis. This element in experience is too large to be put aside merely as misconstruction. (p. 47)

5. Both thinkers rejected the three major worldviews of the modern world. Like Whitehead, Steiner (1968, 17–19), while accepting Descartes's starting point, rejected the Cartesian

dualism between matter and spirit, seeing that it makes the problem of interaction between the two realms unintelligible. He also rejected the two best-known forms of monism—materialism, which denies mind, and monistic idealism or spiritualism, which denies matter. Whitehead affirmed another kind of monism, namely, a pluralistic "panexperientalism" (sometimes called "panpsychism," although neither term was used by Whitehead), according to which all fully actual things experience. In an early writing, Steiner seemed to reject this view (1968, 21). In later writings, however, he seemed to affirm some version of it, saying, "There is no such thing as 'unconsciousness,' but only varying degrees of consciousness. Everything in the world possesses consciousness" (1972, 135). Supportive of this interpretation is Robert McDermott's statement that Steiner and Barfield view "the modern West as a world of outsides without insides" (1984, 293).

6. Closely connected to this notion was the reaffirmation by both thinkers of versions of the old macrocosm-microcosm idea. For Whitehead, the notion that the individual is a microcosm, somehow containing the whole universe within itself, is not limited to human beings but applies to all individuals whatsoever: "each unit has in its nature a reference to every other member of the community, so that each unit is a microcosm representing in itself the entire all-inclusive universe" (1960, 89). The world is thus radically interdependent; there are no wholly independent substances: "The whole world conspires to produce a new creation" (1960, 109).

7. Also closely related to the rejection of dualism was the concern of both thinkers to overcome the subject-object split. Steiner said that the longing to overcome the apparent lack of connection between the subjective and objective worlds was with him from childhood. Whitehead's similar concern is obvious from his doctrine. His panexperientialism is a denial that there are any instances of "vacuous actuality," any actualities devoid of experience, any actualities that are objects of our experience that are *mere* objects, devoid of subjectivity or experience of their own (1978: 29, 167). Each

actual entity is an "occasion of experience." It exists in two modes: It exists first as an experiencing subject; it then exists as an object to be experienced by subsequent subjects. So, anything actual that is an object of our experience was in itself, prior to its being experienced by us, a subject for itself or a society of subjects (for example, a rock as such would have no unified experience, but it would be comprised of billions of occasions of experience). A second feature of Whitehead's overcoming of the gap between subject and object is his doctrine that the objects that one perceives are literally constitutive of one's self at that moment. "The many become one" (1978, 21)—that is, the perceived actualities are, in their objective mode, taken ("prehended") into the new subject and are thereby constitutive of it. I will return to this notion later in discussing perception and the apparent isolation of consciousness.

8. As might be inferred from their ontologies, both thinkers were heavily influenced by romanticism. Owen Barfield documents this with respect to Steiner's thought, referring to it as "romanticism grown up" (1967, 14). In addition, Whitehead devotes a sympathetic chapter in *Science and the Modern World* (1926) to "The Romantic Reaction," saying:

> The nature-poetry of the romantic revival was a protest on behalf of the organic view of nature, and also a protest against the exclusion of value from the essence of matter of fact.... The romantic reaction was a protest on behalf of value. (p. 138)

Whitehead referred to his own view of nature as "the organic view," and said:

> Remembering the poetic rendering of our concrete experience, we see at once that the element of value,... of being something which is for its own sake, must not be omitted in any account of an event as the most concrete actual something. "Value" is the word I use for the intrinsic reality of an event.... We have only to transfer to the very texture of

realization in itself that value which we recognize so readily in terms of human life. (p. 89)

9. In line with their rejection of materialism, both thinkers rejected another cardinal feature of modernity, the denial of divine presence in the world. Steiner's whole position was oriented around the belief that a divine reality is present and active in our experience and, in fact, in every aspect of the universe, making it teleological through and through. Whitehead, after having been an agnostic for most of his professional life, came to affirm the reality of a deity who provides an "initial aim" to every event, thereby grounding the teleology of the universe. "The world lives by its incarnation of God in itself" (1960, 149). For both thinkers, this divine influence in the world was necessary, among other things, to account for the novelty that arises at various levels of the evolutionary process (1972, 89; 1978: 164, 247). This means that both thinkers, while accepting an evolutionary view of the cosmos enthusiastically, rejected the Darwinian interpretation of how evolution occurs (Whitehead 1958, 4–7).

I might add here a word about a particular type of evolution beyond cosmic, geological, biological, and cultural evolution (at least as the latter is often understood), namely, what has been called "evolution of consciousness" by anthroposophists and evolution of the "structures of human existence" in the Whiteheadian tradition. In both cases, the idea—that cultural evolution involves actual changes in the intra-psychic structure of existence—has been developed more by a discipline (Owen Barfield in the former movement, John Cobb in the latter) than by the founder. In the case of Steiner, the idea is clearly and explicitly present, even if not as prominently as in Barfield; in Whitehead, it is present most by implication. But as shown by Cobb's book *The Structure of Christian Existence*, Whitehead's thought lends itself to this development.

10. Closely connected with their divinely rooted teleology, both thinkers provided what can be called, in a broad sense, a

Christian cosmology. In Steiner, this was more explicit. He said, after his conversion experience, that Christ provides the essential clue to understanding the whole evolutionary process (1984, 22). Whitehead, by contrast, did not explicitly speak of his philosophy as Christian, but he clearly regarded his view that "the divine element in the world is to be conceived as a persuasive agency and not as a coercive agency" as consistent "with the essence of Christianity [as] the appeal to the life of Christ as a revelation of the nature of God and of his agency in the world" (1933: 213, 214). This view of divine influence, which is derived from the "Galilean origin of Christianity" and which "dwells upon the tender elements in the world, which slowly and in quietness operate by love" (1978: 342, 343), is an essential feature of Whitehead's reconciliation of theism with both evolution and evil.

11. An especially striking similarity is present in their doctrines of the divine reality. Both Steiner and Whitehead held a "dipolar" doctrine of God. That is, there is both a changing and an unchanging aspect of God. And these two aspects correlate closely with the fact that God not only affects the world (a point already discussed), but the world also affects God in return. (This latter point will be discussed later under the rubrics of the "Akashic Record" and the "consequent nature of God.")

12. Furthermore—and here we come to what is probably the most important point of similarity—both thinkers rejected the sensationist doctrine of perception, according to which our perception of things beyond our own experience is limited to sensory perception. There may be a difference in how the two men rejected this notion. Steiner, on the one hand, spoke of "suprasensory" perception, which may suggest that sensory perception is our basic mode of perception, with nonsensory perception being a "higher" mode. Whitehead, on the other hand, said that sensory perception is a secondary mode of perception, derivative from a nonsensory "prehension" of other things. In any case, both men affirmed the reality of nonsensory perception.

13. In a closely related point, both thinkers rejected the restriction of thought to the limits proclaimed by Kant, limits predicated on the assumption that all perception *is* sensory perception, that theoretical thought is therefore limited to reflection about the resulting appearances, and that knowledge of what things are in themselves is impossible. Steiner indicated his rejection of the Kantian "limitations" often (e.g., 1972, xi, xxxi). Whitehead began his magnum opus by saying that his "philosophy of organism is a recurrence to pre-Kantian modes of thought" (1978, xi), and he later explicitly indicated his rejection of Kant's acceptance of "the sensationalist doctrine of perception" and his related rejection of "the Kantian doctrine of the objective world as a theoretical construct from purely subjective experience" (1978: xiii, 155, 156, 157). By "the sensationalist doctrine of perception," Whitehead meant the view "that all perception is by the mediation of our bodily sense organs, such as eyes, palates, noses, ears," so that the data of perception are limited to "the patterns of sensa provided by the sense organs" (1933: 228, 288). In rejecting this doctrine by affirming nonsenory perception, Whitehead in the first place has in mind simply the fact that, for sensory perception to occur, the mind must prehend the body (the eye, the ear, the brain) in order to receive the data it transmits from the outer world, and that this prehension of the body is not itself sensory perception. Another commonplace example of nonsensuous prehension is memory—at least assuming Whitehead's doctrine that the mind or soul is not a single, numerically one, enduring substance but instead a temporally ordered society of occasions of experience—because memory is thereby an example of the perception by one actuality of another, numerically distinct actuality (1933: 231–35, 283–84). (I will deal in the next section with the kind of nonsensory perception that is *normally* suggested by the term "extrasensory perception.")

14. This allowance for nonsensory perception enabled both thinkers to have what Steiner called an "epistemological

monism." That is, what are often distinguished as "facts," "qualities," and "values"—otherwise known, respectively, as primary, secondary, and tertiary qualities—are all known in the same way. Modem dualism has supposed that only the purely quantitative aspects of perceived objects, such as shape and mass, which it called "primary qualities," were really there in nature to be known through sensory perception. So-called secondary qualities, such as colors and scents, were said to be purely subjective, somehow produced by the perceiving mind out of purely quantitative data. Moreover, values, sometimes called, tertiary qualities, were said not in any sense to be perceived, so that they had to be explained as innate ideas divinely implanted in the human mind or else explained away as wholly invented. Whitehead and Steiner replace this epistemological dualism with an epistemological monism, thanks to their acceptance of nonsensory perception, through which the affective and valuational features of reality can be directly perceived.

There are yet other commonalities of concern and doctrine in the thought of Whitehead and Steiner, but the foregoing list is sufficient to indicate that the two positions do have enough in common to make an encounter between them promising.

II. Whiteheadian Support for Some of Steiner's "Occult" Notions

In this section, I deepen the discussion of the commonalities between the two systems by showing that Whitehead supported at least some of that side of Steiner that is probably most responsible for the widespread neglect and rejection of his thought—his concern with "occult" realities. To affirm occult qualities and powers is to challenge modernity at its very center because nothing was more central to the founding of the modern worldview than the rejection of "occult" qualities and powers, a point I have discussed at length elsewhere.[1] Evidently a number of motives

---

1. See the introduction to David Ray Griffin, ed., *The Reenchantment of*

combined to generate the intensity of this concern, such as the desire to rule out claims of witchcraft, the desire to protect the supernatural character of the church's miracles by ruling out the possibility that such events could occur through occult but natural powers, and the desire to make nature (and later reality as a whole) entirely accessible to study by sensory perception and its magnifying instruments. However, whatever the motives, modernity began with the rejection in principle of "the occult," and this rejection has remained central to the modern mind to this day. One of the most significant commonalities between Steiner and Whitehead, therefore, is the fact that Whitehead, although he did not use the term "occult," did affirm some qualities, powers, and relations that the modern mind has been taught to consider occult in a pejorative sense.

A. Occult Qualities and Powers

Steiner defined the "occult" as that which is secret or hidden in the sense of that which "is not perceived in external nature" or, more precisely, that which is not "grasped...by means of the senses and the intellect bound up with them" (1972: xiii, 5). Given that definition, Whitehead affirmed occult powers, qualities, and relationships throughout every level of the actual world. He sometimes defined "nature" as "the world as interpreted by reliance on clear and distinct sensory experiences" (1968, 128). But nature in this sense, which is "nature lifeless" (the title of the chapter from which the quotation is taken), gives us a mere abstraction from the full reality of nature (1968: 154, 158). In reality, each unified event in nature is, in and of itself, an occasion of experience. Each occasion of experience enjoys values received from prior experiences (which Whitehead called the occasion's "physical pole") and makes a self-determining response thereto (which Whitehead called its "mental pole"). We should, in other words, think of each actual entity by analogy with a moment of our own experience. Just as we know that we are something for

---

Science; ch. 6 of my *God and Religion in the Postmodern World;* and my "Philosophy and Parapsychology: A Whiteheadian Postmodern Perspective," *Journal of the American Society for Psychical Research.*

ourselves that is hidden to the sense perceptions of the behavioral psychologist, we should assume that every individual has this hidden side.

This side of nature—this inside—is not *entirely* hidden, however. Although it is hidden to sensory perception, it is not in every case hidden to nonsensory prehension. That is, in that portion of nature that constitutes our own body, we can directly feel the feelings of natural entities, namely our bodily cells. And this perceptual experience of our own body includes the "direct feeling of the derivation of emotion from the body" (1968, 160). This experience provides us with a perceptual clue as to what natural entities are in themselves, namely, centers of emotional experience, because we can generalize from those entities composing our bodies to entities in nature at large.[2] We can then combine this perceptual knowledge of the nature of nature with intellectual arguments, such as: Mind and body could not interact if

---

2. The inside of individuals (meaning their experience) is actually even more "hidden" than the discussion in the text indicates. Whitehead's view is that each occasion of experience is first a subject, which exists for itself, and then, after its moment of subjectivity has passed, it becomes an object for others. While it is a subject for itself, it exists *wholly* for itself, being in principle not available to the perception of others, whether sensory or nonsensory. Only after an occasion of experience's moment of subjectivity has passed does it become an object for others. It is at this point that the distinction between sensory and nonsensory perception becomes relevant. Sensory perception not only perceives large aggregates rather than individuals (for example, a rock big enough to be seen is comprised of billions of individuals); sensory perception is also an extremely indirect mode of perception (billions of photonic events occur between the rock and one's eye, and then billions of neuronic events bring the information from the retina to the brain). Because of these features of sensory perception, it abstracts greatly from the nature of things, even in their mode as objects. Nonsensory perception, however, involves a direct perception (which Whitehead calls a "prehension") of objects. It can, therefore, give a fuller revelation of their natures. In particular, in one's nonsensory perception of one's own bodily parts and of one's own past occasions of experience (that mode of perception that we call "memory"), we become aware of the emotional nature of the objects that we perceive. Accordingly, although the subjective moment of an occasion of experience is hidden in principle from all perception, nonsensory perception gives a much better clue than does sensory perception as to what this hidden nature is like.

bodily cells were wholly different in kind from human experience; human experience, or animal experience in general, could not have emerged out of entities that are wholly devoid of experiences. Through this combination of direct experience and intellectual reflection, we can conclude that natural entities must, in themselves, be centers of experience.

Whitehead agreed with Steiner, therefore, that there is a side to things that is necessarily hidden to sensory perception and intellectual reasoning based on it alone. And he agreed that the way to go beyond this view of a dead nature is through a recognition that our perception is not limited to sensory perception. Whitehead said, "sense perception for all its practical importance is very superficial in its disclosure of the nature of things.... My quarrel with modern epistemology concerns its exclusive stress upon sense perception for the provision of data respecting nature" (1968, 133). The problem with this sensationalist doctrine of perception is that it "only deals with half the evidence provided by human experience" (1968, 154). With a larger view of perception, we arrive at a doctrine of "nature alive," a nature with enjoyment, aim, and creativity (1968, 154).

One feature of the difference between a "nature lifeless" and a "nature alive" involves the issue, raised above, of so-called secondary qualities. The Cartesian ontological dualism between experiencing and nonexperiencing actualities led to an epistemological dualism between objectively perceived features of things (primary qualities) and subjectively created features said to be imposed on perceived things (secondary qualities). Whitehead, the defender of the romantic poets, mocks this view of nature in an oft-quoted passage (1926), in which he spells out the consequences of Locke's epistemology, according to which sensory qualities, which are "purely the offspring of the mind," are "projected by the mind so as to clothe appropriate bodies in external nature."

> Thus nature gets credit which should in truth be reserved for ourselves; the rose for its scent: the nightingale for his song: and the sun for his radiance. The poets are entirely mistaken. They should address their lyrics to themselves, and should turn them into odes of self-congratulation on the excellency

of the human mind. Nature is a dull affair, soundless, scentless, colorless; merely the hurrying of material, endlessly, meaninglessly. (p. 80)

Whitehead's alternative to this dualism does not revert to naive realism, according to which sensory qualities as we perceive them exist in nature apart from our perception of them. He agrees that, for example, red as we see it does not exist in the rose apart from its being perceived. Red as we see it *is* a "secondary quality," in that it is produced by the physiological and psychological functioning of the perceiver (1978: 63–64, 122). But Whitehead did not hold, as did Locke, that this secondary quality was somehow produced, miraculously, out of "primary qualities" alone, meaning out of purely quantitative data. Rather, it was produced out of "tertiary qualities," meaning values. That is, red as it exists in cells and molecules is a value, a subjective form of feeling, a way of feeling. Molecules and cells can feel redly. The mind receives these red feelings from its brain cells and then transmutes them into red as a qualification of an external region of nature, in order to produce red as we see it. In this way, Whitehead recognizes the creativity of the human mind in sensory perception, thereby avoiding naive realism, without succumbing to the view that nature in itself is devoid of qualitative values.

B. *Extrasensory Perception*

I have thus far, in this and the previous section, limited the discussion of nonsensory prehension to memory and one's direct prehension of one's own bodily parts. Although these types of nonsensory perception are, technically speaking, examples of perception of "occult" qualities—namely, qualities not perceivable by the physical senses—most people would not classify them as "occult perception." The kind of perception generally intended by this phrase is *extrasensory* perception, generally taken to mean the direct, conscious perceptual experiences of actualities beyond one's own body without employment of the bodily senses. This is at least part of what Steiner means by "suprasensory" or "clairvoyant" perception (taking "clairvoyance" broadly to include what parapsychologists generally distinguish as telepathy, clairvoyance, clairaudience, and so on). Extrasensory perception in this sense involves perception at a distance, in that there is (by hypothesis) no chain of contiguous events connecting the perceived event and the perceiver. Whitehead also supported Steiner's "occultism" in this sense. Making this point requires going further into Whitehead's view of perception.

As indicated earlier, each occasion of experience arises out of the entire past world. This means that the occasion prehends the whole past, not just the contiguous past. When the "many become one," the "many" is comprised of the whole past universe, not just the past universe that is spatially and temporally contiguous with the percipient occasion—although the causal influence from contiguous events is normally much more powerful than that between noncontiguous events. To be sure, not everything from the past is *positively* prehended. Prehensions are distinguished into positive and negative. A positive prehension is synonymous with a "feeling" (one of Whitehead's "romantic" terms); in a feeling, the datum is included within the prehending experience. A negative prehension is said to "eliminate from feeling" (1978, 23). Nevertheless, the distinction between positive and negative prehensions does not coincide, respectively, with the distinction between contiguous and noncontiguous prehensions. There can be feelings, or positive prehensions, of noncontiguous objects. Accordingly, action at a distance and—the reverse side of this—prehensions at a distance are occurring all the time. Given this view, the only thing unusual about extrasensory perception as normally understood is that in it the prehension of distant objects rises to the level of *conscious* perception.[3]

Consciousness, according to Whitehead's analysis, is a "subjective form," meaning that it is *how* certain data are prehended. And it is a subjective form that illumines only a few of an occasion of experience's prehensions. If we prehend the whole past, we obviously are conscious, when we are conscious, of only a miniscule percentage of the things we are prehending: consciousness

---

3. I have treated the relation between sensory, nonsensory, and "extrasensory" perception at much greater length in "Philosophy and Parapsychology: A Whiteheadian Postmodern Perspective" (see note 2).

is highly selective. Another way to put it (the remainder of this paragraph contains my own explanation, not to be found explicitly in Whitehead's writings) is that the competition to decide which of the data of experience will rise to *conscious* experience is fierce. Only those data that have been prehended with great intensity have a chance; the rest remain in the unconscious portion of experience. We tend to be conscious primarily of two types of data: those that have come from our own past (through that mode of nonsensuous perception that we call "memory") and those that have come to us through our physical senses. These are the ones that we usually receive with the greatest intensity. We receive data from our own past with great intensity because these experiences were powerful, because we are connected with our past through a contiguous chain of experiences, and because we identify with our own past so closely. We receive the data from our sensory organs with great intensity because these data are connected to us through a chain of contiguous events (in vision, a chain of photonic events from the object to the eye and then neuronic events from the eye to the brain) and because (as mentioned above) the influence between contiguous events is normally much more powerful than that between noncontiguous events. But there is no reason in principle why we cannot become conscious of our direct prehensions of noncontiguous events other than those constituting our own past. Consciousness of any prehension is possible because, in Whitehead's words, "the knowable is the complete nature of the knower" (1978, 58). "Understanding is limited by its finitude. Yet...there is nothing finite which is intrinsically denied to it" (1968, 44).

The simple classification of perceptions into sensory and nonsensory is misleading. It can easily suggest the common view that sensory perception is fundamental and natural, while nonsensory perception is somehow derivative and unnatural, an exception to the normal course of things. The truth, Whitehead's analysis suggests, is that *all* conscious perception, whether sensory or extrasensory, arises out of nonsensory prehension. The first phase of an occasion of experience is entirely constituted by nonsensory prehensions of past actualities (prehensions of other actualities are called "physical prehensions," a distinction from "conceptual prehensions," defined below). The data of some of these are data that were delivered to the brain from sensory organs; the data of other prehensions come from other portions of the brain; the data of still other prehensions are given to the experience directly, without being mediated through the brain. In this first phase of the occasion of experience, the various types of data are on all fours, and there is no consciousness—it cannot arise until the fourth phase. The second phase is that of "conceptual prehensions," in which the datum of each prehension is not an actuality but a pure possibility, called by Whitehead an "eternal object." This eternal object is a form derived from a physical prehension. This phase begins the mental, or self-determining, part of the occasion of experience. The third phase is one of "propositional feelings," in which the physical and conceptual prehensions are integrated. The fourth phase, if it occurs, involves an integration of the propositional feelings with the original physical feelings. These are called "intellectual feelings," and consciousness arises as, and only as, the subjective form of an intellectual feeling. "Conscious perceptions" constitute one of the two types of intellectual feelings, along with "intuitive judgments" (1978, 266).

One moral of this exposition is that the objects of conscious sensory perception are largely created by the experiencing subject. On this point, Whitehead agreed with Kant's emphasis on the constructive activity of the process of experience (1978, 156). The idea that sensory objects as consciously perceived are simply *given* to experience is an illusion; they are more created than given. Sensory data belong to what Owen Barfield calls the "specious Given" (1967, 250). But Whitehead disagreed with Kant's assumption that this constructive activity totally obliterates all characteristics possessed by objects of experience that are actually given to experience (what Barfield calls the "net Given") beyond the bare fact *that* something is given. Whitehead agreed with Kant, to be sure, with regard to sensory perception. It was Whitehead's acceptance of *presensory* prehension that allowed him to say that perception can tell us something about things as they really are.[4]

The distinction in question was termed by Whitehead the distinction between "perception in the mode of causal efficacy" and "perception in the mode of presentational immediacy." In the latter, a sensory object is immediately present to our conscious awareness. It, as Hume said, tells us nothing about a real world beyond ourselves. It, as Kant said, is a construct of our own making. But it, Whitehead said, is not our only or even basic form of perception. Our perceptual knowledge, therefore, is not limited to what we can learn from it. It is derivative from perception in the mode of causal efficacy, which is a synonym for what I have been calling (nonsensory) physical prehension. In this form of perception, we directly perceive *(contra* Hume) other actualities, and we *(contra* Hume and Kant) directly perceive their causal efficacy upon us. And we thereby directly experience an example of real interconnectedness. I will turn to this point later.

For now, the second moral of the story is most germane. This moral is that "conscious perceptions" can arise whether the actually given objects are given indirectly, via the senses, or directly, apart from the sensory organs. If and when the latter occurs, we have an example of conscious telepathic or clairvoyant perception. It may be extraordinary (especially in our period of history) for this to occur, because, as Steiner said, our extrasensory perceptions are usually smothered by sensory perceptions (1986, 158); but it is not supernatural.

C. The "Akashic Record"

Another controversial but essential feature of Steiner's system is his idea that the remote past can be directly perceived. This kind of perception is usually called "retro-cognition" in psychical research circles. The *distance* involved in this form of perception at a distance is more temporal than spatial distance. Claims about

---

4. I have treated the issue of a "given" element in experience at greater length in the introduction to David Ray Griffin, ed., *Founders of Constructive Postmodern Philosophy: Peirce, James, Bergson, Whitehead, Hartshorne.*

this kind of perception are controversial not only because the perception involved is necessarily nonsensory, but also because of the widespread opinion that the past no longer exists. Even if extrasensory perception were possible, many think, the past is not anywhere to be perceived.

Steiner's view was that "the facts even of the remote past have not disappeared" (1972, 104). At least the "spiritual forces" of the past have not disappeared; rather, they have left "their impressions, their exact counterparts, behind in the spiritual foundations of the world" (1972, 104–105). The result is "a mighty spiritual panorama, in which all past world-processes are recorded." This panorama, or "Akashic Record," is "the spiritually permanent element in universal occurrences, in contradistinction to the transient forms of these occurrences." Knowledge of the past is possible through spiritual perception, that is, "by reading the...'Akashic Record'" (1972, 105; see also *Cosmic Memory*, 1981).

Whitehead had a similar doctrine, which he called the "consequent nature of God" (1978, 345). In the consequent nature, "there is no loss," and through it the transient flux of the world acquired permanence (1978: 346, 347): "The consequent nature of God is the fluent world become 'everlasting' by its objective immortality in God" (1978, 346). It is only because of the consequent nature of God, furthermore, that there is a truth about the past: "The truth itself is nothing else than how the composite natures of organic actualities of the world obtain adequate representation in...the 'consequent nature' of God" (1978, 12). Whitehead did not speculate about the possibility of our having conscious perceptions of the contents of the consequent nature of God. But he did say that this aspect of God (which is really God as a whole) influences the world, which means that the individuals of the world prehend it (1978, 351). His position, accordingly, allows in principle for the possibility that one could have knowledge of the truth about the past by prehending the consequent nature of God.

D. Divine Influence

The other side of the God–world relation, namely the influence of God upon the world, is also a central and occult feature of Steiner's position. That is, he said that suprasensory perception allows one to see the influx into individual beings of spiritual influences, which originate ultimately in the divine reality. This influence, if I understand correctly, is a prototype (1972, 52), or archetypal image, which draws the individual toward its ideal destiny. And it is through this divine influence that novelty enters the world (1972, 89).

Again, Whitehead's doctrine is similar. He suggested that God's "primordial nature" is a primordial envisagement of the infinite realm of eternal objects, with appetition for their realization in the world in due season. God's influence on each finite occasion of experience involves an ideal aim, or initial aim, which lures the occasion toward the best possibility open to it, given its situation in the world. ("Initial aim" is short for "initial subjective aim.") Each occasion has a subjective aim, which is the aim it settles on for itself and in terms of which it harmonizes its various prehensions into a unified experience. To say that God provides an *initial* subjective aim, rather than the subjective aim itself, is to indicate that the finite occasion has the power of self-determination even vis-a-vis God. God's power is persuasive, not coercive. It is only through this divinely rooted initial aim that novelty, meaning eternal forms that had not previously been realized in the world, can enter the world (1978, 247).

E. *Life after Death*

A final aspect of Steiner's system to be dealt with in this section involves his ideas about life after death. Late modern thought, which is materialistic (in distinction from early modern thought, which was dualistic), necessarily considers the very idea of life after death impossible because the person is not distinguishable from his or her body. And even if the mind were thought to be somewhat distinguishable from the brain, as in epiphenomenalism, life after death would still be unthinkable because the mind's perceptions are said to be wholly dependent upon the physical body.

Whitehead's philosophy, however, allows for the possibility of life after death. The psyche is not simply identical with the brain or some of its functions but is numerically distinct from it. The brain is a spatiotemporal society involving billions of brain cells (and their constituents), whereas the psyche is a purely temporal society of occasions of experience of a much higher type than those occasions of experience constituting the brain cells. (In a purely temporal society, there are not spatial relations among the members because there is only one member at a time.) It is this temporal society of "dominant" occasions of experience that accounts for the psychophysical organism's unity of experience and action. Furthermore, although these dominant occasions of experience unify the various experiences received from the brain cells into an experiential unity, these dominant occasions are not, as already stated, limited to data coming from the brain. These occasions of experience directly prehend other actualities beyond the body. It is possible in principle, therefore, for the psyche to exist and perceive apart from its physical body. Whitehead himself recognized this (although he himself evidently did not believe in life after death), saying that his philosophy is neutral on the question, meaning that the question should be answered by empirical evidence, if any be reliable (1960, 107; 1933, 267). I have dealt with this question at much greater length elsewhere.[5]

III. WHITEHEADIAN BASES FOR WITHHOLDING AFFIRMATION FROM SOME OF STEINER'S IDEAS

Whereas in the previous section I have pointed out several respects in which some of the "occult" features of Steiner's position could be supported from a Whiteheadian perspective, in the present section I will point out reasons in Whitehead's philosophy for withholding affirmation from some of Steiner's ideas. One can withhold affirmation from an idea in one of two ways: by positively rejecting the idea or by remaining agnostic about it. I will indicate why one convinced by Whitehead's general position would need to reject some of Steiner's ideas and also why

---

5. See "Postmodern Animism and Life after Death," which is chapter 6 of *God and Religion in the Postmodern World,* and "Parapsychology and Philosophy: A Whiteheadian Postmodern Perspective," in the *Journal of American Society for Psychical Research.*

one could remain agnostic about some of Steiner's clairvoyantly derived ideas while affirming others.

Steiner himself seemed to think of all of his ideas as being of a piece, so that there would be no basis for accepting some while rejecting, or at least remaining agnostic about, others. He seemed to think that his suprasensory perception of occult realities provided virtually infallible information about the whole range of topics that he discussed (even if he did often exhort his listeners not simply to accept his ideas blindly but to verify them for themselves). He often said, for example, that his method was purely empirical, being based on perceptions, not speculative hypotheses, and that as such it provided certainty, not mere probability (1986, 90). He spoke of "the one true opinion" about occult matters (1986, 129), indicating that others developing the capacity for his type of clairvoyance would all reach the same opinion (1986, 14). Against those who suggested that at least some of his so-called suprasensory perceptions might in fact be hallucinations, he declared that he could clearly tell the difference between objective realities and products of his own imagination (1972, 280).

Not all admirers of Steiner, however, seem compelled to take an all-or-none approach to his teachings. Owen Barfield, for example, says that Anthroposophy is *not* "believing...everything that Steiner chose to say" (1967, 76). Lionel Adey advises the reader of Steiner to "learn to discriminate between Steiner's method of discernment, the strange things supposedly discerned, and the often admirable outcome of Steiner's teachings" (1978, 25). And Robert McDermott speaks of "Steiner's radically ambitious and generally suspect claims to historical knowledge" (1984, 168). I will, in this section, indicate why I, as a Whiteheadian, reject some of these claims and remain skeptical about still others, even while rejecting the notion of clairvoyant perception as such.

The basic ontological difference between Whitehead and Steiner involves the relationship between the divine reality and the world. Both thinkers held that we and the divine reality are, so to speak, composed of the same stuff. In Steiner's words, "the 'I'...is the same nature and essence as the Divine"

(1972, 35). In Whitehead's words, "God is not to be treated as an exception to all metaphysical principles.... He is their chief exemplification" (1978, 343). Both thinkers, in other words, agreed with Scotus, against St. Thomas, that "being" is to be predicated univocally of God and the creatures. But Whitehead affirmed this in a pluralistic and pan-en-theistic way, distinguishing God from being itself, while Steiner, if I have understood correctly, was finally monistic and therefore pantheistic, equating God and being.

In Whitehead, the word for being itself, understood to be the "material cause" of all things (in the Aristotelian sense of a universal stuff that is in-formed in actual things), is creativity. Creativity is that process or activity by which "the many become one, and are increased by one" (1978, 21). It is the twofold process by which an occasion of experience (1) creates a unified experience out of the many efficient causes upon it (self-creation, self-determination, self-causation, final causation) and then (2) exerts influence upon subsequent occasions of experience (efficient causation, other-determination). God is the primordial embodiment of creativity. But God is not, never was, and could not be, the only embodiment of creativity. Creativity is also necessarily and eternally embodied in a plurality of finite actual entities. God is the all-inclusive embodiment of creativity, in the sense that all finite events are in God. But they are in God only in their objective mode, after their moment of self-creation has passed. During the mode of self-creation, their creativity is their own (1978):

> An actual entity...is *causa sui*.... All actual entities share with God this characteristic of self-causation. For this reason every actual entity also shares with God the characteristic of transcending all other actual entities, including God. (p. 222)

It is this double fact, that God has a self-determining capacity through which God is an individual over and beyond the totality of events constituting the world, and that each finite event likewise has a self-determining capacity with which it transcends God, that makes this position pan-en-theistic rather than pantheistic. And it is because each finite event has its own self-determining power that God, while influencing all finite occasions, can fully determine none of them, meaning that the divine influence is persuasive, not coercive. All creatures have the capacity to deviate, more or less widely, from the divinely given initial aim.

A point of clarification: This panexperientialist, neoanimistic view, that all finite individuals embody creative experience, is often rejected without further ado with the rhetorical questions, "Do rocks have feelings? Do rocks act creatively?" Such questions ignore a basic distinction, going back at least to Leibniz, between true individuals and clusters of individuals. The contention is only that all *true individuals* embody creative experience. Besides primitive individuals (perhaps quarks, if not electrons, are such), there are "compound individuals" (e.g., atoms, cells, animals with central nervous systems), in which a higher-level, temporally ordered society of "dominant" occasions of experience gives the organism as a whole a unity of experience and activity. However, things such as rocks and typewriters are mere aggregates of individuals, in which there is no higher-level, unifying members, so the thing as such has no experience and exercises no creative responses to its environment. Because of this distinction, incidentally, Whiteheadians would respond to Spinoza's analogy between the behavior of a stone and that of a human being somewhat differently than did Steiner, who declared the difference to be that an adult human being has "a consciousness of the causes" by which he or she is led. Steiner thereby seemed to allow Spinoza's analogy to stand with regard to a child or a drunk (1968, 6–10). In any case, given the distinction between aggregates and true individuals, the idea that all individuals embody creative experience is not as self-evidently counterintuitive as many materialists and dualist like to think.

In contrast to Whitehead's pluralistic pan-en-theism, Steiner's view seems to be monistic and thereby pantheistic. In saying that the statement that the I is "of the same nature and essence as the Divine" does not simply *identify* the I with God, Steiner asks rhetorically: "Would anyone contend that a drop of water is the sea when he says that the drop is of the same essence or substance as the sea?" And he adds that "the drop of water has the same relationship to the sea that the I has to the Divine." This analogy does not suggest that we have any self-determining power vis-a-vis God by virtue of which we transcend God. Rather we seem to be *simply* parts of the divine reality. Our "innermost being is drawn from the Divine" (1972, 35). Whereas Whitehead's position is pan-en-theistic, in that it distinguishes between God and being itself, understood as creativity itself, so that we and God both transcend each other by virtue of having our own creativity, Steiner's position finally seems to equate God and being itself, so that in participating in being itself we are *simply* parts of God.

Steiner's whole teaching about sense-free thinking seems to depend upon this pantheistic position. His view is that "the thought world has an inner life" (1972), and that when one understands correctly,

> one says to oneself: "There is something in me that fashions a thought organism: I am, nevertheless, at one with this something."... The observer who has surrendered himself to sense-free thought feels the spiritual reality announcing itself as though it existed *within him;* he feels himself one with it. (p. 295; italics in original)

One gets to a condition in which "one may then say...'I surrender myself to what "thinks in me."' Then one is fully justified in saying, 'Something possessing the nature of being acts within me'" (1972, 296). A monistic view of the relation between the Divine Reality and the world also seems reflected in Steiner's view that "the physical Earth planet has evolved out of a spiritual cosmic being," and that in matter in general "we have before us transformed parts...of the primeval spiritual substance" (1972, 103).

One reason for preferring the Whiteheadian view (alluded to earlier) is the problem of evil that results if the creatures do *not* have freedom vis-a-vis the Divine Reality. If they *do* have their own nonoverridable creativity, with which they can both exercise self-determination and exert efficient causation upon others, then the evil of the world does not imply evil in its

Divine Creator, and we can believe that our impulses towards truth, beauty, and goodness are unambiguously supported by the supreme power of the universe. But if finite matter and spirits are simply parts of the Divine Reality (parts that have no self-determining transcendence vis-à-vis the Divine Reality as a whole), then either the evil in the world must be declared, implausibly, to be only apparently, not genuinely, evil, or else the mixture of good and evil in the world must betoken ambiguity in the Divine Reality itself. And this latter conclusion would imply that there is no more divine sanction for our good, creative inclinations than for our evil, destructive impulses.

This problem of evil does seem to be a real problem in Steiner's position, due to his pantheistic tendencies. He (rightly) held that ethics is not independent from cosmology, that morality must be based upon an idea of the world (1984, 17). He also (rightly) held that "the forces at work in the world are both destructive and constructive" (1986, 75). And, finally, he (rightly) encouraged us to cultivate "a love for all living creatures, yes, for all existence...and the inclination to refrain from all destruction as such." Our "joy must be in growth and life," and we must lend our hand to destruction only when we are "able, through and by means of destruction, to promote new life" (1986, 126). Although I support Steiner on all three points, what I do not find is an explanation of *why*, if our "idea of the world" is that the Divine Reality is equally at the root of all destruction as well as all creation of life—we should side only with the creative forces in the world. Perhaps Steiner's answer is that the Divine Reality is *always* "able, through and by means of destruction, to promote new life." But this would return us to the position that there is no genuine evil, that all apparent evil is *only* apparently evil, because it is all in the service of a higher good that would not have been possible without it. Such a position is not only implausible; it is also, I hold, impossible to hold in practice because we all, in practice, presuppose that things happen that are worse, all things considered, than other things that could have happened.[6] Also, the denial that

---

6. For Whitehead, those notions that we inevitably presuppose in practice,

Steiner's Anthroposophy and Whitehead's Philosophy

anything genuinely evil happens would undercut Steiner's call for us to serve only creative, as opposed to destructive, forces because there would *be* no (genuinely) destructive forces.[7]

The distinction between the pan-en-theistic and pantheistic visions is relevant not only to the problem of evil and ethics, but also to the issue of method and certainty discussed earlier. Whitehead believed that no pure empiricism is possible, especially when that which is to be interpreted is the whole universe. Philosophy, therefore, is necessarily speculative, and "speculative philosophy embodies the method of the 'working hypothesis'" (1933, 286). One seeks probability, Plato's "likely story," not certainty. But Steiner, as we saw, believed that we can get beyond speculative probability to certainty. This belief was based, evidently, on the twofold assumption that (1) there are suprasensory conscious perceptions that are not significantly the product of the perceiver, but

---

even if we deny them verbally, should be considered the ultimate criteria against which every theory is evaluated. The "metaphysical rule of evidence," he says, "is that we must bow to those presumptions, which, in despite of criticism, we still employ for the regulation of our lives" (1978, 151). Examples of such notions are as follows: there is a real world beyond our present experience; every experience is causally influenced by prior events; there is a distinction between the past, which is settled, and the future, which is partly unsettled; our present experience is partly free, being not wholly determined by prior events; some things are better than others, and some events happen that are worse than others that could have happened instead. Most philosophers have agreed that we must in practice presuppose the truth of these "commonsense" beliefs about an external world, causation, time, freedom, values, and evil. But those philosophers who have rigorously limited perception to *sensory* perception have generally held, with Hume, that these beliefs cannot be theoretically justified; Santayana, for example, said that they belong to our "animal faith." And even those contemporary philosophers who, speaking of them as "basic beliefs," say that they belong to our knowledge, provide no answer as to *how* we know them. But Whitehead, in regarding nonsensory perception as prior to sensory, can say that we know of these things because we directly perceive them.

7. I have discussed the problem of evil in *God, Power, and Evil: A Process Theodicy*, and *Evil Revisited: Responses and Reconsiderations*. The notion of evil in God is discussed especially in chapter 16 of the former and chapter 9 of the latter, and also in the discussions by and of Frederick Sontag and John Roth in Stephen Davis, ed., *Encountering Evil*, to which I am one of the contributors.

that instead fairly directly reflect the received data, and that (2) there can be human thinking that is not significantly the product of the thinker but that is, at least for the most part, simply divine thinking. The essential point behind both parts of this twofold assumption is the same. It is that human beings can reach a state in which conscious experiences, be they perceptions or thoughts, are not significantly created by the (conscious and unconscious) constructive power of the human mind but are, quite directly, reflections of something simply *given* to the individual's mind. On the basis of this assumption, Steiner can assume that suprasensory perception and sense-free thinking can almost perfectly reflect *the* truth about reality, that they can be virtually free of distortions introduced by individual, sexual, racial, religious, and species-wide biases.

From a Whiteheadian perspective, Steiner's assumptions are not possible. Each occasion of experience has its own creativity, with which it transcends the divine creativity initially provided it. An influx of divine creativity influences, but cannot determine, an occasion of experience. Those occasions of experience that rise to *conscious* experience, having conscious perceptions and thoughts, have even more capacity to transcend the divinely rooted initial aims than do lower-grade occasions. With regard to thinking, therefore, we must repeat the biblical disclaimer, "Our thoughts are not God's thoughts." Conscious *perceptions* may, at least in some cases, not be *as* created by the experiencing subject as is its thinking, but even here the self-creating power of the subject must be recognized. Whether the data received by the psyche be from the sensory organs or not, several phases of self-constructive activity occur between what is actually given and the "specious given"—between what is received in the mode of causal efficacy and what is consciously perceived in the mode of presentational immediacy. In those intervening phases, there is ample space for one's own lenses—honed by species-wide, cultural, sexual, and individual psychodynamic factors—significantly to shape the final product. This is not to say that particular forms of spiritual discipline cannot help one reduce the distortion, so that what one creates will correspond more closely to what is actually given. But it does mean that conscious perceptions will always in large part be *creations* of the finite experiencing subject and thereby suspect.

Steiner's claim to be able clearly to distinguish genuine "spiritual perceptions" from self-produced visions (1972, 280) must be treated with extreme skepticism. Our conscious sensory perceptions are largely self-produced, and yet they *seem* to be simply *given* to us, to be simply *observations* of given realities. Yet, in reality, as Barfield reminds us, they belong to the "specious given," not the actually given. They are in large part products of the creativity of our bodies and minds. Nonsensory perceptions can also become conscious with a similar clarity and force. The fact that they *seem* simply given to a person, as given as one's sensory perceptions, is no reason to believe that they *are* actually given, rather than largely created.

In sum: The fact that some of a person's thoughts and/or perceptions have turned out to be true does not justify the issuance of a blank check. New creativity surges up in every new occasion of experience. Any person's deliverances must be treated as hypotheses, to be evaluated in terms of their self-consistency, adequacy, and illuminating power.

There is yet another way in which the distinction between God and creativity is relevant to this issue. This has to do with how, if one accepts the Jungian idea of "archetypes" of the "collective unconscious," one explains their origin. Jung himself wavered between at least two explanations. One explanation fits with Jung's monistic, pantheistic tendencies, according to which the archetypes reflect the (unconscious) ideation of deity itself. Other statements by Jung, suggesting a more pluralistic ontology, explain the existence of an archetype in terms of innumerable repetitions by former creatures, sometimes going back far into prehistory, of a particular form of feeling, thought, or behavior. It is the fact that the form has been repeated many times that gives it power to impress itself upon the experience of people today.

Steiner evidently, assuming that Owen Barfield represents his position on this issue, supported the first explanation. According to Barfield, "the collective unconscious is really understood only if you see it...as something out of which the human individual and his physical body arose," not as "something which arose out of the aggregation of a number of experiences had by individual human beings" (1976, 14). Barfield cites Jung's tendency to endorse the latter explanation as evidence of a "residue of unresolved positivism" (1976, 14). The issue of positivism, therefore, seems in the thinking of Barfield (who refers here to his own position as "objective idealism") to be closely related to the distinction between pluralism and monism. The latter, pluralistic explanation is, as I have discussed elsewhere,[8] supported by the philosophy of Whitehead (which is what the reader of Barfield should expect, since Barfield sees Whitehead as also guilty of this same residue of unresolved positivism) (1976, 14). This pluralistic explanation of the origin of the archetypes would lead one to suspect that those collective images and thoughts that well up spontaneously and powerfully into one's conscious experience are so powerful not simply because they are divine images and thoughts (they may or may not be that), but because they have been experienced many times in the past.[9]

Another consideration supportive of caution with regard to the manifold ideas Steiner "saw" about the past involves the Akashic Record. It would seem that if there is a record of the past that is in principle perceptible (extrasensorily) by us, this record would hold not only everything that has actually happened, but also everything that has been thought, said, and written *about* what has happened—or, more precisely, included in "what has actually happened" is everything that has been thought, said, and written about what has happened. (As Steiner rightly said,

---

8. See the introduction to David Ray Griffin, ed., *Archetypal Process: Self and Divine in Whitehead, Jung, and Hillman* (Evanston, IL.: Northwestern University Press, 1990).

9. This explanation of archetypal images, patterns, and behaviors in terms of innumerable repetitions in the past is at the root of Rupert Sheldrake's views, as explained in *A New Science of Life: The Hypothesis of Formative Causation;* and the *Presence of the Past: Morphic Resonance and the Habits of Nature.* I have, in a review of the earlier book, discussed Sheldrake's position in the light of Whitehead's philosophy in *Process Studies* 12: 1 (spring 1982), pp. 38–40.

thoughts are deeds.) This realization would imply that the record of the past—whether we call it the "Akashic Record" or the "consequent nature of God"—would include all sorts of opinions and speculations as well as what we normally mean by "actual facts." If so, then if someone *were* able to tap into this record, perceiving its contents in an extrasensory way, one would likely receive a wild mixture of fact and fancy. Accordingly, the fact that a person had through extrasensory perception come up with previously unknown truth about the past would not imply that all of that person's nonsensory deliverances about the past should be accepted as true.

These reflections about the nature of the record can be taken one step further on the basis of a generalization of the Whiteheadian explanation of the origin of Jungian archetypes. Forms classified as "archetypes" need not be involved. The more genera point is that any form repeated numerous times will, all other things being equal, tend to impress itself upon the present with more power than do other forms. Accordingly, if one seeks to receive in an extrasensory fashion an answer to a question about the past, the answer one is most likely to receive would be: the answer that had been given the most times. The mere repetition of the answer would give it extra intensity. For example, Edgar Cayce (who also spoke of the Akashic Record), while in clairvoyant trances, was asked what Jesus was doing during the so-called missing years (the year between ages twelve and thirty, about which the gospels of the New Testament say nothing). Now, the answer most often given to this question has probably been "learning Oriental wisdom and practice in India." That, accordingly, is the answer Cayce gave—not because it is true, but because it has been given so many times and therefore impresses itself upon present experience more strongly than other answers. Through this hypothesis, one can reconcile skepticism about such pronouncements with the fact that some of Cayce's clairvoyant deliverances, such as his "medical readings," were evidently amazingly accurate.

To summarize: The belief that Steiner did sometimes intuit truths about the past on the basis of a direct, extrasensory perception of the record of the past is reconcilable with skepticism about some of his deliverance said to arise from clairvoyant perception, on the basis of two assumptions. Not only can we assume that between Steiner's conscious pictures and the record as given there was always a creative process in which distortions and fancies could arise, we can also assume that the record itself may contain fancy as well as fact.

Acceptance of the distinction between God and creativity would lead one to withhold affirmation from—and here again in the stronger sense of rejecting—yet another feature of Steiner's position. Here I have in mind some of his statements about the future, those that imply that the course of the future, even the quite remote future, is now knowable, which means that it is already determined. These statements seem to contradict the basic principle of Whitehead's philosophy, namely, that all events embody creativity and therefore an element of self-determination. This principle entails that future events are not fully determined by present patterns of events and are therefore not knowable—which means that even divine omniscience does not include knowledge of future events. (Freedom in the sense of self-determination is not compatible with foreknowledge, and the divine experience is not thought to be above or outside of time.) By "future events" I mean the events in all their concreteness. They are not knowable in advance because, by hypothesis, every event includes a self-determining decision that is made only in the moment.

It might be, however, that Steiner affirms only the kind of knowledge about the future that Whitehead's philosophy allows. For Whitehead, certain abstract features of the future are knowable in advance insofar as those features are already determined by the past and present configuration of events. Also, other abstract features of the future are, while not strictly determined by the present, rendered more or less probable by it, and these probabilities are knowable. Accordingly, divine omniscience can, by knowing the past and present, know certain abstract features that will characterize, either definitely or probably, the future. And a human mind with acute clairvoyant capabilities could in principle have a share of this knowledge, either directly or by telepathically tapping into the divine knowledge. This hypothesis is one of many ways in which Whitehead's philosophy of universal creativity can be made compatible with apparent precognitive experiences.[10]

The question here is whether Steiner's statements about the future are compatible with this outlook. It would seem not. He speaks of "communications about the future," and even of confronting "future events" (1972, 351). A strong element of determinism is suggested by his statement "what must happen will happen" (1972, 356).

It is possible, however, that Steiner is not speaking of events in their concreteness, but only of certain abstract features of the world. A Whiteheadian would agree for example, that how the Earth's existence will be ended (say, by falling into the sun) is already determined and is therefore now knowable in principle. And indeed, Steiner in speaking of "future events" usually seems to have events of this nature in mind. An example is his statement that, "after the seventh cultural period has run its course, the Earth will be visited by a catastrophe that may be likened to what occurred between the Atlantean and post-Atlantean ages" (1972, 359). He indicates, in fact, that he distinguishes between such geological events and events in which human freedom is involved. His statement that "human freedom is...compatible with foreknowledge and predestination of the future condition of things" (1972, 363) might at first glance appear to be an affirmation of an unacceptable (to Whiteheadians) compatibility—between human freedom, on the one hand, and divine determination and foreknowledge of human actions, on the other. Actually, however, he is distinguishing between natural and human events and saying that, although predestination and foreknowledge of natural events do limit human freedom, they do not eliminate it. Steiner confirms this interpretation by saying that the "outer world and the world of soul

---

10. I have offered thirteen alternative (to true precognition) explanations of apparently precognitive experiences in the aforementioned essay "Parapsychology and Philosopy: A Whiteheadian Postmodern Perspective" (see note 2).

and spirit form, within certain limits, separate evolutionary streams" (1972, 365).

Even with this interpretation, however, problems remain. One problem is whether the natural and human events can be as separate as Steiner's assertions about the future imply. From a Whiteheadian point of view, there can be no dualism between human and so-called natural events. Human occasions of experience are greatly different in degree from molecular, cellular, and even chimpanzee occasions of experience, but they are not different in kind. Furthermore, enduring individuals of every level interact and are therefore interdependent. This latter point has become increasingly accepted in our century, as human activity has changed the face of the Earth drastically and now threatens to bring itself and much of the rest of the life of the planet to a grossly premature end. Steiner's statements about natural events in the future seem to presuppose that, although nature could affect human freedom, human freedom could do little to affect the course of nature. In this, Steiner shared what was still the common opinion at the beginning of this century. But we who, at the end of the century, think in terms of global warming, a growing hole in the ozone layer, and a possible "nuclear winter" realize that the future course of nature is not as independent of human freedom as Steiner evidently supposed. If the future course of human history is radically contingent, so is the future course of the planet as a whole, therefore, to a considerable degree.

A second problem with Steiner's statements about the future is that they are not, in fact, limited to the course of nature. He said, for example, "the wisdom of the Grail," meaning the hidden knowledge that he was imparting, "will take hold of [humankind] more and more in the future" (1972, 356). It was, in fact, about this predicted development that he wrote the above-quoted statement "what must happen will happen." He made statements, furthermore, about the "soul state...to be developed by a sufficiently large number of human beings of the sixth cultural period" (1972, 358), which is to occur thousands of years hence. And he went even further into the future, telling us what human souls would experience in the "seventh cultural period," and then in the next seven periods (1972, 359). This suggests a degree of determinism that goes far beyond anything a Whiteheadian could accept.

This issue, perhaps more than any other, brings out the radical difference between Whitehead's pan-en-theism and Steiner's pantheism. Steiner evidently believed that, by knowing the Divine Being's intentions, one could know what was actually going to happen. In Whitehead's pluralistic view, however, in which creaturely creativity is distinct from and not fully controllable by divine creativity, even knowing God's desires would not provide one with knowledge of what is actually going to occur.

IV. STEINER'S SUGGESTION OF A SPIRITUAL DISCIPLINE APPROPRIATE TO WHITEHEADIANS

In the previous sections, I indicated how Whitehead's and Steiner's philosophies are both similar to and different from each other in terms of their epistemologies, onotologies, and theologies. My intention was not only to provide an objective comparison of the two systems, but also to indicate how Whitehead's philosophy could provide support for various aspects of Steiner's philosophy. Section III is, of course, not so obviously supportive, and it will probably not be perceived as such by those who find the aspects of Steiner's philosophy discussed therein unproblematic. But those who are attracted to some aspects of Steiner's philosophy but find other aspects problematic, especially those aspects discussed in Section III, may find that section supportive in an indirect way, in that it, in conjunction with the earlier sections, suggests that Whitehead's philosophy may provide a framework in terms of which one could retain those aspects of Steiner's philosophy regarded as valuable while rejecting some aspects of it and remaining agnostic about still others.

In any case, in the present section I reverse the relationship, suggesting a way in which Steiner's thought could be helpful to Whiteheadians. I suggest that it presents a type of spiritual discipline that would be appropriate for and could be helpful to Whiteheadians (and others of like mind with respect to the relevant issues). It is appropriate because it is based on an understanding of the human psyche that is similar to Whitehead's and because it envisages goals of spiritual discipline that are both possible and desirable from a Whiteheadian point of view. It could be helpful because it brings out aspects of these issues that are less explicit in Whitehead's writings and suggests practices that are not present in these writings at all.

As I mentioned in the introductory comments, Steiner's central concern was human transformation, whereas this concern is for the most part only implicit in Whitehead's writings. Whitehead's understanding of the human self does provide a way for understanding how the human psyche can be transformed through divine–human cooperation, a way that is in continuity with the course of progressive evolution in general. But Whitehead does not develop this point. Steiner, by contrast, makes the capacity for transformation central, saying, for example: "Man has it in his power to perfect himself and, in time, completely to transform himself" (1986, 10). Whitehead (1960) does point out, in his discussion of religion, that religious belief can transform one.

> Religion is force of belief cleansing the inward parts. For this reason the primary religious virtue is sincerity, a penetrating sincerity. A religion, on its doctrinal side, can thus be defined as a system of general truths which have the effect of transforming character when they are sincerely held and vividly apprehended. (p. 15)

But Whitehead did not suggest methods to increase the "sincerity" and "vividness" with which religious truths are apprehended in order to increase their transforming power. This Steiner sought to do.

Steiner also stressed, in a way Whitehead did not, the importance to the world in general of self-transformation, saying that the state of one's soul affects not only one's future self and those upon whom one has bodily effects, but the world as a whole. Whitehead does point out that every private fact becomes a public fact (1978, 290) and that every event affects, to some degree, the entire future. And, as discussed in Section II, he allows that every occasion of experience influences the noncontiguous future not only indirectly, through a route of contiguous occasions, but also directly, so that influence at a distance occurs. This means that a moment of human experience influences other souls not only directly, through the person's bodily movements and sound, but also directly, soul to soul. These latter points, however, are hardly thematized; most Whitehead scholars have not even noticed them. Steiner, on the other hand, makes these points explicitly. He says "every feeling produces an effect, just as does every action of our hand" (1986, 122). Accordingly, "a wrong thought in [one's] mind may have as devastating an effect upon other thoughts that spread life in the thought world as the effect wrought by a bullet fired at random upon the physical objects it hits" (1986, 42). Therefore, one's thoughts and feelings are as important for the world as [one's] actions. It must be realized that it is equally injurious to hate a fellow being as to strike him. The realization will then follow that by perfecting ourselves we accomplish something not only for ourselves, but also for the whole world. The world derives equal benefit from our untainted feelings and thoughts as from our good demeanor. (p. 121)

> Through spiritual discipline, Steiner (1972) says, one comes to see that the welfare and misfortune of the individual is intimately bound up with the welfare or misfortune of the whole world. The human being comes to understand that he injures the whole universe and all its beings by not developing *his* forces in the proper way. If he lays waste his life by losing the relationship with the suprasensory, he not only destroys something in his own inner being—the decaying of which can lead him finally to despair—but because of his weakness he creates a hindrance to the evolution of the whole world in which he lives. (pp. 15–16; italics in original)

Besides stressing the possibility and importance of spiritual discipline, Steiner portrays goals of spiritual discipline to which Whiteheadians can assent. As mentioned in Section I, both Steiner and Whitehead want to overcome the gap between subject and object. For both Steiner and Whitehead, the problem is that, although our soul is not really separate from the rest of the world, our *conscious* experience seems to itself to be isolated. Barfield (1967) describes Steiner's view as follows:

> The Consciousness Soul indicates the maximum point of self-consciousness, the point at which the individual feels himself to be entirely cut off from the surrounding cosmos and is *for that reason* fully conscious of himself as an individual. He has attained complete self-consciousness—at the cost of practically everything else. (p 72)

Whitehead's explanation for the isolation felt by consciousness depends upon the analysis of the phases of experience described before. According to this analysis, consciousness arises, if it does arise, only in the fourth phase, when the integration of the products of earlier phases produce intellectual feelings. Accordingly, "consciousness arises only in a late derivative phase of complex integrations" (1978, 162). The reason consciousness seems cut off from the world is the fact that "consciousness primarily illuminates the higher phase in which it arises, and only illuminates earlier phases derivatively, as they remain components in the higher phase" (1978, 162). That is, our experience in its totality is *not* cut off from the world. In the first phase of an occasion of experience, in which perception in the mode of causal efficacy occurs, the past world flows into the new experience and, in fact, is constitutive of its first phase. And in this phase there is a conformity of subjective form: the feeling of the past experience is felt with sympathy (1978, 162); that is, the present experience has the same emotion as the past experience had. But, although this is the reality, most of this reality is lost in what appears clearly and distinctly in consciousness because consciousness primarily lights up the final phase, rather than the first phase, of a moment of experience.

> Consciousness only dimly illuminates the prehensions in the mode of causal efficacy, because these prehensions are primitive elements in our experience. But prehensions in the mode of presentational immediacy are among those prehensions which we enjoy with the most vivid consciousness. These

prehensions are late derivatives in the concresence of an experient subject. (p. 162)

In other words, the physical phase of an occasion of experience, which is constituted by physical prehensions, or perceptions in the mode of causal efficacy, is truly connected with the past world. But once this phase has occurred, the monad's windows are closed, as it were, and the mental phases of the occasion begin. In these mental phases, the occasion is autonomous, self-determining, self-constructing. Consciousness, when it arises, illumines primarily the final phase of this autonomous mentality. This means that *it illumines the experience primarily insofar as the experience is self-constructed and therefore independent,* leaving in the dark the fact that the occasion was initially constructed by the past world and therefore dependent upon the totality of the past. In seeing mentality as autonomous, cut off from the surrounding world, then, consciousness is not deluded. The occasion's mental pole really is autonomous. An illusion occurs only insofar as we equate ourselves with our mental experience alone, losing sight altogether of the physical experience from which it arose.

Whitehead's chief criticism of modern philosophy is that it has lost sight of this physical perception of other actualities. As fashioned by Descartes, Locke, Hume, and Kant, this philosophy has accepted a subjectivist view of the datum of experience, according to which the datum can be analyzed wholly in terms of eternal objects, otherwise called forms, universals, or sensory data (1978, 157). This subjectivist principle implies solipism, the position that we have no knowledge of the existence of other actualities. It leads to Descartes's treatment of the mind as an independent substance, meaning "it requires no other actual entity to exist" (1978, 160). It leads to a world of "individual substances, each with its private world of qualities and sensations" (1978, 160). This is an illusion, but it has been a very powerful illusion, one that modern philosophy, far from overcoming, has accentuated.

A central purpose of Whitehead's philosophy is to explain how this illusion arises and how to overcome it. "Philosophy," he says, "is the self-correction by consciousness of its own initial excess of subjectivity" (1978, 15). By this "initial excess of subjectivity," he means just what was explained above, the fact that consciousness initially, when it first arises, creates the sense that the experiencing subject is wholly subjective, not rooted in objective reality. Whitehead (1978) says that it is the task of consciousness, thinking philosophically, to "recover the totality" from which the occasion of experience arises *"and which it embodies,"* thus overcoming this initial excess of subjectivity and thereby the sense of isolation. The complete statement is as follows:

> Philosophy is the self-correction by consciousness of its own initial excess of subjectivity. Each actual occasion contributes to the circumstances of its origin additional formative elements deepening its own peculiar individuality. Consciousness is only the last and greatest of such elements by which the selective character of the individual obscures the external totality from which it originates and which it embodies. An actual individual, of such higher grade, has solidarity with the totality of things by reason of its sheer actuality; but it has attained its individual depth of being by a selective emphasis limited to its own purposes. The task of philosophy is to recover the totality obscured by the selection. It replaces in rational experience what has been submerged in the higher sensitive experience and has been sunk yet deeper by the initial operations of consciousness itself. (p. 15)

A question this passage raises is whether philosophy by itself is sufficient to overcome the sense of alienation that is thereby inevitably produced, at least in our present period, in which we tend to identify our self with our consciousness. In his analytical index, Whitehead refers to this passage as "Subjectivity and the Metaphysical Correction" (1978, xvii). But is a metaphysical, in the absence of an experiential, correction sufficient? Can the deep divorce between experience and nature, with the resulting emotional, aesthetic, and religious impoverishment, be healed simply by making the correction in "rational experience"? Must not the recovery go deeper? Whitehead is correct that his philosophy "abolishes the detached mind" and recovers "the solidarity of the universe" (1978, 56). But must not this abolition and recovery sink deeper than our thoughts, becoming basic to the very way we experience ourselves in the world? This was Steiner's view, and he proposed his method of spiritual discipline largely to overcome the felt gap between consciousness and reality.

Besides the other benefits that this experienced sense of connection with "the totality" would bring, it can lead, as most religions stress, to a transformation from egoism to a sense of love and concern for others, even for all things. Whitehead sees this goal as the only solution to the problem of morality. "The antithesis between the general good and the individual interest can be abolished only when the individual is such that its interest is the general good" (1978, 15). Steiner (1986) presents this attitude as the result of his method of spiritual discipline:

> The individual frees himself from everything which depends only upon the faculties of his own personal nature. He ceases to view things from his own separate standpoint, and the boundaries of his own narrow self, fettering him to this point of view disappear.... This is liberation.... It is from this personal manner of regarding things that the student must become liberated and free. (p. 174)

Over and above the fact that the goals of Steiner's spiritual discipline are attractive to a Whiteheadian, the presuppositions of his method are harmonious with Whitehead's views about the nature of experience and the divine purpose. I begin with the nature of experience; the key notion here is the rejection of faculty psychology.

The first step in the training Steiner advocates is training in devotion. This is the soul's first transformation. "[The student's] entire inner life is flooded by this basic feeling of devotion for everything which is truly venerable.... Just as the sun's rays vivify everything living, so does reverence in the student vivify all feelings of the soul" (1986, 12). Steiner then comments:

> It is not easy, at first, to believe that feelings like reverence and respect have anything to do with cognition. This is due to the

fact that we are inclined to set cognition aside as a faculty by itself—one that stands in no relation to what otherwise occurs in the soul. In so thinking, we do not bear in mind that it is the soul which exercises the faculty of cognition; and feelings are for the soul what food is for the body. (pp. 12–13)

The rejection of faculty psychology is also central to Whitehead's philosophy, so central that it is included in the list in the preface of *Process and Reality* (1978) of nine "prevalent habits of thought" that are repudiated by his philosophy (p. xiii). Cognition, or knowing, is not something that occurs in a separate department of the soul that is sheltered from the rest of the soul—its feelings, desires, and purposes. To say that it is the "cognitive faculty" that knows would be to commit the "fallacy of misplaced concreteness" (1926, 75), because one would be equating an abstraction with a concrete actuality. It would be to violate the "ontological principle," which says that only actualities can act—that all activities are performed by full-fledged actual entities, never by abstractions therefrom (1978: 24, 43, 256). It is the occasions of experience as a whole that act, and this includes the activity of knowing. The soul as a whole knows, and this means that knowing is not divorced from feeling. Knowledge, in fact, says Whitehead the cryptoromantic, is only a particular kind of feeling—an intellectual feeling. And by the category of subjective unity, "each of [the feelings of an occasion] is conditioned by the other feelings" (1978, 233). Accordingly, the highest type of feelings, those intellectual feelings that we normally refer to as "thoughts," are not separable from those emotional responses that are normally indicated by the word "feelings."

This approach to spiritual discipline is in harmony with Whitehead's views on the relations among intensity, desire, and self-transformation. To see this requires a technical discussion of one more concept in Whitehead's philosophy, that of "hybrid physical feelings." A physical feeling in general, as explained earlier, is a feeling in which the datum is a previous actuality (in contrast with a conceptual feeling, in which the object is a possibility, an eternal object). Physical feelings are then distinguishable into two forms, pure and hybrid. In a *pure* physical feeling, the previous occasion of experience is felt in terms of *its* physical pole (1978, 245–46), which means in terms of data that it had simply taken over from the past and repeated. In a series of pure physical feelings, no novelty is introduced. Each occasion of experience simply repeats what it received and passes it on to subsequent occasions. Nonliving, enduring individuals, such as molecules, maintain their stability, century after century, through this method of self-perpetuation. In a *hybrid* physical feeling, by contrast, the prior occasion of experience is felt in terms of its mental pole (1978: 107, 246). It is in the mental pole with its self-determination, that novel forms may arise. The rate with which novel forms (or eternal objects) arise in the mental poles, the novelty of these forms (that is, the extent to which they diverge from received forms) and the intensity with which they are entertained are the measures of an enduring individual's grade. In low-grade, nonliving individuals, such as atoms and ordinary molecules, novelty is rare and entertained with little intensity. It is with the rise of what we call "life" that novelty arises often and is felt with considerable intensity. In any case, in a hybrid physical feeling, the novelty that was felt mentally in the prehended occasion is felt physically by the prehending occasion.

To explain further: A form or eternal object is a pure possibility. To feel an eternal object mentally is to feel it *as a possibility*. It is to feel it as an appetition. In fact, a conceptual feeling can also be called an "appetition" (1978, 32–33). When occasions of experience comprising an enduring individual feel an eternal object conceptually, or with appetition, that eternal object is an ingredient in the enduring individual, but only in a *restricted* way. It is realized only as a mere possibility, and thereby it does not confer definiteness upon the individual (1978, 290–91). It does not really change its shape (whether literally or metaphorically). But when a hybrid physical feeling occurs, the eternal object that was previously felt only with appetition is now felt physically, so that it is *unrestrictedly* realized. It now does confer definiteness upon the individual. The novel possibility is no longer simply felt appetitively as a possibility; it now actually characterizes the experience.

It is the difference, for example, between wanting to love all sentient beings and actually loving them.

Once the hybrid physical feeling has occurred, so that the novel possibility is felt physically, it can then be appropriated by subsequent occasions of that enduring individual simply by means of pure physical prehensions. The novel possibility has then become "canalized" (1978, 107–08). This is the way that progressive evolution in general occurs and the way the growth and transformation of the human soul in particular occurs. And, of course, it occurs much more regularly and rapidly in a human soul than in biological evolution. In fact, a "living person" is defined by Whitehead in terms of the prevalence of hybrid physical feelings. Any enduring individual, whether a human soul or a proton, is a "person" in the most general sense (1978, 90). A person is a *living* person if, and to the degree that, the prehensions connecting occasion to occasion are *hybrid* physical prehensions (1978, 107). This is the case supremely, on our planet in any case, in human beings. The fact that we relate to our past occasions of experience by means of hybrid as well as pure physical feelings means that the novel possibilities entertained appetitively in one moment can become actual features of our existence in the next moment, so that we can continually be transformed by novelty. Whitehead, in fact, defines human beings in terms of this relationship of our souls to novelty: "The definition of mankind is that in this genus of animals the central activity has been developed on the side of its relationship to novelty" (1968, 26).

The point to stress in relationship to Steiner's method of spiritual discipline is that intensity of thought, feeling, and desire is crucial. It is when the novel possibility for one's own existence is felt with sufficient desire or appetite that a hybrid physical feeling can occur. Entertaining the thought and feeling about this novel possibility with sufficient intensity and for a sufficient time allows them, in Steiner's words, "to bore themselves into the soul."

Accordingly, although there are some aspects of Steiner's method of spiritual discipline that a Whiteheadian might reject or ignore, the basic approach is one that seems fully appropriate. It is this side of Steiner's writings, I suggest, from which Whiteheadians and others of like mind might have the most to gain.

The previous quotation from Steiner (1986) ended with the notion that feelings are food for the soul. He continued:

> If we give the body stones in place of bread, its activity will cease. It is the same with the soul. Veneration, homage, devotion are like nutriment making it healthy and strong, especially strong for the activity of cognition. Disrespect, antipathy, underestimation of what deserves recognition, all exert a paralyzing and withering effect on this faculty of cognition.... A soul which harbors feelings of reverence and devotion...receives intelligence of facts in its environment of which it had hitherto no idea. Reverence awakens in the soul a sympathetic power through which we attract qualities in the beings around us, which would otherwise remain concealed. (pp. 13-14)

The idea expressed here, that reverence will allow us consciously to perceive new things extrasensorily, is not explicitly stated by Whitehead. But it is certainly consistent with his principles. The idea that the soul feeds on feelings is for him a literal truth: each occasion of the soul's life is nothing but a creative synthesis of a multitude of feelings. And the idea of sympathy is not foreign. Whitehead (1978) said:

> The primitive form of physical experience is emotional—blind emotion—received as felt elsewhere in another occasion and conformally appropriated as a subjective passion. In the language appropriate to the higher stages of experience, the primitive element is *sympathy*, that is, feeling the feeling *in* another and feeling conformally *with* another. (p. 162; italics in original)

Given this primacy of sympathy and the fact, previously discussed, that Whitehead allows prehension at a distance, it is not much of a jump to infer that reverence and devotion for other souls would, by increasing one's sympathy for their feelings, open one to receiving their feelings with more intensity and thereby to becoming conscious of their feelings. Love is a tie that binds; in this case it would bind souls together telepathically. From this point, it is not a great jump to reach Steiner's point, that reverence for beings in general might open us up to conscious knowledge of qualities of beings in general of which we had previously no conscious knowledge. This is a possible truth that Whiteheadians could learn from Steiner, and, if it is an actual truth, it is one that they might verify for themselves, by following Steiner's method of spiritual discipline.

A central feature of Steiner's method that makes it peculiarly appropriate for Whiteheadians is that it begins by intensifying certain thoughts and feelings. Many forms of spiritual discipline are predicated on the belief that spiritual growth can occur only through the diminishment, perhaps elimination, of all thoughts and feelings, including all emotional responses. This puts these forms of spiritual discipline at odds with a Whiteheadian outlook, according to which the divine aim is directed towards the intensification of experience (1978: 105, 249; 1968, 94). But Steiner's approach is different. In *Knowledge of Higher Worlds and Its Attainment* (1986), he says:

> [No] fantastic, mysterious practices are required for the attainment of higher knowledge.... [A] start has to be made with the thoughts and feelings with which we continually live.... Everyone must say to himself: *"In my own world of thought and feeling the deepest mysteries lie hidden, only hitherto I have been unable to perceive them."* (p. 59; italics in original)

Here, there is agreement with Whitehead's view of experience, as discussed earlier. Each occasion of experience arises out of the whole past universe and is a microcosm, containing that universe, including God, within itself. If we could become fully conscious of the feelings at the base of our experience in each moment, we would indeed know "the deepest mysteries." The way to deeper knowledge is through, not around, our feelings.

Steiner then suggests particular contemplative practices, in which one is to "form with intensity the right kind of thoughts, and through these thoughts develop certain feelings" (1986, 60). In this practice, there is no denigration of thought, as in many forms of meditation. Thoughts as such are not regarded as inauthentic, as distractions, or as merely epiphenomenal. Rather, thoughts entertained with intensity are seen to be capable of making a difference for the better. Compare this estimation of the power of thoughts, held intensely, with Whitehead's statement about religion, which was quoted earlier: "A religion, on its doctrinal side, can...be defined as a system of general truths which have the effect of transforming character when they are sincerely held and vividly apprehended" (1960, 14).

The importance of intensity is emphasized over and over by Steiner (1986):

> Particular stress must be laid on the following point: what the student thinks he must also feel with intensity.... And sufficient time must be taken to allow the thought and the feeling which is coupled with it to bore themselves into the soul, as it were. (p. 62)

Steiner says that these thoughts and feelings, held intensely over a period of time, will produce real change. Closely related is Steiner's teaching about desire. In contrast with those who teach that we should overcome all desire, including the desire for enlightenment, Steiner demurs, saying that the proper path is to *educate* the desires. We should not try to eliminate the desire for spiritual knowledge and self-transformation, "for if we are to attain something we must also desire it" (1986, 103). Steiner's position here depends on his belief that "desire will always tend to fulfillment if backed by a particular force" (1986, 103). "We should learn," he says, "to cherish and foster a particular desire in such a way that it brings with it its own fulfillment" (1986, 104).

John Dewey

7

John Dewey's Project for "Saving the Appearances"

Exploring Implications for Education and Ethics

Douglas Sloan

Many persons today, often from very different perspectives, are concerned with the relation between education and ethics. Increasingly, the question is asked, "What and whose is the responsibility within modern education for, as a common expression puts it, 'the teaching of values?'" While much attention is currently given to this question, a deeper, more fundamental issue goes largely unaddressed. This has to do with the relation between ethics and the dominant conceptions of knowledge that determine and guide modern education and consciousness. Still today, as in Dewey's time, the dominant conception of knowledge is that represented and epitomized by the methods of science. As important as they might otherwise be thought to be, ethics, values, and even religion are all usually seen as having little or nothing to do with our ways of knowing and our knowledge as such, and, as a result, their central and primary place in education is always subject to question.

Throughout his life, John Dewey concerned himself with just this split between knowledge, as defined by science, on the one hand, and ethics and human values, on the other. It was a separation that he was convinced worked untold mischief in modern society, and much of Dewey's lifelong thought was devoted in one way or another to overcoming it. "Certainly," he wrote, "one of the most genuine problems of modern life is the reconciliation of the scientific view of the universe with the claims of the moral life."[1] Repeatedly, Dewey identified the gap between man's knowledge of the world in which he lives as given by natural science and "the values and purposes that should direct his conduct" as "the deepest problem of modern life."[2] This split Dewey saw as basic and central among all those dualisms of the modern world that his life's work was devoted to overcoming. My own study of the epistemology of Rudolf Steiner has made me aware that although Dewey addressed the central problem of our time, he was unable to develop his solution to it fully.

This article will explore three things. The first section will look at Dewey's work to overcome the dualism of science and values. The second section will explore what I see to be some of the inherent problems and shortcomings in Dewey's solution to the modern knowledge–value split that must be dealt with, if his solution is to fulfill whatever promise it may have. The last section will suggest that Dewey is forced to assume tacitly a larger, more capacious view of knowing, a qualitative way of knowing, than his explicit solution, strictly adhered to, permits. In this last section, I will look at some of the far-reaching implications for education and culture that result from this larger conception of knowing, especially in its artistic dimensions that Dewey draws upon without acknowledging that he is doing so. Here it will be argued that it is precisely this qualitative way of knowing that must be acknowledged and further developed, if Dewey's own most important intentions are to be fully realized. Throughout all sections of this article, I will be drawing on my understanding of the work of Rudolf Steiner and the well-established experience of Waldorf Education that is grounded in just such a rich and detailed qualitative way of knowing.

---

1. Dewey, *Philosophy and Civilization*, p. 43.
2. Dewey, *Quest for Certainty; A Study of the Relation of Knowledge and Action*. Gifford Lecturer 1929, pp. 255–256, passim.

Reconciling Science and Values—
Instrumental Knowing and Aesthetic Experience

In the autobiographical sketch, "From Absolutism to Experimentalism," which he wrote in 1930, Dewey described how as a young man he read Harriet Matineau's rendering of Auguste Comte's philosophy. Among Comte's notions that Dewey said especially impressed him was "the idea of a synthesis of science that should be a regulative method of an organized social life."[3] Here we see Dewey placing himself in the tradition of modern positivism in the affirmation of certain ideas of one of the greatest of the nineteenth century positivists. But Dewey was not a positivist pure and simple.

To be sure, there have been different varieties of positivism. However, common to all, from nineteenth-century Comteanism to twentieth-century logical positivism, is the assumption that science is the only method for attaining true knowledge of any kind. From this there flows a second assumption that, where in any area of human endeavor true knowledge is to be had, science must be brought to bear. A final assumption that many, though not all, positivists have held is that, because science is regarded as the only source of knowledge, it can provide an all-encompassing view of the essential nature of reality based on its findings, that it can, in other words, be raised from scientific method to a scientific view of the world.[4] Dewey accepted the first two assumptions of positivism but rejected the third. It was this last assumption that he saw as fundamentally responsible for the knowledge–value split that lay at the bottom of the ethical-meaning crisis of the modern world.

Although the story of the origins of the modern knowledge–value split is a familiar one, its full implications are still too

---

3. Dewey, "From Absolutism to Experimentalism," in *The Philosophy of John Dewey*, vol. 1, p. 8.
4. Yet another assumption, so deeply ingrained that it remains almost never questioned, even in those rare instances when it is brought to light, is that there is only one method possible of scientifically studying nature, namely, that method based on quantitative measurement and abstraction. As I hope this article suggests, even this assumption need not remain sacrosanct.

seldom grasped and understood. Let us, therefore, briefly recall that story as Dewey himself told it, for his account not only goes to the heart of the matter, it also lays the basis for understanding his own attempted solution.[5]

Modern science had its origins partly in the decision that, as a method for understanding nature, it had to exclude from its purview all qualities and forces that could not be directly perceived through the senses and interpreted in terms of physical cause and effect. As early as Galileo, the distinction was made between primary qualities and secondary qualities in experience. The primary qualities—including size and extension in space, number, weight, or mass, motion, and time—were regarded as alone belonging to the world and accessible to observation, experiment, and measure. The secondary qualities—all those qualities thought to pertain to sensation: color, taste, smell, form, and so forth, as well as larger concatenations of these—were held to exist only in the mind of the observer, not in the world to be observed. Hence, even if regarded as real, they were not considered accessible to being known scientifically. From the beginning, modern science was based on a method that, by definition, could deal only with the primary qualities, that is, with quantity. As claims were increasingly raised during the nineteenth century that natural science constitutes the only method for knowing anything at all, the very reality of the secondary qualities began to be called into question.

If science is taken as the source of our fundamental view of the world, then only those quantities and physical relationships with which it is capable of dealing are accorded reality. All else—life, qualities, meaning, values—are regarded as, at most, subjective. "If the physical terms by which modern science deals with the world are supposed to constitute the world, it follows as a matter of course," Dewey wrote, "that qualities we experience and which are the distinctive things in human life, fall outside of nature."[6] For example, he said, "It tends to be assumed that

---

5. See Dewey, *The Quest for Certainty* (chapter 3, pp. 49–73); also Whitehead, *Science and the Modern World*, pp. 71–82.
6. Dewey, *The Quest for Certainty*, p. 233. Modern science asks questions

because qualities that figure in poetical discourse and those that are central in friendship do not figure in scientific inquiry, they have no reality, at least not the kind of unquestionable reality attributed to the mathematical, mechanical, or magnetoelectric properties that constitute matter."[7] "Since all value traits are lacking in objects as science presents them," he pointed out, "it is assumed that *Reality* has not such characteristics." The result is to deny to our view of nature just "the traits that give life purpose and value." In their place arises "the belief that nature is an indifferent, dead mechanism." "We eliminate the distinctively human factor—reduction to the physical ensues."[8]

Another way of putting the problem is that science, to the extent that it takes physics as its determinative branch, deals only with the microscopic and submicroscopic worlds (whether it conceives of those worlds as made up of particles or waves, or wave particles, or purely formal, causal relations for which wave particles are but useful, functional pointers and markers). At the same time, the macroscopic world, "the world as experienced," fades away. In the scientific worldviews, the macroscopic, experiential world is a world of *mere* appearance—it moves from being a world of phenomena to that of epiphenomena.

Yet, it is precisely the macroscopic world, the world of appearances, in which is to be found (whether conceived of as subjective or objective) those qualities and values that are the source of all life and meaning, of both nature and human beings. The central

---

that can only be answered in terms of relationships among quantities. It makes little difference whether the answers are given in statistical formulations or otherwise. It is perhaps important to note also that it makes little difference whether science has abandoned, as it increasingly has in the twentieth century, the older, cruder notions of primary qualities, dealing in their stead only with purely formal, quantitative relationships like number, motion, and force, modern science cannot, by definition, deal with or speak of qualities (except in the subsidiary sense as signs of an underlying quantitative substratum).

7. Dewey, *Experience and Nature*, p. 25.
8. Dewey, *The Quest for Certainty*, (pp. 137, 233, 21–22, 216). Cf. Whitehead, "Nature [in this view] is a dull affair, soundless, scentless, colorless; merely the hurrying of material, endlessly, meaninglessly." *Science and the Modern World*, p. 80.

task, then, becomes establishing the reality and primacy of "the world as experienced"—the macroscopic world of phenomena, of appearances. The central task becomes "saving the appearances," for it is in the macroscopic world of the appearances that, as Owen Barfield has put it, "we live and sense and have our being."⁹

All his life, Dewey worked to save the phenomena, that is, to keep the fullness of experience in all its qualitative richness either from being bypassed as unimportant or from being reduced away as nonexistent. The threat to the phenomena, as Dewey saw it, was twofold. On the one side, as we have seen, was the widespread view that science is capable of giving us an exhaustive picture of reality. On the other side, and just as much a threat in Dewey's view, were all systems of abstract rationalism that held that reality and meaning are to be found in a world of ideal essences or forms. One way of understanding many of the idealist philosophies of the nineteenth and early twentieth centuries is as attempts to maintain the reality of a world beyond or within the world described by science in which meaning could still be found and secured. For Dewey, however, all such rationalistic systems paid the high price of losing contact both with science and with the world of ordinary experience. In Dewey's view, all

---

9. "Saving the phenomena" or "Saving the appearances" is not Dewey's expression or one that he used. The expression is the Greeks *Sozein ta phainomena* and one that figured centrally in Western philosophy and science in connection with astronomy down to the time of Copernicus. To see Dewey in relation to it is to underscore his taking up one of the central and most venerable issues in the Western philosophic tradition. The expression has had different meanings. At one end of the spectrum of meanings, "saving the appearances" was understood to mean that the hypotheses of natural philosophy should accord with appearances without necessarily claiming to say anything about the underlying reality of them. See the discussion of *Simplicius* and the Copernican theory in Olson, *Science Deified and Science Defied*, pp. 242–267. At the other, more ancient end of the spectrum, the expression meant that the phenomena were to be saved so as to reveal the concealed depths of reality that they manifest. For an example of a statement of this meaning, see Corbin, *The Concept of Comparative Philosophy*, pp. 4–5. What I have called Dewey's project to save the appearances touches in its own way on the meanings at both ends of the spectrum. The most penetrating discussion of the issue, historically and in its contemporary importance, is Barfield, *Saving the Appearances*.

rationalistic idealism served only to widen rather than to heal the split between knowledge as determined by science and meaningful, value-laden experience.

Overcoming this split was further complicated for Dewey by his own acceptance of the identification of knowing solely with the methods of science—with "reflective intelligence" or "organized intelligence," as he was fond of describing science. For Dewey, the task of "saving the appearances" had to be carried out without sacrificing science as *the* way of knowing in the modern world. In order, therefore, to understand the nature of Dewey's attempt to ground the value and qualitative dimensions of life, it might be well to recall the privileged place science held for him.

In the first place, science in general epitomized human knowing as organized inquiry and intelligence. Herein, for Dewey, lay the possibilities of human freedom. Part of Dewey's hostility to rationalism was his feeling that it offered an escape from the responsibilities entailed in concrete experience, as well as an opening for religion and what he feared as a rationale for the exercise of arbitrary ecclesiastical authority at the expense of human freedom and responsibility. As organized intelligence, science, for Dewey, was also the possibility and the safeguard of human freedom.

In the second place, biology more specifically was also paradigmatic for him. He once reported having, as a young man, discovered in reading Huxley the concept of organic unity. This biological notion of organism provided a kind of scientific underpinning for the demands of unity which, throughout his life, Dewey sought and stressed as essential to survival and satisfactory existence. Dewey, furthermore, also found in Darwin a biological foundation and explanation for his conception of instrumental inquiry. The notion of the interaction of the organism in its environment offered to Dewey an explanation for the origins of thinking. It also offered a seminal image for describing the nature and role of thinking in human life.[10]

---

10. Dewey's "From Absolutism to Experimentalism," in *The Philosophy of John Dewey*. See for example, essays in Dewey, *Human Nature and Conduct;* also, for a discussion of this Darwinian notion of knowledge

In the third place, science was a central concern for Dewey because science in the modern era had, as nothing else, affected the whole of human experience. The worlds of culture, of social institutions, of man's relations, and of his own self-understanding had been, and, more important, continued to be, decisively reshaped by scientific discovery and its associated technological applications.[11] Dewey saw this clearly, and he never relinquished his hold on the insight that any attempt to claim the importance of values and qualities without dealing with the question of knowing, in this case with science as the dominant way of knowing in the modern world, was doomed.

A two-realm theory of truth—a realm of knowledge as defined by science and a realm of values vouchsafed by feeling, belief, or tradition, but cut off from knowledge—would not work. Whatever reality might initially be accorded to values, meanings, purposes, and the qualities of life, if these were not in some fashion integrally related to knowing, then the dominant form of modern knowing would continue to produce a world of experience increasingly without them. Or, if cut off from knowledge but fed by irrational prejudices and passions, value assertions would become dogmatic, willfully enforced, and violently fought over.[12] Our world today is not lacking in examples of both moral vacuity and moral dogmatism, and the baneful consequences of both.

Dewey's effort to overcome the knowledge–value split involved his two key and closely intertwined concepts of instrumental inquiry and of experience.[13] A glance at the former can recall for us Dewey's ever-present concern for the role of values in knowing.

---

in the context of Dewey's wider conception of experience, see Dewey, *Creative Intelligence: Essays in the Pragmatic Attitude* (1917), reprinted in *The Philosophy of John Dewey*, vol. 1, pp. 58–99. See also Dewey, *Philosophy and Civilization*, pp. 13–35.

11. For one of his latest statements to this effect, see Dewey, *A Common Faith*, pp. 32–33.
12. See Dewey, *Theory of Valuation*, pp. 1–18.
13. Dewey's important essay, "The Reflex Arc Concept in Psychology" (1896), contained more than an adumbration of both concepts. Dewey, "The Reflex Arc Concept in Psychology," repr. in McDermott (ed.), *The Philosophy of John Dewey*, vol. 1, pp. 136–148.

And more important, it can also indicate why it became increasingly necessary for Dewey, in the 1920s and 1930s, to develop in a more full-blown fashion his concept of experience that had been implicit in his work all along.

The essentials of Dewey's notion of instrumentalism are well known, and we need here only to underscore certain aspects of it. As noted, at bottom Dewey's conception of knowing, of thinking, is biological. It begins with the living organism responding to problems posed by its environment. The environment is in part structured and enduring, in part, fluid and changing. As long as the environment permits, the organism repeats its activity habitually. A change in the environment produces an obstacle to habitual behavior, and a response is demanded. For the human being, part of the necessary response is to recognize the situation for the problem it is and to envisage ways of resolving it satisfactorily. Suggestions, hypotheses, and possible actions are entertained. Ways of reacting are tested and tried out, and those that are successful become habits. Habits can be harmful and beneficial. They are harmful if they are rigid; then they fail to yield in problematic situations where new responses are demanded. They are beneficial when they preserve a supporting relationship with the environment and thus release energies and attention for the solving of new problems that may arise.

In this view, intelligence, mind, is not substantive but is to be understood as purely functional. It is an aspect of the response to the problem and of the action involved in reaching a solution. Mind, "reflective intelligence," is instrumental intelligence arising in a problematic situation and directing action toward a suitable end.[14] Likewise, the ends of this active inquiry and problem solving also lie within the process, not outside it. Nor do they stand independently of the means employed for their attainment. Means and ends are mutually implicated, interrelated, and interdependent. As "ends-in-view," they represent hoped-for outcomes of the situation. As such, ends must be constantly reevaluated in relation to the means involved, and the means must be appropriate to the ends sought.

---

14. For example, *The Quest for Certainty,* pp. 224–15.

There is one overriding aim of inquiry, however, that does not change, for it characterizes successful inquiry as such—that is the aim of control. Knowing, for Dewey, is a method of gaining control over an otherwise unstable, or too stable, environment. Science is the method of instrumental intelligence in its most complete, organized, and systematic development. This means that for Dewey, cognition, theoretical knowledge, is defined solely in terms of instrumental, problem-solving reason. Knowing "is a way of employing empirical occurrences with respect to increasing power to direct the consequences which flow from things." In short, for Dewey, "knowledge is power."[15] This means, further, that science, as the method par excellence of instrumental reason, is concerned solely with establishing, effecting, and experimentally and directly controlling those relationships of cause and effect that will most efficiently ensure the desired aims. In *The Quest for Certainty,* he further sharpened and narrowed his instrumental conception of knowing by adopting Percy Bridgman's notion of scientific knowing as purely operational.[16]

It is important to note that his is a severely restricted and narrowed view of cognition. Nothing else counts for Dewey as knowing and knowledge—at least when he is speaking self-consciously about the issue. This also constitutes an extremely narrowed conception of science. For Dewey, science is important not primarily for its content and conclusions about reality but as a method for controlling experience of reality. The importance of this for Dewey's effort to secure the full significance and meaning of human life will become apparent.

There are other aspects of Dewey's view of inquiry that from the beginning anticipated, and in a sense, demanded his attempt to develop a complete metaphysics of experience. One is that, for Dewey, inquiry is *participatory.* Dewey rejected objectivistic conceptions of knowing, or what he called "the spectator view of

---

15. Dewey, *Creative Intelligence,* in *Philosophy of John Dewey,* vol. 1 (p. 88). Also, see Dewey, *The Quest for Certainty,* esp. chap. 4, "The Art of Acceptance and the Art of Control," pp. 74–107.
16. Ibid. (pp. 111–112, passim); in 1938, he extended operationalism to his theory of logic and inquiry. Dewey, *Logic: The Theory of Inquiry,* in part in *Philosophy of John Dewey,* vol. 1. pp. 223–239.

knowing."[17] All knowing, for Dewey, involves an active interaction between knower and the known in which each affects the other in the process. Here, in Dewey, is a central legacy from idealism. As much as did the idealists, Dewey rejected any notion that we can have knowledge of any so-called brute facts that stand apart, undetermined by our engagement with them in the knowing process. Unlike the idealists, however, Dewey denied that it is consciousness as such that determines the object of knowing. For him, this would accord too much to the powers of the mind apart from concrete experience. Rather, the participation of knowing for him becomes one of action and reaction in which reflective intelligence is a part of the whole process. What is known is always "funded" with the ideas involved in the act of knowing; these in turn, however, are not derived from some realm apart from the process, of knowledge but arise as a function within it.

Moreover, inquiry for Dewey is always in itself *valuation*. There is no such thing for Dewey as value-free thinking. Thinking is always shot through, permeated, with values and value choices. This insight was basic to pragmatism and is itself central to Dewey's project to save the appearances.[18] Because by its nature Dewey's conception of thinking is purposive, values, far from being extrinsic to the process of means, ends, consequences attained, and further consequences sought are present at every point.

With respect to science specifically as the method of reflective intelligence, this enabled Dewey to emphasize that science is not value free. Science is made possible by the ideals that pervade, sustain, and guide it—cooperation in the scientific community, respect for evidence, experimental openness, and so forth. In this sense, science itself depends upon wider relations, ideal relations, in fact, that extend beyond those immediately present within the focus of any particular inquiry. However, for Dewey, because the process of inquiry is a relationship, both internal and external, ends do not have value in themselves but only within the larger context of experience. That is, ends as values ought not to be abstracted from the larger context of experience. They have

---

17. Dewey, *Creative Intelligence, op.cit.*, p. 91.
18. See Smith, *Themes in American Philosophy*, pp. 7–25.

to be, as Robert Neville has put it, "articulated in the broad scope of experience."[19]

This points to yet a third characteristic of Dewey's notion of inquiry important to note. Inquiry, finally, requires a *context*. And the context is experience itself. It is only an awareness of the wider context and a taking of it fully into account, for example, that keep instrumentalism from collapsing into a crass utilitarianism, a danger that Dewey acknowledged. What Dewey called "capricious pragmatism based on escalation of personal desire," "the shortcut pragmatism congenial to natural man" for whom "importance" and "efficacious power" are synonymous, the subordination of rational thought to "particular ends of interest and profit"—these were the ever-present ordinary threats to an instrumentalism unrelated to the larger context.[20] To be more technical, the process of valuation itself demands this context. In Dewey's terms, for example, the seeking of what is "satisfying," the beginning of inquiry, must be joined at every step with a concern for the "satisfactory," the culmination of successful inquiry. Raw "prizing" must not be separated from constant critical "appraisal."[21] This activity of evaluation is only possible within a larger context of experience where the notions of satisfactory and desirable can have meaning because they have a wider reference than the immediately satisfying and desired.

As Dewey developed his concept of experience, especially in *Experience and Nature* and *Art as Experience*, this context became ever richer.[22] And it was essential in his effort to secure the significance of the qualitative and value dimensions of human life against all threats that would subordinate or reduce them to something else. Together with his conception of knowing and cognition as strictly instrumental, it enabled him to provide his full answer to the question, which he said "set the main problem

---

19. Neville, *Reconstruction of Thinking*, p. 101.
20. Dewey, *Experience and Nature*, pp. 242, 384; Dewey, *Philosophy and Civilization*, pp. 15–16, passim.
21. See Dewey, *Theory of Valuation*.
22. Dewey, *Art as Experience*.

for modern philosophy": "How is science to be accepted and yet the realm of values to be conserved?"[23]

At its most basic level, experience, said Dewey, is *precognitive*. He called this level primary experience. At this level, experience cannot be fully grasped in thought, nor adequately talked about, nor explained away. It is simply "had"; or in the form of expression Dewey was fond of using, "Experience means primarily not knowledge, but ways of doing and suffering"; it is "primarily a process of undergoing."[24] The scope of experience is inclusive. What is "had" at this level is not primarily objects of perception but qualities and relationships. In fact, objects of perception already contain within themselves a conceptual element (the idealist insight again) and so belong to the dimension of secondary experience—the dimension of our ideas, memories, habits, social and cultural outlooks and assumptions with which primary experience merges unbrokenly.[25] Primary experience is *qualitative and relational*. Dewey invoked William James's "radical empiricism" in its stress that we are given in experience the relations and conjunctions that are the essence of things.

Primary experience is *irreducible*. The qualities of experience are as objective as they are subjective; "they are as much qualities of the things engaged as of the organism."[26] Experience bridges nature and the organism so that what is experienced is as much in nature as in the organism. "Experience," said Dewey, "reaches down into nature; it has depth." "*Things,*" he said, "are beautiful and ugly, lovely and hateful, dull and illuminated, attractive and repulsive."[27] He even made his notion of instrumentalism witness to the objective, irreducible quality of experience. The true problematic situation of knowing arises not merely because the subject is psychologically perplexed and confused, but "we are doubtful because the situation is inherently

---

23. Dewey, *The Quest for Certainty*, p. 41.
24. Dewey, *Experience and Nature* (p. 4). Dewey, *Creative Intelligence*, in *Philosophy of John Dewey*, pp. 63ff.
25. Ibid., pp. 4–5.
26. Ibid., p. 259.
27. Ibid., p. 108.

doubtful."²⁸ Primary experience is, therefore, *participative*. The organism and nature are in constant interplay and interaction, and any separation of the two can only be admitted as a limited abstraction, useful, perhaps, for certain purposes but misleading if taken for the full reality.

Dewey demonstrated that all instrumental knowing is suffused from beginning to end with values. He made clear, as perhaps few others have, how important it is to realize that things represented as values are conditioned by the larger connections of means, ends, and further consequences in which they and our striving for them are enmeshed. Dewey himself, therefore, denied that values can be abstracted from this means-ends context without their either losing relevance for concrete experience or of doing violence to it.

Nevertheless, Dewey also came to emphasize the role of consummatory experiences, characterized by the experience of harmony and wholeness, that bring inquiry to a certain close and lend to it a kind of intrinsic, self-contained worth of its own. The criterion for such consummatory occasions was the degree of harmony and wholeness attained. Although he emphasized it more and more, this seeking for unity and harmony was a primary concern of Dewey's throughout his life. He once described how, as a young student at the University of Vermont, he underwent a personal crisis in which he experienced a deep sense of cleavage and alienation within his own person.²⁹ This inner experience he saw as a reflection within of a similar fragmentation in the social and thought world around him. As he developed in his own outlook—from that of his evangelical family, through the liberal, New England Transcendental Theology and NeoHegelian idealism of his student and early teaching years, to the final scheme of naturalism that he had essentially adopted by 1900—the search for unity and

---

28. Dewey, *Logic, op. cit.*, p. 227.
29. "The sense of divisions and separations that were, I suppose, borne in upon me as a consequence of a heritage of New England culture, divisions by way of isolation of self from world, of soul from body, of nature from God, brought a painful oppression—or rather, they were an inward laceration." Dewey, "From Absolution to Experimentalism," in *Philosophy of John Dewey*, p. 7.

harmony of experience was his life's guiding *telos*.[30] And in the 1920s and 1930s, the consummatory experiences of harmony and wholeness figured ever more prominently in his philosophy.

This emphasis is further reflected in Dewey's depiction of primary experience as also *holistic*. "What makes sense," Dewey wrote, "is the whole immediately apprehended."[31] Dewey did not mean that we can ever grasp at once the whole of reality. That he thought impossible, and trying even to conceive of the whole of reality has the danger of landing us in some form of absolute rationalism that posits an abstract whole apart from experience. He did mean, however, that in the immediacy of experience, connection and wholeness are primary and that the parts, rather than being the ultimate constituents of reality, receive their significance from their place in the whole. It is, he wrote, "the sense of an extensive and underlying whole" that is "the context of every experience."[32] Experience, therefore, contains within it an *intrinsic* worth. This provided him with an answer to the charge that his emphasis on the process of inquiry never could result in anything worthwhile in and of itself. The primacy of the whole enabled him to say that within the means–ends continuum there are experiences in which things come together in harmonious, integrated wholes as "consummatory experiences" (that these may also in turn be instrumental to further consummatory experience is secondary). The striving for wholeness and harmony, for "total integral experiences that are intrinsically worthwhile," is, for Dewey, the real lure of human existence.[33]

Finally, because of its holism, experience is at bottom *aesthetic*. Aesthetic experience is the grasp of qualities in their immediacy, their wholeness, and their harmonious interconnectedness. Thus, "esthetic experience is experience in its integrity ... esthetic experience is pure experience."[34] The implication,

---

30. See Kuklick, *Churchmen and Philosophers, From Jonathan Edwards to John Dewey*.
31. Dewey, *Experience and Nature*, p. 261.
32. Dewey, *Art as Experience*, p. 194.
33. Ibid., p. 37.
34. Ibid., p. 274.

which we shall have to examine, is that the necessary context for knowing (in the narrow sense that Dewey defines it) is aesthetic experience, and that, therefore, the necessary, primary, and indispensable context for instrumental knowing is art. Thus, he writes: "To esthetic experience, then, the philosopher must go to understand what experience is."[35]

Now we can see Dewey's most complete answer to how value-qualities, all the things that make life significant, can be secured in the face of a scientific knowledge that has no place for them. What is essential, Dewey said, is that we realize that the only kind of knowledge or cognition worthy of the name is instrumental, operational knowledge as he has described it. Instrumental, operational knowledge as perfected in the methods of science deals only with abstract, cause and effect, sequential relationships for purposes of control. Nothing else counts as knowledge. To suppose otherwise is to commit the "fallacy of intellectualism," which carries over from traditional rationalism the delusion that it is through knowing that we grasp reality. But knowing defined as purely instrumental—and this, insists Dewey, is all that counts as knowing—allows us only to manipulate and control, not to describe or understand the world as it "really" is.[36] If we hold fast to this strict and narrow definition of knowledge, Dewey argues, some important things ensue.

For one thing, we will not disparage the world of appearances, of "everyday qualitative experience, practical, esthetic, moral" as unreal or purely subjective simply because science does not deal with it. The trouble comes, he argues, when the abstract operations and objects of science are taken to give us knowledge of the world. "When real objects [objects of experience] are identified, point for point, with knowledge objects [concepts of science], all affectional and valuational objects are inevitably excluded from the 'real' world, and we are compelled to find refuge in the privacy of an experiencing subject or mind."[37] It is principally this confusion, and the false idea

---

35. Ibid., p. 276.
36. Dewey, *The Quest for Certainty*, p. 131.
37. Dewey, *Experience and Nature*, p. 27.

entailed in it that knowledge, properly speaking, is more than instrumental and other than abstract, that causes us to neglect or regard as secondary all "the things we experience by way of love, desire, hope, fear, purpose and the traits characteristic of human understanding."[38] The problem disappears, Dewey thinks, if we give up the notion that science really gives us a grasp or envisagement of the world. All that science deals with is nature "in its instrumental character."[39] Science does not even give us knowledge of nature in her inner being; it gives us only control of nature.[40]

At the same time, according to Dewey, this narrow definition of knowing permits us truly to appreciate science itself. As the method of control par excellence, science enables us to set up the conditions for controlling the appearance of qualitative experiences that we deem most important or "to endow the objects of experience with other qualities which we want them to have."[41] The qualities themselves are "had"; "they are not themselves things known."[42] But the method of science as control enables us to make them more secure from the vissicitudes and uncertainties arising from an always risky, as Dewey says, "aleatory" existence. Hence, Dewey argued that a true unity between science and the non-scientific realms could be achieved.

Here we can understand most clearly, perhaps, Dewey's insistence that science be extended into all areas of life and all studies of life, even the most qualitative. This extension of science was not to supplant the qualitative by the quantitative or to reduce the one to the other, but to establish the conditions for the sustained appearance and preservation of the most desirable value-qualities in every dimension of experience. Knowledge is control—that is the definition of knowledge for Dewey, and to that definition he insists we adhere.

---

38. Ibid. (p. 135); *The Quest for Certainty*, p. 219.
39. Dewey, *Experience and Nature*, pp. 135, 137.
40. Dewey, *The Quest for Certainty*, p. 131; *Creative Intelligence, op. cit.*, pp. 85–88.
41. Dewey, *The Quest for Certainty*, p. 137.
42. Dewey, *Experience and Nature*, p. 140.

But this demanded that the full context of experience be preserved. "Science," he said, "is not a final thing. The final thing is appreciation and use of things of direct experience."[43] If we understand this, we will not think and act as though the world of things and relationships beyond the world of science is less real or important. On the contrary, without the larger context, there would be no science.

Dewey's attempt to save the appearances and to move beyond the two-realm theory of truth had certain, clear strengths. If taken seriously, it accomplished at least part of what Dewey intended. It showed that modern science has limits set to it, limits within which it has great power and potential usefulness but when modern science is extended beyond these limits, it is misleading and destructive. The proper domain of science, in Dewey's view, is precisely the quantitative and mechanical dimension of reality. Because every aspect of experience has this dimension within it, Dewey urged the extension of science as the method of knowing and thus of gaining direction and control over the qualitative dimensions most desirable to human welfare. "Nature has mechanism" he wrote. "This forms the content of the objects of physical science for it fulfills the instrumental office to be performed by science." But it is a false extrapolation from this to conclude that "nature *is* a mechanism and only a mechanism."[44]

Here Dewey was able to make use of what he called the principle of "selective emphasis." Selective emphasis is necessary, Dewey argued, for all reflective, intelligent inquiry, for selection from the total has to be made, the problem isolated, and abstractive analysis brought to bear upon it. Every inquiry proceeds from some kind of prior selection and abstraction from the whole. The "fallacy of selective emphasis" is committed, however, when scientific concepts and relationships are identified with reality itself.[45] When this happens, then the qualitative world, the world of distinctively human interests, disappears.

---

43. Dewey, *The Quest for Certainty*, p. 222.
44. Ibid., pp. 247–248.
45. Dewey, *Experience and Nature* (pp. 25–28). This seems to have been

John Dewey's Project for "Saving the Appearances"

Dewey's solution underscores the absolute necessity that instrumental reason as embodied in science must have a context not itself. Without such a context, science runs amok. Equally clear is that this context for quantitative, mechanical instrumental knowing must be qualitative through and through. It is the ability of science to deal with nature in terms of its mechanical, quantitative dimensions and in terms of formally quantitative, functional abstractions that permits the manipulation and control of nature. "But the qualities are still there," Dewey insisted, "are still experienced, although as such they are not the objects of knowledge."[46] And it is precisely the qualities that are for Dewey the reality, and the indispensable context for science.

But he was equally insistent that this qualitative context of experience itself is not known; rather it is felt. Knowing and knowledge, that which alone constitutes cognition has been strictly consigned to the instrumental methods of science. And because cognition in this sense has by definition extruded the qualitative, it can only be instrumental. Treating "all experience of worth" as inherently Cognitive—the great "intellectualistic fallacy"—is the basic reason, Dewey thought, why we lose the world of qualities. For Dewey nature does have an "inside," but science as cognition can only deal with the outside of nature, and it is the outside alone that we can, in the strict sense of the word, know. The *inside* of nature and experience, "the intrinsic nature of events," Dewey maintained, "is revealed in experience as the immediately *felt* quality of things."[47] And, while science itself cannot reveal this inwardness, it is this qualitative inside of things that is the fundamental, indispensable context for all science and its applications that are to be humanly beneficial.

Dewey's version of Whitehead's "fallacy of misplaced concreteness."
46. Dewey, *The Quest for Certainty*, p. 219.
47. Dewey, *Experience and Nature*, p. v.

Problems in Dewey's Solution to the Knowledge-Value Split: The Lack of Qualitative Ways of Knowing

Now the question arises: Is Dewey's solution satisfactory? Putting it pragmatically, does it work? Is Dewey's solution, grounded as it is on this extremely narrow view of knowledge, adequate, or does it not contain within it problems which threaten his whole attempt to save "experience of worth"?

There are serious problems to be raised about Dewey's narrow conception of knowing itself. All are connected with the definition of knowledge exclusively in terms of "knowledge as power." One such question has to do with the view and treatment of nature that is involved. From the vantage of "knowledge as power," nature can only be known on its surface, its outside. In fact, in this view, from what we can know, nature has no inside; it is only outside, externally related. We have, Dewey writes, "to surrender [the] traditional view that knowledge is possession of the inner nature of things and is the only way in which they may be experienced as they really are."[48] Dewey intended this as an affirmation and protection of the inner reality of nature from its being subsumed and reduced by an abstract, quality-less theoretical knowledge.

But *does* it protect? Or does it not, more likely, serve to deliver nature unprotected and all the more vulnerable to unrestrained manipulation and dismantling? Everything we see in nature, Dewey stressed as an instrumentalist, "is now something to be modified, to be intentionally controlled."[49] Since Dewey does not really develop the notion of feeling by which, as we have seen, he says the inner reality is grasped, what is involved in feeling remains vague and inchoate and retreats into the background. By contrast, knowing as instrumental is clear, powerful (by definition); it produces results and is in our command. It moves to the forefront. The tendency becomes overwhelming to extend into everything the essentially Darwinian notion of instrumental reason so that all that nature presents is interpreted exclusively in

---

48. Dewey, *The Quest for Certainty*, p. 131.
49. Ibid., p. 100.

John Dewey's Project for "Saving the Appearances"

terms of its utility for adaptation.[50] Any awareness and respect for the intrinsic inner reality of nature then tends to disappear altogether. Nature becomes fair game, theoretically and practically, for being taken apart, rearranged, and used up, without regard for its own inwardness, which is denied to it.[51] And it is difficult to see that Dewey's exclusive and narrow definition of knowing, contrary in part to his intention, does not serve really to further, rather than to restrain, this destructive approach to nature.

A second problem has to do with knowledge of other persons. There is nothing in Dewey's view, strictly interpreted, that can be properly called personal knowledge. There is only either aesthetic experience of the other or control of the other. A larger sense of anything that might be called qualitative knowing, embedded in aesthetic experience and capable of providing a context for instrumental reason, finds no place in this scheme. Dewey feared that to give more meaning to knowing than that of instrumental action threatened to make knowing something substantial, and, thereby, to introduce a realm of mind too close for comfort to the idealistic rationalism that he rejected. Apart from the fact that abstract rationalism need not be the only alternative to exclusive instrumentalism, Dewey's solution has its own problems. The felt appreciation of the other is surely a good. If, however, it does not include, as integral to the experience, the possibility of a genuine knowing of the other that is more than instrumental, can relations between persons in Dewey's scheme involve anything other than either manipulative control of the other or an equally exploitative, aesthetic "enjoyment" of the other? An exclusive definition of knowledge as power rules out any possibility of

---

50. The Darwinian and Neo-Darwinian notion of adaptation is itself highly problematic. See, for example, Richard C. Lewontin, "Adaptations," *Scientific American* 239, (Sept. 1978), pp. 212–230; S. J. Gould and R. C. Lewontin, "The Spandrels of San Marco and the Panglossian Paradigm: A Critique of the Adaptationist Programme," *Proceedings of the Royal Society of London. Series B. Biological Sciences,* 205 (1979), pp. 581–598.
51. That this need not be the only way to understand nature, see the works of Adolf Portmann for a nonutilitarian, nonadaptationist scientific approach to the study of the inwardness of nature. Most recently, Adolf Portmann, "What Living Form Means to Us," *Spring* (1982), pp. 27–38.

a deeper and more embracing knowledge of the kind, say, that stems from love. Such a personal knowledge (knowing the other as person) would require as its essential condition a capacity for change in the knower—an ability to enter empathetically into an understanding of the other in his or her own right. Such a change would not even entertain the question of controlling the other. On the contrary, it would most likely arise from a willingness to relinquish control and to take on a vulnerability to the other (the more complete the vulnerability, the more penetrating the knowing). That possibility does not seem to be present in Dewey's position, if we take it in the strict sense in which he often presents it. But without some conception of a genuine knowing of this wider and deeper kind, it is difficult to conceive of self-and-other relationships in which any sense of personhood remains.

Moreover, the lack of any notion of knowing that includes genuine knowing of persons seems also to be reflected in Dewey's neglect, even frequent strong disparagement, of self-knowledge. The ancient admonition, "Oh Man, Know Thyself," is not a leitmotif of Dewey's work. Dewey is suspicious of all talk about the self for fear that it implies positing a separate absolute, an entity sufficient unto itself; hence, his well-known distaste for contemplation and self-examination. (Such a self, Dewey seemed to fear, would not only render concrete experience essentially irrelevant but would make communication impossible).[52]

Yet Dewey cannot entirely avoid the self. It makes its appearance when he talks about imagination and inventiveness in science and the arts. Dewey recognizes that imagination and inventiveness, whereby alone newness enters human thought and culture, are indissoluably connected with individuality.[53] The self also appears as an unavoidable concept when in *A Common Faith* Dewey addresses the "religious" as the striving of self for unification and harmony.[54] And some notion of the self seems implied in the emphasis Dewey gives to the categories of language and communication. Both are almost, we might say, basal categories for

---

52. Dewey, *Experience and Nature*, p. 168.
53. For example, ibid., pp. 211, 239.
54. Dewey, *A Common Faith*.

Dewey,[55] and neither is scarcely conceivable, except in the most denatured or Pickwickian senses, unless someone is speaking and communicating with someone else.

In every case, some conception of an active self seems to be implied, indeed, demanded, by Dewey's analysis of experience, if it is to be intelligible. But in every case, rather than dealing directly with what seems to be implied by his own assumptions, Dewey substitutes a notion of self as a kind of functional unity reducible ultimately to empirical, biosocial determinants. In every case, there remains the sense of a crucial question begged.[56] To be sure, at some levels this functional notion of self is appropriate and useful, but that it is sufficient and that it can carry the burden of communication, language, inventiveness, and religious striving (even, or especially, in Dewey's sense of the religious) is highly questionable.[57] There is, however, perhaps an even more important consequence of this lack of a conception of person and personal knowledge. Dewey has little to say on what has become one of the central and most excruciating questions of our century: the integrity of the self in the face of myriad threats from without

---

55. See especially, Dewey, *Experience and Nature*, pp. 166–204.
56. That the biosocial empiricism Dewey appealed to at such points is closer to the naive realism of nineteenth-century science and twentieth-century popular scientism than it is to much in his own discussion of experience is also a problem.
57. The same question, of course, is to be raised with respect to Dewey's related, functionalist conception of mind. In part, his functionalist view of mind can be seen as an aspect of his participatory description of knowing, and he shied away from any conception that to him threatened to break the continuity between mind and matter, mind and action (see Dewey, *Experience and Nature*, p. 74). However, to the contrary, exclusive functionalism does not follow from a thoroughgoing participatory conception of knowing. In Dewey's case, the exclusively functionalist, derivative status of mind is an inference from a specific scientific theory, that of Darwinian evolutionism. Consequently, at every point where Dewey's own rich description of experience calls, at the very least, for a more rigorous analysis of mind, he collapses everything back into a biologizing, functionalist mode. Just as things start to get interesting, the central question is begged. Thus, Dewey is able to have things both ways: some mind and consciousness, so that communication and inquiry can be intelligibly talked about but not so much that their radical implications have to be pursued.

and within to its identity. On the most important issues involving our self-hood—conscience, integrity, loyalty, alienation, anxiety, the need for self-sacrifice, courage—we must go elsewhere than to John Dewey for help.[58]

The definition of cognition as exclusively instrumental has a further related consequence. It encourages the seeing of all human problems as purely scientific and technological problems. All problems of human life that cannot be cast in scientific and technological terms, and dealt with accordingly, tend to be lopped off or dropped from view. But are there not crucially important human problems, indeed, we might say, the definitively human problems, that have *no* solution, let alone a technical solution? These are issues that lie at the heart of distinctively human experience—issues involving, for instance, self-identity, commitment, loyalty, courage, sacrifice, and so on, and their sources. These have no solution in any instrumentalist, technical sense of the word. The central human issues are probably better thought of not as problems at all but rather more as life-tasks and challenges. They call not so much for explanation and solutions as they do, in Dewey's terms, for "undergoing, suffering," and for understanding. Dewey's notion of experience encompasses them; but his definition of cognition excludes our *understanding* of them.

Sometimes Dewey speaks of instrumental knowing in terms of scientific, experimental inquiry, which he insists is to be extended into and made regulative in every dimension of human life. Again difficulties arise. John Smith has also pointed out, for instance, that there are many modes of primary experience—friendship, love, vengeance, and forgiveness are examples that he gives—that would be seriously disrupted, if not destroyed, by the intrusion of experimentalist-controlled "inquiry" into them.[59] There are, more-

---

58. Among those, otherwise representing a broad diversity of philosophical positions, who seem to support this judgment in their own ways, are Sidney Hook, "Reflections on the Metaphysics of John Dewey: Experience and Nature," in Caws, *Two Centuries of Philosophy in America*, p. 165; Hartshorne, *Creativity in American Philosophy*, pp. 92–101; Rosenstock-Huessy, *The Christian Future, or the Modern Mind Outrun*, pp. 43–53; Smith, *Purpose and Thought*, pp. 88–89.

59. Smith writes, "The question is: Can one live through, suffer, undergo

over, for example, dimensions of primary human relationships in which experimentation is not the appropriate form of knowing—in which such experimentation can only be destructive and impoverishing.[60] The implications here for much of the dominant, modern educational research orientation are fairly obvious.[61] (Actually, Dewey often attempts to disarm critics by playing on the ambiguity of the word inquiry—sometimes exploiting its meaning as a general sense of adventurousness, which would seem to be unexceptionable in many contexts, while invoking at the same time the prestige of its more precise scientific, experimental meaning.)

Dewey's narrow conception of knowing also seems to pose problems for his value theory itself. We have noted the stress that Dewey placed on consummatory experiences of harmony and wholeness. Yet, as Robert Neville has pointed out, while Dewey seeks and commends such consummatory experiences, he never provides an adequate, analytical account of harmony and wholeness. As Neville puts it, Dewey's contribution was "to show in detail how we come to value these experiences and to describe the experience of valuing"; "his failure was that he did not ask about the structure of harmony, inquiring why consummatory experiences are valuable.[62] But how could he have from a conception of knowing that was strictly instrumental-operational? Thus Dewey could only assert the value of harmony and wholeness, but beyond that all remained vague.

---

the experience of vengeance or forgiveness, and yet 'know' nothing of what they mean? This seems quite absurd on the face of it, and yet it is precisely what is implied by the view that knowledge properly so-called can be nothing but the outcome of controlled inquiry. And to make the matter worse, one has but to consider that many such instances of primary experience would be transformed or even destroyed if an attempt were made to introduce 'inquiry' into the situation in which these experiences are realized" (Smith, *Purpose and Thought*, pp. 65–66).

60. Smith, for example, writes, "The point is that there are human problems in connection with which the concept of *control* is not appropriate, and these problems signal the limits of instrumental intelligence" (ibid., p. 89).
61. See John Davy, "The Social Meaning of Education," *Teachers College Record*, 81 (spring 1980), pp. 345–359.
62. Neville, *Reconstruction of Thinking*, p. 101.

Perhaps this may also help to explain, at least in part, other related issues that have perplexed and, at times, infuriated critics of Dewey. Although Dewey maintained that his value theory was itself instrumental, many of the actual values Dewey espoused throughout his life seemed anything but instrumental. Many students of Dewey have demonstrated that Dewey's own most cherished values and ideals were precisely those of the liberal Christian and idealistic traditions of his own background.[63] As Bruce Kuklick has recently written, "Dewey and his successors ruled out the supernatural, but only when they imported its values into the natural.[64] While eschewing axiology, Dewey, in his own concrete value commitments, drew covertly on the fruits of those traditions that were unabashedly axiological and teleological, and it is hard again to see how, from a purely instrumental conception of knowing, he could have done otherwise, if he was interested in values other than those having to do with power and power relationships, the only kind intrinsic to instrumentalism as such.

A last illustration of the difficulties posed by Dewey's narrow problem-solving conception of cognition is to be found in his final inability to resolve, or even address, fundamental ambiguities inherent in modern science itself. Science is ambiguous at several levels; and this sometimes made difficulties for

---

63. Jude P. Dougherty, "Dewey on Religion," in *Two Centuries of Philosophy*, pp. 174–184; Rosenstock-Huessy, *The Christian Future*, pp. 43–53; Steven C. Rockefeller, "John Dewey: The Evolution of a Faith," in Wohlgelernter, *History, Religion, and Spiritual Democracy*, pp. 5–34; William M. Shea, "The Supernatural in the Naturalists," ibid., pp. 53–75; Ralph W. Sleeper, "John Dewey's Empricism and the Christian Experience," and Robert C. Pollock, "Process and Experience: Dewey and American Philosophy," *Cross Currents*, 9 (fall 1959), pp. 341–378; Kuklick, *Churchmen and Philosophers*, pp. 230–253.

64. Ibid., pp. 256. In naturalizing these values, Dewey never convinced his critics that he had not also uprooted and denatured them. "My objection to John Dewey," wrote Rosenstock-Huessy, "is that he takes his healthy heritage for granted, that he thinks these qualities to be man's Nature while they are the fruits of 1,900 years of our era, and that he goes on from there as though nothing could jeopardize this assumed 'Nature' of Man. Dewey has never a word of gratitude for the powers which gave him the strength and the unity and the wholeness" (Rosenstock-Huessy, *The Christian Future*, p. 44; also, for example, Urban, *Beyond Realism and Idealism*, pp. 210–212, passim.

John Dewey's Project for "Saving the Appearances"

Dewey, while at other times it enabled him to avoid certain hard problems. Dewey's main concern, to recapitulate, in trying to reconcile science, the dominant mode of modern knowing, with human values and the qualities of life, was to try to place science firmly within his concept of experience. In the primordial encounters and relations of primary experience, Dewey had a point where ideals and qualities could make their appearance as constituents of reality; in the holism of experience, he had a vision that could challenge the assertions of reductionism as anything more than methodological abstractions; in the aesthetic grasp, he had something fundamentally intrinsic within which to place the utilitarian and instrumental. Furthermore, his conception of reflective intelligence as itself instrumental, as arising out of and entering back in to guide action, also promised to locate cognition fully within concrete experience. In his identification of science with *the* method of reflective intelligence in action, he seemed to have thought that he had established a fundamental unity between the abstractions of science and the richness of experience.

Thus, it was a problem for Dewey when he observed that science as it is actually practiced in the twentieth century is highly abstract and formal. He recognized the procedural usefulness of abstraction, but he was, nevertheless, suspicious of its remoteness from ordinary experience. The sense of suspicion toward mathematics and formal logic that sometimes surfaces in Dewey's writings has been noted and commented upon frequently.[65] Dewey had a number of reasons for his suspicion toward the abstract and mathematical nature of modern science. If not attended to, it tended in itself, as Dewey saw it, to move away from experience and thus to reinforce the dualism that was Dewey's central concern to resolve. The world of mathematics and formal relationships also smacked a little too much of those notions of ideal and rationalistic essences that were anathema to Dewey and in which he saw some of the historical reasons for the modern alienation from experience. Finally, the abstract nature of science, if not anchored in and

---

65. For example, Dewey, *Experience and Nature*, pp. 35–36, 57.

made accountable to ordinary experience, had patently undemocratic tendencies. It fostered an esoteric knowledge inaccessible to the public and controlled by an elite, who because of the actual connection between science and technology threatened to become not merely an intellectual elite but also a power elite.[66]

Sometimes, therefore, Dewey tried to ground science in ordinary, common experience by speaking of science as essentially arising out of actual trial and error everyday activity. In this sense, science was simply a more systematic way of working with the hands. When he talked this way, he tended to identify the craftsman, the old artisan, "the intelligent mechanic," rather than the mathematician, for instance, as the true scientist. The scientist as craftsman, as artisan, deals with problems that arise out of everyday experience. Furthermore, he produces knowledge that feeds back into the community and is accessible to its control.[67] This was in keeping with instrumentalism, and it left science close to experience.

However, the artisan notion of science did not do justice to the actual formalism and abstraction of science. Dewey's most complete treatment of the problem, therefore, the one that we have focused on as the linchpin in his attempt "to save the appearances," was to embrace entirely the formalism of modern science. In doing this, Dewey was then able to maintain that science does not tell us anything about the world in its qualitative reality; science only enables us to act, to operate on the world. In *The Quest for Certainty* Dewey accepted the most extreme form of scientific formalism as it appeared in the operationalist theory of the physicist Percy Bridgman.[68] Operationalism in its extreme form, as represented by Bridgman, is science at its most formal. It is entirely a method for manipulating, not for understanding, reality. We have seen how Dewey used this concept in attempting

---

66. Dewey, *Experience and Nature*, p. 296; *The Quest for Certainty*, p. 251; Dewey, *The Public and Its Problems*, pp. 173–78; Dewey, *Freedom and Culture*, pp. 131–54.
67. Dewey, *Experience and Nature*, pp. 128, 161–165, 383; *The Quest for Certainty*, pp. 84–85; *Art as Experience*, pp. 5–6.
68. Dewey, *The Quest for Certainty*, pp. 110–111.

to overcome the central dualism of modernity and some of the difficulties it brought with it.

What needs to be pointed out further, however, is that this embrace of operationalism brought some of the unresolved ambiguities of modern science itself directly into Dewey's scheme of things. Operationalism from its beginning has not been an uncontroversial interpretation of what science is about. In the first place, it means relinquishing the venerable tradition of science as a search for truth and knowledge of the nature of things, without which it is difficult to understand the emergence of science at all, and the dogged commitment of earlier generations of scientists. Furthermore, the relationship between the purely formal mathematical operators and the informal language of macroscopic experience has been one of the thorniest and most hotly debated issues in the philosophy of science since the 1920s.[69] Operationalism, rather than unambiguously settling the problem of scientific knowledge, seems only to have further exacerbated it. One thing does seem clear, however, and that is that operationalism, fully as much as (if not more so than) Dewey's artisan conception of science, underwrites the exclusive conception of "knowledge as power," and it tends further to encourage confounding science and technology.

From time to time, Dewey did seem to have sensed that the concept of "knowledge as power" entailed some difficulties. He frequently complained that the control of science in the modern world is too much in the hands of elites of privilege and power.[70] He always attributed such abuse of science and technology, however, to faulty social and economic arrangements, bolstered often by an outmoded individualism. He never raised the question whether there might be something about science as control that in itself favors those already in charge. He did not ask whether an exclusive definition of knowledge as power may carry by its very nature a built-in affinity for power and the powerful. Despite his

---

69. See Powers, *Philosophy and the New Physics*, pp. 6–12; Kolakowski. *The Alienation of Reason*, pp. 189–191; Urban, *Language and Reality*, pp. 532–534.
70. See note 66.

concern that science not be the monopoly of intellectual power elites, he never entertained the possibility that even a truly democratic science and technology might by their very nature have an unavoidable shadow side.

The ambiguity in the meaning of natural science was not resolved by Dewey. In fact, it is an ambiguity that Dewey frequently took advantage of, and traded upon. Dewey never tired of invoking natural science—as Bruce Kuklick has put it, almost talismanically—as "the one sure road of access to truth," "the one method for ascertaining fact and truth," "the sole dependable means of disclosing the realities of existence," "the sole authentic mode of revelation."[71]

Yet in all of this, it was never clear what science Dewey really meant. He had expressly set himself against the mechanistic, deterministic science of the nineteenth century. He was basically suspicious of a primarily mathematical science. The artisan science that he favored, with its possible implications of a kind of tacit knowing—this he never really developed beyond a problem-solving instrumentalism, and the science of operationalism, which excluded any connection between cognition and truth, an exclusion that Dewey made one of the pillars of his most rigorous and complete attempts to overcome the dualism of science and value-qualities, carried problems of its own. Most important, a strict conception of cognition as control, on the one hand, and, on the other, a conception of value-qualities as apprehended, as "had" noncognitively, did not solve the central problem. Rather, it left the basic dualism of modernity, which exercised Dewey all his life, more firmly entrenched than ever.[72]

Unanswered Questions

Yet we must ask, Did Dewey himself in the end really hold resolutely to his own explicit and narrow definition of cognition as exclusively the controlled inquiry of pure operationalism? Are there not, throughout his analysis of experience,

---

71. Kuklick, *Churchmen and Philosophers*, p. 253; Dewey, *A Common Faith*, pp. 32–33.
72. See Dewey, *Experience and Nature*, p. 140.

intimations of a deeper, more capacious, and more fundamental, conception of knowing? Indeed, does not the very process of describing experience, art, education, the public, ideals, wholes, harmonies, all the things of central concern to Dewey, assume a view of knowledge that is far more than operationalism? To even describe and talk about such things assumes some possibility of understanding, implication, and interpretation that is more than "the tested instances of controlled inquiry." To restrict knowledge to the purely operational begs the question even of how any communication of nonoperational meanings is possible.[73] After all, pure operationalism, in the strict sense, says nothing about anything; it only operates.

Dewey's Unacknowledged Conception of Qualitative Knowing: It's Implications for Education and Culture

At point after point, Dewey actually trenches on a view of knowing that is much broader than is contained within his severely restricted, explicit notion of cognition. Even in speaking about science as the paradigm for knowledge as "tested instances" of instrumental inquiry and control, Dewey, at times, nevertheless, had to appeal to a kind of scientific knowing in a more "general and generous sense."[74] Likewise, in other contexts, he had to say that while science may signify "tested instances of knowledge," "knowledge also has a meaning more liberal and more humane": "It signifies events understood"; "it means comprehension, or inclusive reasonable agreement."[75]

Dewey actually moves back and forth between a narrower and a broader notion of knowing. Explicitly, the only meaning

---

73. Dewey even speaks of "non-cognitive meanings." Such an expression is either nonsensical, an oxymoron, or it is forced upon Dewey as a way of reserving cognition to describe only formal operations, while suggesting the reality of a larger conception of knowing that is not narrowly cognitive—but this, too, comes close to a violation of language. Such is the bind Dewey was in. *Experience and Nature*, p. 339.
74. Dewey, *A Common Faith*, p. 33.
75. Dewey, *Experience and Nature*, p. 161.

he allows to the term cognition is the narrow one, but when necessary, and without acknowledging what is happening, he also draws implicitly on a broader, "more liberal and humane," meaning. Thus, he was able to have it all—a constant appeal to modern science as determinative in every human domain and a world of experience rich in value-qualities and occasions of intrinsic worth and meaning—but only by moving back and forth between a narrow and larger conception of knowing, drawing on the latter covertly, and repeatedly begging central, crucial issues that doing so involved.

To point out this use of two conceptions of knowing is not meant entirely as criticism, for it is just this vacillation alone that enabled Dewey to analyze and describe the realm of experience and art (and to some extent religion), with all the richness of detail and insight that characterized his accounts. This suggests an all-important possibility that Dewey's conception of experience need not be tied inseparably to his instrumentalism, but that it can be considered and developed in its own right. From this perspective, then, Dewey's attempt to secure the values and qualities of the macro-world of ordinary experience is more fundamental and far-reaching in its promise than his own strict interpretation of the relation between operationalism and aesthetic experience suggests (an interpretation, which we have seen, despite Dewey's intention, leaves the fundamental modern dualism between knowledge and value-qualities unbridged). Something of what the promise entails can, perhaps, be glimpsed in pointing to some of the implications that his description of experience and art have for education—implications for an education quite different in many respects from that commonly associated with Dewey's problem-solving, utilitarian emphases.

One aspect of Dewey's description of experience that has great importance for education is his emphasis on the centrality of the precognitive. This emphasis appears in different guises throughout Dewey's work. We have seen it especially in his insistence that qualities are directly "had," rather than cognitively grasped. In this instance, Dewey made two crucial points: one is that of the primacy of lived experience over conceptual, theoretical, and technical knowing, and the derivative nature of this knowing from lived experience. Dewey stressed that "cognitive experience must originate within that of a non-cognitive sort."[76] A related implication, then, is that all purely intellectual knowing requires a context of lived experience, which it must respect and take its guidance from, lest it become irrelevant, escapist, or destructive. It is only from precognitive experience that the bright light of consciousness and the sharp focus of intellectual cognition emerge.

It is true that there are some weighty problems involved in talking about the precognitive and the cognitive in this way. On the one side, Dewey did want to talk about the precognitive without investing it with any foothold for the abstractions of idealistic rationalism, or for what he took to be a supernaturalism divorced from experience. To do so, he almost invariably employed the language of the Darwinian biological organism. This, however, gave priority of privilege to physicalist reductionism, and it had the effect of introducing just the kind of questionable objects of a naive scientific realism that in other contexts he wanted to avoid. Because all the things that Dewey did want to draw attention to and to ascribe to experience—value, quality, meaning, person, communication and so forth—outran the categories of organism as biological mechanism, he did appear repeatedly to be begging important questions. On the other side, however, if we accept the sharp distinction Dewey also wanted to make between the cognitive and the precognitive, there are all the difficulties that we have seen of avoiding some kind of final dualism.

However, as we have seen, Dewey did seem repeatedly to employ a broader conception of knowing that makes his conception of the precognitive available and of immense importance to education. He seems again and again to imply a kind of knowing that, like experience itself, is holistic, participative of meanings larger than the operational, and itself bordering on the qualitative.[77]

---

76. Ibid., p. 23.
77. From this point of view, the precognitive always includes the unknown, as does all lived experience. But the unknown need not be in principle unknowable; there need not be a Kantian-like separation in principle between the precognitive and the cognitive.

Consider Dewey's instrumentalism from this point of view. Recall Dewey's frequent, unfavorable comparison of the abstract methods of pure science with the concrete methods of an applied, hands-on kind of science and scientist. "Applied science," wrote Dewey in this vein, is "more truly science than what is conventionally called pure science" because it is not concerned with "just instrumentalities" but "instrumentalities at work...in behalf of conclusions that are reflectively preferred." "Thus conceived," he added. "knowledge exists in engineering, medicine and the social arts more adequately than it does in mathematics and physics."[78] There is more than one notion of knowledge implied here. There is abstract operationalism. Then there is an applied kind of knowing that is the more scientific, in his view, because it is directly involved with the macroscopic context of lived experience, from which it arises and to which it must be accountable. It can be held accountable because there is yet another kind of knowledge that has to do not merely with what is preferred but with what is preferable. This determination of the preferable arises directly from a participative involvement with experience. It is a knowing by doing in which direct participation, exploration, action, and acquaintance are primary.

Was not Dewey, perhaps, edging here toward that kind of deep participative knowing that—by doing that, Michael Polanyi has developed and described in terms of "personal knowledge" and "tacit knowing"?[79] There are three aspects of this "tacit" knowing that Dewey seems very close to. First, it is a knowing by doing, a participative, active knowing. It is an embodied knowing, mortised and tenoned into experience. Second, it is a knowing that lies primarily in what Lawrence Kubie and others have called the "preconscious," that realm lying between the inaccessible unconscious and the waking consciousness.[80] But it is a

---

78. Dewey, *Experience and Nature*, p. 161.
79. Polanyi, *Personal Knowledge*; and *The Tacit Dimension*.
80. Kubie, *Neurotic Distortion of the Creative Process*. Much of Dewey's discussion of the place of habit—active, preconscious—as the ground of cognition may be understandable in terms of tacit knowing. Whether all cognition results as Dewey would suggest from the Darwinian notion of habit obstructed is questionable but is another issue.

genuine knowing, and, as Polanyi shows, is always presupposed by more abstract, intellectual knowing. Third, tacit knowing is holistic; it provides the indispensable context of the whole within which alone the parts are to be understood and within which, in fact, they are even to be recognized. "Unless macroscopic things are recognized," wrote Dewey, "cells, electrons, logical elements become meaningless. The latter have meaning only as elements of."[81] It is precisely in the participation of embodied, tacit knowing that the whole is primary.

From this perspective, Dewey's emphasis on the precognitive has several important implications for education.[82] As Piaget, Philip Phenix, Rudolf Steiner, and others have emphasized, it is the form of knowing that first awakens in the young child.[83] It is a kind of knowing in the young child that is experienced primarily through physical activity, imitation of others and of the environment, and in play. In this active knowing, furthermore, the basis is laid for later cognitive learning in its narrower sense. "All cognition," writes Kurt Fisher, "starts with action.... The high level cognitions of childhood and adulthood derive directly from these sensorimotor actions."[84] It is also a know-

---

81. Dewey, *Experience and Nature*, p. 144. Compare Frederdick Ferres' Polanyi-based, similar observation: "Before we begin to analyze an interesting whole, we must first be able to recognize the whole as interesting. Any consciousness operating by analysis alone could never recognize the difference between the atoms of the frog and of the fly and of the air and water surrounding them. We must—logically must—move *from* holistic awareness of significant unities, *then* to the detailed parts that find their meanings and importance in the wholes within which they function, if we are to understand the universe as it is." Ferre, *Shaping the Future: Resources for the Post-Modern World*, p. 33.
82. It is precognitive only in the narrow sense of cognition as formal, operational thinking.
83. Philip Phenix, "Promoting Personal Development through Teaching," *Teachers College Record* 84 (winter 1982), pp. 301-316; "Iona Ginsburg, Jean Piaget and Rudolf Steiner: States of Child Development and Implications for Pedagogy," ibid., pp. 327-338; Frommer, *Voyage through Childhood into the Adult World*.
84. K. Fischer, "Theory of Cognitive Development," *Psychological Review* 87 (1980), p. 481; quoted in Authur Zajonc, "Computer Pedagogy? Questions Concerning the New Educational Technology," in Sloan, *The Computer in Education*, p. 33.

ing that encompasses the aesthetic and the moral, for it involves participation with the environment and other persons and shows their deep connection with the narrowly cognitive. It is a kind of knowing in which the *being* of the knower is involved and which is the essential foundation for what Phenix has called "learning to live well as persons."[85]

As the major mode of knowing for young children, this active knowing requires that the educator's primary task is, as Rudolf Steiner urged, to provide an environment and persons worthy of the child's imitation and interaction. It suggests the importance of a socially, an aesthetically, and a morally rich and nourishing "field of experience." Negatively, it suggests that every attempt at premature conceptual thinking, "hothousing" young children to read and calculate, even a misconceived deliberate emphasis on problem solving at an ever earlier age, is an intrusion that threatens the development of the tacit knowing necessary to truly powerful, creative cognition later on.[86]

A second aspect of experience with deep implications for education is Dewey's concept of art. It is not too much to say that his whole philosophy culminates in his conception of "art as experience." Art (as including both artistic creativity and aesthetic appreciation) becomes one of the central pieces in his project to save the appearances, to secure the reality and value of ordinary experience. It is in the artistic experience that qualities and qualitative relations are grasped in their full reality. As the most complete union of the instrumental with the consummatory and the intrinsically worthwhile, "art represents the culminating event of nature as well as the climax of experience." "Esthetic experience," he says, "is experience in its integrity." And, if art is "the final flowering of experience, the crown and culmination of nature...then it is the artist who represents nature and life at their best."[87]

---

85. Phenix, "Promoting Personal Development," pp. 301ff.
86. See David Elkind, *The Hurried Child* (Reading, MA: Addison-Wesley, 1981); for a good account of the scope of Rudolf Steiner's educational insights, see Harwood, *The Recovery of Man in Childhood.*
87. Dewey, *Experience and Nature,* p. ix; *Art as Experience,* p. 274; John Dewey, "Experience, Nature and Art," in Dewey, Barnes, et al., *Art and Education,* p. 23.

Art is the indispensable context for all experience and knowledge in which meaning, value, the qualitative, and the humane are guarded and nourished—and this includes not only science but philosophy and education. In fact, art actually tends to become, for Dewey, not only contextual but, at times, paradigmatic for all of these—and he will speak of "scientific inquiry as an art" and of "education as an art" and of philosophy guided by art.[88] We may well ask: Why is it that, with all the devotion and attention given to Dewey in twentieth-century American education, his central emphasis on art has found scarcely an echo there? The question becomes even more puzzling if we look briefly at some of the specific educational dimensions of art as Dewey describes it.

In presenting us the qualitative, art opens to us, as nothing else does, the structures and dynamic relationships of experience. It is art that "keeps alive the power to experience the common world in its fullness."[89] Artistic experience is the best educator that we can have for developing the capacities that life offers and demands of us. It is in art, for example, that we encounter and learn to balance and unite the many polarities of experience and to be schooled by them: the "material" and the "spiritual," freedom and discipline, movement and structure, the fixed and the spontaneous, tradition and innovation, substance and form, and so forth. Art also reveals the deep rhythms at the heart of nature and experience and enables us to develop the sensitivity and balance to participate in them creatively.[90] And it is art that presents, as does nothing else, the reality of wholeness as prior and primary to all partial experience. Reflective and reductive analysis, as useful as these may be, are abstractions from the whole, and a culture that tears them from context and regards them as final, is, Dewey says, nothing less than *mad,* "insane!"[91] It is art that makes possible the integration of the self in the larger meaning of

---

88. Dewey, *Experience and Nature* (pp. ix, 358); *Art and Education*, p. 7; *Art as Experience*, p. 26; Dewey, *The Sources of a Science of Education* in *John Dewey*, pp. 6–7, 33.
89. Dewey, *Art as Experience*, p. 133.
90. Ibid., pp. 147ff, 163ff.
91. Ibid., p. 194.

the whole. "We are, as it were," writes Dewey, "introduced into a world beyond this world which is nevertheless the deeper reality of the world in which we live our ordinary experience. We are carried out beyond ourselves to find ourselves."[92]

Art is further, and more specifically, fundamental to education because as the prime medium for grasping and working with qualities and qualitative relations, it provides the essential foundation for all creative knowing more narrowly defined. "To think effectively in terms of relations of qualities is as severe a demand upon thought," says Dewey, "as to think in terms of symbols, verbal and mathematical.... The production of a work of genuine art probably demands more intelligence than does most of the so-called thinking that goes on among those who pride themselves on being intellectuals."[93] Whether Dewey here means knowing in the narrow sense is not at all clear. At one point in *Art as Experience,* he does expressly disavow any notion of art as a form of knowing.[94] Yet his whole discussion throughout is redolent of a kind of knowing that is genuinely and primarily qualitative; and it is this capacity in art to think in terms of relations of qualities, what he himself calls "the *kind of intelligence* that is exercised in perception of qualitative relations" (my italics) that gives his conception of art its central educational importance.

For one thing, the full development of operational thinking itself requires an education in which art is central, if for no other reason than that the formulae and quantitative relations of science and mathematics are themselves abstracted from the deep structures and rhythms of nature first encountered in precognitive and aesthetic experience. Not to ground the education of instrumental reason in an artistic education may very well mean handicapping the full development of powerful and creative conceptual thinking later on.

Moreover, art as a kind of qualitative thinking involves an education of the feelings. It is the feelings that give us qualitative

---

92. Ibid., p. 195.
93. Ibid., p. 46.
94. Ibid., p. 289.

experience; it is, therefore, the feelings that are most in need of education.⁹⁵ This is why Dewey says that taste, commonly thought beyond the pale of education, is the one thing above all worth educating.⁹⁶ Art as education involves an education of the emotions and an education through the emotions. Not to educate the feeling life is to leave individuals at the mercy of undirected, unformed passions and desires, and it is to deprive them of the most important way of knowing the most important dimensions of life.⁹⁷

To have a whole society in which the feeling life is not developed through an artistic education is to deprive it of any sense of social priorities and possibility of real social feeling and cooperation. To neglect an education of the feelings, and of the priorities that they make possible, while instrumental, technical reasoning skills are stressed at all levels, is not only to tie that society to technologies driven by all kinds of undirected, unformed desires and passions but to deliver it more and more into the hands of those who control the science and technology. More than once Dewey maintains that art and aesthetic experience provide the most penetrating critique of a society's social arrangements and worth. Aesthetic experience, he writes, provides "the ultimate judgment upon the quality of a civilization."⁹⁸

Finally, it is only in art that imagination comes fully into its own. By implication, it can only be through an artistic education that imagination can be properly nourished and best developed. It is in his work on art that Dewey provides his most well-worked-out conception of imagination. It is in art that imagination is seen to be precisely that grasp of wholeness in all its qualitative relationships, which is the essence of a sense of beauty. "It is a *way* [Dewey's emphasis] of seeing and feeling things as they compose an integral whole." The whole person also is involved, for imagination is what happens "when varied materials of sense quality,

---

95. Ibid., pp. 67, 119, 212.
96. Dewey, *The Quest for Certainty*, p. 262.
97. See Macmurray, *Reason and Emotion;* Peter Abbs, "Mass Culture and Mimesis," *Tract*, no. 22, n.d., pp. 3–29.
98. Dewey, *Art as Experience*, p. 326; *Experience and Nature*, p. 204.

emotion, and meaning come together in a union that makes a new birth in the world." Because the whole person is involved, there is to imagination an integral moral definition: "Imagination is the chief instrument of the good."[99]

This conception would seem to call for an education in which the whole person, thinking, feeling, and willing, is involved. It would also suggest that an artistic education—education in which sound, tone, stories, poetry, music, movement, painting and colors, and direct acquaintance with other people and living nature permeate the pedagogy and curriculum—is especially crucial for school-age children for whom the feeling life is their main mode of experiencing and knowing the world.[100]

John Dewey was keenly aware of the consequences of allowing the intrinsic meaning and value-quality of the world of ordinary experience to disappear. In his attempt to save the appearances for the human being, he was unwilling to challenge the basic positivist assumption that natural science is the only source of all that can properly be called knowing and knowledge, but he tried to draw strict limits around the meaning of knowledge. Sticking to this narrow definition, he thought, would make clear (1) that science on principle cannot provide a world view and (2) that quantitative science, if it is not to be utterly destructive of "all that is humanly worthwhile," has to be placed within, and guided and restrained by, a larger, qualitative context. Nevertheless, in attempting to describe experience as this context, and even, as we have seen often in invoking science, Dewey, in fact, had to make use of a larger conception of knowing, but without acknowledging that he was doing so. That he did do so enabled him to underscore the primacy of experience, and to give a rich

---

99. Dewey, *Art as Experience*, p. 348.
100. Waldorf Education, based on the work of Rudolf Steiner, is unique in having a full-fledged conception, in curriculum and pedagogy, of "education as an art." While Dewey's *Art as Experience,* I argue here, provides insights that support the Waldorf concept, the latter has quite different, independent sources and is worked out in a detail that Dewey never began to approach. For introductory treatments of Waldorf Education, see Harwood, *The Recovery of Man in Childhood;* Henry Barnes, "An Introduction to Waldorf Education," *Teachers College Record* 81 (3) Spring 1980, pp. 332–336.

and detailed account of it. That he did not acknowledge, and often denied, his using this larger meaning of knowledge also meant that he left untouched any possibility of further developing it or of drawing the full implications from his use of it. Occasionally Dewey seems to have sensed that to save the appearances, the realm of the qualitative, would require the full-fledged development of qualitative ways of knowing. Dewey never took up this task, most of the time denying both its possibility and necessity.[101] That Dewey avoided considering seriously a larger conception of knowing beyond the purely instrumental, however, left his attempt to save the appearances, despite all his intentions to the contrary, still immured in the central dualism of modernity—and, as becomes steadily more evident, fully vulnerable to all the incursions of an instrumental reason run rampant.

In our times, instrumental reason has expanded into the all-consuming worldview of an instrumental rationalism become its own context. "Knowledge as power" has become "truth as power."[102] The central human questions—economic, political,

---

101. In his chapter, "Qualitative Thought" in *Philosophy and Civilization*, Dewey does address the possibility and necessity of qualitative thought for grasping the qualitative dimensions of reality. He even entertains the notion of intuition as underlying all reflection and explicit reasoning. However, the development of qualitative thought never gets under way. At crucial junctures, functionalism is invoked in such a matter as to foreclose further inquiry. At the end of the chapter, he does present in capsule form the approach to saving the appearances that we have examined: the affirmation of "the existential reality of qualitative things" as the essential background, context, and regulative principle for scientific quantitative thinking. But, sensing almost, it seems, that even for his own account more is needed, he concludes by also affirming artistic creation as being "as much a case of genuine thought as that expressed in scientific and philosophical matters." So we are left again with the acknowledgement of the necessity for a larger conception of cognition than the instrumental/operational, without its being explored and pursued or more said. On the possibility of the genuine development of actual ways of qualitative knowing in physical science itself, see Arthur Zajonc, "Fact as Theory: Aspects of Goethe's Philosophy of Science," *Teachers College Record*, 85 (winter 1983): 251–274; also, Barfield, "Science and Quality," in *The Rediscovery of Meaning and Other Essays*, pp. 176–186.

102. On some of the consequences of "Truth as Power," see Weizenbaum, *Computer Power and Human Reason*.

educational, spiritual—are more and more cast in exclusively scientific and technological terms, or simply go unasked and unattended. The mechanistic philosophy is more pervasive than ever.[103] Intelligence as control continues to produce a technology that shows every sign of being increasingly out of control. The management of knowledge as power by vested military and corporate interests has continued in just the ways Dewey feared. John Dewey might just as well have never written *Experience and Nature* and *Art as Experience* as far as American education is concerned. Of art in education we have had but little, of "education as an art" there is scarcely a trace.

Dewey's work on experience and art contains rich resources and radical implications for modern education and culture. Will it be possible to tap and develop them fully, while also freeing them from the last vestiges of the positivism in which they are lodged?

---

103. The renowned Harvard biologist R. C. Lewontin has recently pointed this out in writing: "It is no exaggeration to say that most scientists simply do not know how to think about the world except as a machine." R. C. Lewontin, "The Corpse in the Elevator," *The New York Review of Books,* July 20, 1983, p. 34.

Alice Walker (left), author, poet, and activist, writes on race and gender issues. Her best-known work is The Color Purple, *for which she won the National Book Award and the Pulitzer Prize.*

Sandra G. Harding (right), is a philosopher of feminist and postcolonial theory, epistemology, research methodology, and the philosophy of science. She is a professor at the UCLA Graduate School of Education and Information Studies.

8

Rudolf Steiner's Activist Epistemology and Feminist Thought in America

Gertrude Reif Hughes

In this chapter, I will describe Rudolf Steiner's epistemology and at the same time suggest its pertinence to feminist thought and to the urgent social and cultural difficulties that feminist thought identifies and seeks to ameliorate. Although most academics remain unaware of him, as both an academic feminist and a student of Steiner, I am in a position to explore the relevant connections between the two bodies of theory.

When feminist critics challenge what Mary Hawkesworth has called "male-stream thinking,"[1] they often discover one or more of the practices known as universalizing, gendering, and othering. These practices reveal the operation of a normative individualism usually associated with bourgeois and capitalist values. A redefined individualism, one that is not normative, lies at the heart of Rudolf Steiner's epistemological writings, and therefore his work illuminates and deepens the feminist analyses referred to in this article.

Steiner is best known as a cultural reformer who lived in Europe from 1861 to 1925. He is recognized outside academia for providing the basis of transnational initiatives in numerous fields, including education (Waldorf or Steiner schools), agriculture

---

1. Mary E. Hawkesworth, "Knowers, Knowing, Known: Feminist Theory and Claims of Truth," *Signs: Journal of Women in Culture and Society* 14,3 (spring 1989), pp. 533–57.

(biodynamic farming and soil enrichment), and care for those with handicaps (the Camphill movement). Although Steiner was a white, European male who was writing before most of the events of the twentieth century had occurred and although the feminist analyses discussed here are mostly American and from the last third of the century, I propose to demonstrate the social and cultural relevance of Steiner's epistemology by showing how it pertains specifically to universalizing, gendering, and othering.

Universalizing projects the experience of a single person or group—usually Anglo-Saxon males of some economic independence—and designates this experience as "what everyone knows." Everyone knows, for example, that motherhood is fulfilling, but tell this to an impoverished, unmarried teenage mother trying to provide for "her" infant. *Gendering* creates oppositional pairs that masquerade as complementary partners but are in fact asymmetrical—equal versus different, for example; or objective versus subjective; not to mention masculine versus feminine. Such pairings actually are made up not of two individuals but of an individual and a something else. Indeed, gendering entails the practice called "othering." *Othering* constitutes a Self by marginalizing some Other. Perhaps the Other is cast as unusually emotional, sensitive, and caring; perhaps unusually exotic, otherworldly, or enticing; perhaps unusually civilized or, alternatively, unusually sexual. The question to ask is, "unusual compared to what?"

Obviously, all three of these practices can be used to exploit. They frequently are. Most important for their connection with Steiner, all depend on a network of unexamined assumptions about individualism—that it must conflict with collectivity and that it must always function normatively. These unexamined assumptions block a more radical view—that "individual" really does, or can, mean "unique" and that this meaning can operate accordingly in practical, social life.[2]

Steiner bases his epistemology on precisely such a radical view. He takes a threefold approach to individualism understood as uniqueness. First, he interrogates the assumption that

---

2. For a related view by a feminist critic, see Eisenstein, *The Radical Future of Liberal Feminism*.

there are principled as well as practical limits to knowledge. In doing so, he combines questions of cognition with those of individual responsibility, authority, and freedom, as I will show in part one of this article. In part two, I will describe how Steiner finds an instance where an asymmetrical opposition between subjective and objective does not apply. There he locates the starting point of epistemology, which turns out to be experienced in an act that each individual can claim as her or his own, while also identifying it as fully shared by all other individuals. He then shows how those moves suggest "ethical individualism," a practicable idea in which the unique and the social harmonize rather than oppose. I describe this part of his argument in part three.

Part One: Are There Limits to Knowledge?

Like feminist theories of knowledge, Steiner's theory links knowledge questions with questions of power. His epistemology challenges human beings to see that settling for belief where knowledge is possible, at least in principle, means surrendering agency in favor of obedience to authority. Steiner suggests that when one accepts principled limits to what human beings can know, one also accepts principled limits to human freedom.

In their critiques of universalizing, feminist analyses find social and ethical dimensions in the construction of knowledge. Universalizing practices generalize while silently erasing crucial specificity. For example, what gets taught as "history" should really be called male history. Alternatively, universalizing practices may treat particulars as though they had the same value for all groups, regardless of degrees of privilege. What is represented, for example, as an androgynous human figure often looks very much like a prepubescent white male. In a similar vein, what counts as "news" privileges violent events over peaceable ones; what is called "work" excludes or undervalues various tasks of nurturance.

Feminist critiques expose such practices and the operations of privilege in them. What one knows is always inflected by one's situation—psychological, spiritual, political, cultural, physiological. This positionality constructs knowledge. If one fails to see the constructed quality of knowledge, one unadmittedly universalizes what is really particular, naturalizes what is really sociocultural, and essentializes what is in fact individual.

On the other hand, focusing on positionality can have a misleading result. It can produce a tendency to universalize positionality itself. The focus should, I think, be more on acknowledging positionality than on accepting it as a principled limit. That is where Steiner's way of constructing the problem of knowledge can be illuminating.

The discovery that all knowledge is contingent could produce the following question: If all knowledge is contingent, then can human beings be free? But as far as I know, feminists have not gone in this direction, probably because working with such large questions as freedom seems to lead toward the very universalizing that gender analysis has so prominently and effectively exposed as a form of colonization. Moreover, talk of freedom can seem to lead to the flip side of universalizing-individualism, which in its rugged and ruthless forms has been implicated in so much of the oppression and arrogance that gender analysis exposes and feminists want to challenge. In any case, Steiner does start by relating the question of principled limits to knowledge with the question of whether human beings are free in principle.

One's situation or psychophysical organization may prevent one from full and certain knowledge at a given moment in history, but does this situation entail *principled* limits to knowledge, Steiner asks? It does not. Differently situated, one might know much more fully. Surely anyone's knowing is contingent upon circumstances, including material ones, but it does not follow that no certainty exists. Indeed, certainty on that point would constitute the very universalizing of a particular situation that feminist thought wisely opposes.

When one fails to notice that one is projecting identified individual limitations as universal ones, one institutes a limit that one fails to interrogate. Steiner does interrogate it and with far-reaching results. In his early work, *The Philosophy of*

Freedom: The Basis for a Modern World Conception,[3] which he first published in 1894 and revised in 1918, he points out the obvious but overlooked fact that setting principled limits to what is knowable has a significant consequence: It sets principled limits to human freedom as well. By insisting on the connection between cognition and freedom, Steiner connects epistemology on the one hand and ethics and politics on the other. I call it an activist epistemology.

The Philosophy of Freedom is directed at two questions: first, whether one can find a starting point for epistemology prior to any decisions about what can or cannot be known, that point being itself not doubtable. If such a starting point can be found, then even if erroneous knowing occurred in particular cases and even if uncertainty might therefore always accompany a particular instance of knowing, the existence of this starting point would mean that certainty was possible at least in principle.[4] Second, it addresses whether we human beings have our own free will (again, in principle) or are in some essential way bound to a will that controls us but, though it may sometimes be hidden from us, sometimes gives us an illusion of freedom.

Conceding that some readers might accuse him of linking these two kinds of questions merely for his own theoretical purposes, Steiner discusses the relationship between them by putting a certain responsibility for their connection on the person wishing to make it or to deny it. His words earnestly invite his readers to read his book not passively, but with commitment and engagement, and with warm, active concern for the stakes. Further, he asserts that a concern with such questions characterizes a fully mature phase of a person's soul development. In *The Philosophy of Freedom*, he says:

> It is no artificial tissue of theories that provokes this question [of free will]. In a certain mood it presents itself quite

---

3. Rudolf Steiner, *The Philosophy of Freedom* (1894), cited hereafter as *Philosophy* in parentheses in the text. Note that I have silently changed gender-exclusive language in the translation.
4. This formulation follows chapter 4 of Rudolf Steiner, *Truth and Knowledge* [1892], pp. 51–62, cited hereafter as *Truth* in parentheses.

naturally.... And one may well feel that if the soul has not at some time found itself faced in utmost seriousness by the problem of free will or necessity it will not have reached its full stature. This book is intended to show that the experiences which the second problem causes one's soul to undergo depend upon the position one is able to take up towards the first problem. An attempt is made to provide that there *is* a view which can support the rest of knowledge; and further, that this view completely justifies the idea of free will, provided only that we have first discovered that region of the soul in which free will can unfold itself. (p. 22)

Pointedly, Steiner suggests that he addresses only those individuals for whom the question of freedom and necessity arises; he speaks to readers for whom the question, Are there limits to knowledge? Are feminists such readers? Not necessarily, of course. But by virtue of their insights into the unacknowledged limits that universalize Northern European good looks as "beauty" and bourgeois families as "the" family, feminists do seem crucially situated to engage Steiner's work. In any case, Steiner specifies what sort of readers he means to address and he provides such readers with an epistemology, a work about cognition, that is at the same time an ethics, a work about freedom and thus about moral decision, because his work shows that questions of cognitional certainty are also questions about who could set principled limits to knowledge.

Who but a human knower could know the supposed limits to human knowledge, he argues, and what activity besides human knowing could identify them as such? As soon as cognition identifies a principled limit to knowing, that limit is known and therefore no longer a limit to the knowable. It would have to be set by an extra-human agent, and that act would at the same time set principled limits on human freedom because some extra-human authority would be controlling what humans could and could not know. Thus Steiner connects questions of cognition with the question of freedom.

Steiner's epistemological standpoint is "interested" in the sense of "engaged," not "biased," to use Sandra Harding's helpful distinction.⁵ Instead of talking about epistemology in a vacuum, he situates epistemological and ethical questions as mutually dependent and mutually illuminating. This attitude informs all his epistemological works.⁶ Steiner wants to involve his readers, not just address them. He wants readers to apply his argument to their own potential for knowing and doing. His is not just an elegant, self-contained ethics or epistemology but a guide to living cognitively with urgent questions.

PART 2: EPISTEMOLOGICAL IMPLICATIONS OF GENDERING—SUBJECTIVE AND OBJECTIVE

I shall develop Steiner's argument further by connecting it to the practice that feminist analysis problematizes as gendering. Gendering, recall, constructs oppositional and asymmetrical pairings like male–female, subjective–objective, or different–equal. In such pairings, one member is usually conceived in terms of the other but not vice versa.⁷ According to the dynamics of such pairings, you can choose either member of the pair but not both. Summarizing Jean Baker Miller's analysis of how this works for constructions of masculinity and femininity, Coppelia Kahn has called it "the catch-22 of gender definition as both sexes experience it, a self-defeating complementarity of traits and frustrations."⁸

For the past decade or so, feminist critics of scientific inquiry have been showing that such dichotomizing underlies the

---

5. Sandra Harding, *The Science Question in Feminism* (Ithaca: Cornell University, 1986), p. 148.
6. These include *Truth and Knowledge*; *The Philosophy of Freedom*, 1894 and 1918; *A Theory of Knowledge Implicit in Goethe's World Conception*. See also his survey of individualism in Western philosophy, *The Riddles of Philosophy*; and his 1920 lectures on Thomas Aquinas, *The Redemption of Thinking*.
7. For a discussion of a racialized version of gendering, see Brooks, *Report from Part One*, pp. 82–83, where Brooks notes in detail the asymmetry of dictionary definitions of "white" and "black."
8. Copelia Kahn, "The Hand That Rocks the Cradle: Recent Gender Theories and Their Implications," in *The (M)Other Tongue* (Nelson Gamer, et al., eds., p. 78.

traditions of androcentric and Eurocentric thought. It sponsors male-derived definitions of women and conceptualizes scientific problems within limits that are seen as natural and thus inevitable, rather than constructed and thus implicated in social relations of power relations that can in principle be changed. Sandra Harding[9] quotes Elizabeth Fee to this effect:

> We...construct rationality in opposition to emotionality, objectivity in opposition to subjectivity, culture in opposition to nature, the public realm in opposition to the private realm. Whether we read Kant, Rousseau, Hegel, or Darwin, we find that female and male are contrasted in terms of opposing characters: women love beauty, men truth; women are passive, men active; women are emotional, men rational; women are selfless, men selfish—and so on and on through the history of western philosophy. (p. 123)

Similarly, in an assessment of feminist analyses of the Sears case, a case in which the Equal Employment Opportunities Commission charged discriminatory practices because Sears hired more men than women for fulltime sales commission jobs, Joan W. Scott[10] deconstructs the quality-difference antithesis to show how the dynamics of such a hierarchical pairing work:

> When equality and difference are paired dichotomously, they structure an impossible choice. If one opts for equality, one is forced to accept the notion that difference is antithetical to it. If one opts for difference, one admits that equality is unattainable. (p. 38)

In fact, of course, "the antithesis itself hides the interdependence of the two terms, for equality is not the elimination of difference, and difference does not preclude equality" (ibid.). Scott's argument provides an ideal model for analyzing the pairing, objective/

---

9. Elizabeth Fee, "Women's Nature and Scientific Objectivity," quoted in Harding, *The Science Question in Feminism*, p. 123.
10. Joan W. Scott, "Deconstructing Equality-Versus-Difference: Or, The Uses of Poststructuralist Theory for Feminism," *Feminist Studies* 14, 1 (spring 1988), p. 38.

subjective, that I want to focus on now. I shall follow her moves closely, even using her syntax at a number of points.

When subjectivity and objectivity are paired dichotomously, they structure an impossible choice. Favoring objectivity, for instance, forces one to accept the notion that subjectivity is somehow secondary to it. That binary opposition then produces oversimplified, sentimental claims about the compensatory, even redemptive, value of such marginalized ways of knowing as "intuitive," "connected," "relational," or "right-brain" modes, which are often coded female. But merely celebrating such modes without interrogating the fixed opposition that sponsors their status as Other will replicate the marginalization, not remedy it.[11]

Nor does favoring subjectivity solve anything. It merely results in marginalizing objectivity as the desired but elusive Other. If one constructs the objectivity/subjectivity antithesis this way, one effectively admits that objectivity is unattainable. Steiner argues tirelessly against the validity of making this familiar, usually unrecognized assumption. By constructing objectivity as a desirable but unattainable corrective to the supposedly unavoidable distortions of subjectivity, he says, we project onto reality an effect of our own organization. Since our thinking creates the projection, he goes on to insist, it can also remove it.

He calls this projection "a two-world theory, or *dualism*," and contrasts it with the dynamic monism he advocates.[12] Dualism assumes "that there are two worlds absolutely distinct from one another. It then tries to find in one [and only one] of these two worlds the principles for the explanation of the other" (*Philosopy* 88; emphasis in original). That is, dualism constructs two antithetical *and* asymmetrical worlds. Dualism genders.

---

11. For an excellent analysis of the dynamics involved in reshaping objectivity rather than perpetuating its excesses by compensating for them, see Bordo, *The Flight to Objectivity: Essays on Cartesianism and Culture*, p. 114 and passim.
12. Following standard practice, Steiner ordinarily used "monism" to refer to worldviews classified under materialism, but in *The Philosophy of Freedom* he uses monism to refer to the dynamic whereby subjectivity and objectivity cohere in spiritual perception and conflict only in physical perception. I shall follow that usage.

In contrast, monism avoids the impossible choices and the hidden dependencies and exploitations that such fixed oppositional pairings structure. Monism also sees a duality in human knowing and experience, but for monism this duality is neither original nor final. It is contingent on how humans are organized, and it need not be passively accepted as unchangeable by human activity. "It is due...to our organization that the full, complete reality, including our own selves as subjects, appears *at first* as a duality" (*Philosophy* 88; emphasis added). Reality appears divided into two worlds at first, but whereas a dualist will take these two worlds as "standing apart and opposed," a monist will see them as "two sides of a single reality which are kept apart merely by our organization" (*Philosophy* 88).

Steiner rejects the dualist position because it rests on an unexamined assumption that acquiesces in a pernicious passivity toward the possibilities of both knowing and freedom. Notice that the notion of activity is as crucial to Steiner's epistemology as the idea of freedom. He insists that monism requires not just passive understanding of the relevant ideas but active participation in creating and experiencing them, and he indicates how one can think monistically and thus learn to counteract passivity. He presents the activity of thinking itself as the model for the participatory cognizing that monism requires. In his most elusive and crucial move, Steiner identifies thinking as an exception to everything else in our ordinary environments and activities that human beings can observe and ponder. Thinking "is the unobserved element in our ordinary life of thought," says Steiner in *The Philosophy of Freedom*. (Notably, the German title, *Die Philosophie Der Freiheit* has also been translated as "The Philosophy of Spiritual Activity" and, more recently, "The Philosophy of Freedom, A Spiritual Activity."[13]) In that work and in his reworked dissertation, *Truth and Knowledge,* as well as in his 1920 lectures on Aquinas, published as *The Redemption of Thinking,* Steiner describes thinking as mainly a dynamic, creative activity.[14]

---

13. Steiner, *The Philosophy of Spiritual Activity.*
14. See footnote 6.

Steiner emphatically contrasts this view of thinking with the view he attributes to Kant. Whereas Kant held that the main use of thinking is to portray the sensory world experienced as given, as there, as outside the experiencing subject, Steiner says, "The primary reason for the existence of thinking is not that it should make pictures of the outer world, but that it should bring to full development being. *That it portrays to us the outer world is a secondary process.*"[15]

Steiner does not start with a world already divided into inner and outer, or subjective and objective, or essentially there but only partially known. A proper starting point for a theory of knowledge must be neither objective in the sense of existing independently of a human knower nor subjective in the sense of depending on the organization of a given human knower. Designating such dependence or independence is already a cognitive activity, and the starting point for epistemology must, of course, be precognitive. On the other hand, it must be a point *immediately prior* to cognition so that nothing already, but inadvertently, cognized intervenes.

Steiner seeks a starting point for epistemology. It may assume neither that the content of experience is as we perceive it nor that experience is always being falsified by thinking. The first position he calls naive (or uncritical) realism; the second naive rationalism.[16] Of course no such starting point exists in anyone's experience. Everything is (to adapt Derrida) always already cognized. The directly given world picture—physical or nonphysical—could serve as starting point for epistemology if, in one's experiencing of it, one hadn't always already "thought" about it to the extent of noticing it *as* an it. Steiner resolves this familiar dilemma by remembering that what thinking has added, thinking can remove. We can take our world picture and deduct from it what we ourselves have added and thereby arrive, *in principle if* not *in fact*, at this directly given.

Engaging in the thought process for achieving this deduction constitutes part of following the argument here. At various

---

15. Steiner, *The Redemption of Thinking*, p. 111, emphasis added.
16. Steiner, *Truth and Knowledge*, p. 47 and passim.

points, including this one, it works best to follow Steiner's argument as though you are, say, an actor or a diver and he your director or coach. What constitutes following instructions in such situations is not just listening to them but actually delivering the lines in question or executing the dive. Or, to change the analogy slightly, *The Philosophy of Freedom*, like much of Steiner's work, is written like a musical score: to be performed.

The starting point for epistemology that Steiner seeks, that about which thinking has made no prior claims or assumptions, turns out to be thinking itself. Steiner shows that ordinarily we fail to observe our own thinking; we take it for granted. In a sense, he says, it *is* granted; it is part of the given world picture. It differs, however, in this one respect: Whereas we cannot be immediately certain whether we produced the rest of the "given" world picture, with this one part of it that is our own thinking we *can* be sure that we ourselves produce it. True, people have hallucinations; they sometimes believe that what they are in fact making up has independent sensory existence. But about concepts and ideas we make no such mistakes. "We do know absolutely directly that concepts and ideas appear only in the act of cognition and...enter the sphere of the directly given" through this activity (*Truth* 60). "A hallucination," he says, "may appear as something externally given, but one would never take one's own concepts to be something given *without one's own thinking activity*" (*Truth* 60; my emphasis). Our ideas, our concepts, then, come to us by our own activity of cognition. Our ideas we know we produce.

Notice the paradox. It is crucial. Our cognition is part of the given because we can recognize it directly, that is, without having to draw any conclusions about it first. But (here is the paradox) what we directly know as given when we observe our own thinking is this: that we produce it, we are doing it, it is our own activity! The given or directly known contains an activity, thinking, which we know to be our own activity. So thinking is both given and self-produced in that my self-production of it *is* what I directly know about it.

To use the terms of our fixed antithesis: Thinking is both subjective and objective (for the above reasons). Or to use the terms, "naive realism" and "critical realism": When thinking is observed, *naive* realism is the appropriate attitude. All other observables, physical or spiritual, require *critical* realism, which is achieved by the naive rationalist attitude of assuming the presence of distortions peculiar to our particular organization. With the aid of naive rationalism, critical realism allows for the fact that our thinking may be uncritically mixed in with our observing and may thus be distorting it. But the appropriate attitude toward thinking itself is the very *naive* realism that would be fatally inappropriate in other cases. In the case of thinking, "the object of observation [thinking] is qualitatively identical with the activity directed upon it [thinking]" (*Philosophy* 31). To summarize the exceptional situation that exists when we observe our own thinking: We observe our own thinking *by means of* our thinking, and so we "add nothing to our thinking that is foreign to it, and therefore have no need to justify any such addition" (*Philosophy* 31).

But when and how can we observe our thinking? Can we ever really catch it before it becomes the "already thought"?[17] It is indeed impossible to observe our thinking with ordinary consciousness. At first, Steiner concedes as much. "Productive activity and the simultaneous contemplation of it" are impossible (*Philosophy* 27). But eventually he makes an exception of thinking. He holds that thinking is essentially intuitive. As he uses "intuitive" he means not instinctual or dimly felt but knowable without mediation in the sense I just discussed. Steiner then makes a crucial pronouncement: "Only through an intuition can the essence of thinking be grasped." And he characterizes intuition as "the conscious experience—in pure spirit—of a purely spiritual content" (*Philosophy* 119). In short, intuition is radically self-reflexive and so, as I tried to show in the preceding paragraphs, is the activity of observing thinking. Only because thinking *is* intuitive can it be intuited. This intuiting of the intuitive is an activity independent of physicality; it occurs "in pure

---

17. See Kühlewind, *Stages of Consciousness*, p. x and passim.

spirit," yet one need not be a mystic or an initiate to have this experience "in pure spirit."

(A parenthetical disclaimer is in order here: Steiner is not an idealist, either in the technical sense of one for whom only spirit is real or in the popular sense of an impractical dreamer who commits to unattainable goals. Monism as he constructs it provides a basis for spiritual realism, an epistemological foundation for applying to spirit phenomena a suitable empiricism that can yield precise, shareable understandings comparable to those that the natural sciences can yield for natural phenomena.)

Why does all this epistemological footwork about attending to the activity, rather than the results, of thinking matter? By providing a basis for monism, it provides a basis for refusing dualism. Such dualism is itself the basis for the reductive idea that one must accept fixed antitheses, including those that structure what Nancy Armstrong has called "the gender bind."[18] Monism, remember, recognizes dualities, including those that get antithesized as subjective/objective. But, instead of projecting the bifurcated experience of reality as an inevitable separation between two unrelated and unrelatable worlds as dualism does, monism avoids such reifications. Monism sees these dualisms as constructed. Moreover, this dynamic monism identifies *both* the constructing situation *and* the deconstructing activity as essentially (I use the word reluctantly but advisedly) in human control.

In waking consciousness, humans split reality into two parts: One part is what we observe or perceive or encounter as given; the second part is how we respond. The first we designate as outer; the second as inner, calling the outer "objective" and the inner "subjective" and meaning thereby that the supposed outer

---

18. Nancy Armstrong, "The Gender Bind: Women and the Disciplines," *Genders* 3 (fall 1988), pp.1–23. Pointing out that an increase in the number of female faculty members in universities does not necessarily mean an end to gendered divisions of labor in the academic workplace, Armstrong calls for reconceiving the problem of sexism in universities. The "gender bind," she says, makes us "think that we have taken up an alternative position" while in fact we have remained "within the cultural framework that is already in place" (20).

proceeds independently of us while the supposed inner depends entirely on us and neither refers to the supposed outer nor affects it. All this designating and splitting is ordinarily so transparent to us that we fail to see it and fail to see that we have constructed it, as we might fail to see a glass wall. This glass wall of apparent restriction constitutes a supposed limit that is really an illusion. We create this dualizing ourselves. And we ourselves can stop it. It is not done *to* us but *by* us.

Because our organization—our bodies and sociocultural circumstances—dualizes our experience, splits it as I just described, we may be the instruments of this dualizing, but we are equally the agents. Ignoring or suppressing our own agency brings about the same oppressive results as seeing any human or group only as instruments never also as agents: Real powers and capacities are marginalized as invisible, Other, sublime, dangerous. In the first two parts of this article, I have been suggesting that feminists, who ordinarily challenge dominative tendencies to naturalize what could be changed, sometimes follow the hegemonic practice of accepting as inevitable limitations that have been extrapolated from circumstances which, however coercive, need not be accepted as unchangeable. And I am saying that insofar as one does so, one denies the reality—the existence and the operation—of phenomena that then exist and operate without one's conscious assent and participation. In denying the agency of these realities, one denies the reality of one's own agency; one denies the reality (albeit only a potential reality, to be sure) of one's own freedom.[19]

Steiner's epistemological works address this potential for freedom. By joining instrumentality with agency in the matter of humans' capacity for thinking, Steiner makes individual thinkers responsible for evolving as actuality the freedom that potentially unlimited knowledge makes possible in principle. Steiner links freedom to knowledge and to individual initiative. I have already shown how he makes the connections between

---

19. See Kühlewind, *From Normal to Healthy* and/ or my review of it in *TOWARDS*, winter, 1989–90.

freedom and knowledge. Now I want to conclude by showing how he connects freedom and individualism.

PART THREE: ETHICAL INDIVIDUALISM AND ITS RELATIONSHIP TO THINKING

Steiner's epistemology has the agenda of establishing that all humans are individually responsible and therefore free. Not that Steiner has no politico-social insights, but that agency, for Steiner, is radically human, radically overlooked, and radically individual. In contrast to what many feminists would argue,[20] Steiner's work suggests that we do not need less individuality: we need more.

For many feminists, individualism betokens egomaniacal virtuosos, ruthless go-getters, rugged survivors and prevailers. Such self-styled individualists all thrive at the expense of unacknowledged labor without which their supposedly individual successes would be impossible. Because it is often women and almost always marginalized people—male and female—whose labor sustains these kinds of "individualism," it is no wonder that individualism has a bad name among those who pioneer in identifying such exploitations and trying to stop them. Still, while uncovering and challenging exploitative perversions of individualism, most feminists wisely avoid dichotomizing individual and community or society. Some resist dichotomizing by celebrating collaboratively creative work from quilting to scholarship, others by refusing to assume that, to "do" science or photography means becoming a passive observer arrogantly isolated from what one tries to observe.[21] Both kinds of feminist thinkers about individualism try to avoid constructing impossible choices between autonomy and social responsibility that result when individual and society are locked in a dichotomy.

---

20. See Zillah Eisenstein, footnote 2.
21. Alice Walker and the scholarly partnership of the literary critics Sandra Gilbert and Susan Gubar exemplify the first group; Sandra Harding and Evelyn Fox Keller exemplify the second.

Steiner's epistemology offers a way to see individualism not in conflict with freedom, not even as a means to freedom, but as the expression of freedom. He makes his classic statement of what he calls "ethical individualism" in "The Idea of Freedom," which is chapter 9 of *The Philosophy of Freedom*.[22] There he defines ethical individualism as an epistemological as well as an ethical point of view. He bases it on the idea that individuality expresses itself in conduct that is motivated by a particular person's intuitions as to what she or he should do in any particular case.

What is individual in each of us, says Steiner, is "the sum of ideas which are effective in us, the concrete content of our intuitions" (*Philosophy* 131). These cognitive, moral intuitions that motivate an action may or may not accord with cultural norms for ethical conduct. Steiner insists that general standards—no matter how admirable—can, perhaps, help one *develop* the free will required for intuiting individuated motives and acting on them but they cannot *authorize* free deeds. The appropriateness and content of free deeds can only be intuited by an individual in an individual case, for her- or himself. Habit, inertia, and obedience are all anathema to the conduct of ethical individualism.

Ethical individualism requires individual activity, just as observing one's thinking does—the same individual activity, in fact: intuitive activity. Just as intuiting the intuitive character of thinking eludes our ordinary thinking and requires enhanced activity, so with the moral intuiting of conduct that befits ethical individualism: It doesn't just occur ordinarily, but it can be developed by all who wish to do so. Many of Steiner's works describe this intuitive activity and how it can be fostered. Reading them can constitute a kind of schooling in the necessary consciousness. To try to summarize his indications exceeds the scope of my argument here, so let a brief survey of Steiner's description of "moral intuition" suffice to suggest the quality of cognitional activity and responsibility involved.

---

22. This chapter is readily available in McDermott, ed., *The Essential Steiner*, which is an indispensable anthology.

In the first place, Steiner specifically and emphatically excludes obedience from his description of conduct based in ethical individualism. Such conduct is both moral and free. Instead of constructing morality as obedience and freedom as a problem in constraint the way bourgeois thinking often does, Steiner-like Nietzsche, whose early work he knew well and greatly admired scorns obedience as nothing but automatism:

> If one acts only because one accepts certain moral standards, this action is the outcome of the principles that compose one's moral code. One merely carries out orders. One is a superior automaton. (p. 132)[23]

Accordingly, "It is a moral advance when a person no longer simply accepts the commands of an outer or inner authority as the motive of action, but tries to understand the reason *why a particular maxim of behavior should act as a motive* in him or her" (*Philosophy* 127–128; emphasis added). Instead of the automatism of obedience, Steiner goes on to say, only love for the action itself could motivate a free deed. "Free beings are those who can *want* what they themselves each consider to be right" (*Philosophy* 167; emphasis in original). A motivation other than the warmly interested yet unselfish desire associated with love would, of course, be unfree because it could be coerced, as love cannot be:

> Only when I follow my love for my objective is it I myself who acts. I act, at this level of morality not because I acknowledge a lord over me, or an external authority, or a so-called inner voice;...I have found in myself the ground for my action—namely my love of the action.... Again, I do not ask myself, "How would another...act in my position?"—but I act as I, this particular individuality, find I have occasion to do. No general usage, no common custom, no maxim applying to all..., no moral standard is my immediate guide, but my love

---

23. For a discussion of freedom and its relation to spirituality as against constraints, see Hilde Rein, "Liberating Philosophy: An End To The Dichotomy Of Spirit and Matter," in *Women, Knowledge, and Reality*, Garry and Pearsall, eds., pp. 293–311, esp. 294–5, and her fine definition of spirit as source on page 311.

for the deed. I feel...neither the compulsion of nature that guides me by my instincts, nor the compulsion of...moral commandments. (pp. 132–133)

Of course, students of Steiner's epistemology constantly and vigorously debate the concepts of free deed, love for the deed, moral intuition, and all the other features of ethical individualism. This is not the place to engage in such debates or even try to summarize them. The above explications were intended to suggest that Steiner's ethical individualism involves a cognitive intuition whereby a radically individuated motive directs a conduct based not in obedience but love. Now I want to emphasize those features of ethical individualism that pertain most directly to feminists' characteristic refusal to be trapped into dichotomizing individual freedom and social responsibility.

Steiner discusses individualism without opposing it to socially responsible behavior; his ethical individualism does not structure an impossible choice between the two. Neither does ethical individualism conceive individual and society at one another's expense. Ethical individualism is "ethical" because it is not antisocial; and "social," far from being conceived as arrangements that submerge individuality, is specifically described as arrangements that individuals make so as to serve individuality (*Philosophy* 141–142 and *passim*).

For Steiner, the opposite of individual is not "society" but "genus." He devotes an entire chapter, "Individual and Genus," to this point, arguing that when we view one another generically we cannot hope to understand one another. Fullest understanding of another person comes not by considering the genus but the individuality. Interestingly, Steiner, in *The Philosophy of Freedom*, chooses to make the point via an early formulation of what is now called "the sex–gender system":

> It is impossible to understand a human being completely if one takes the concept of genus as the basis of one's judgment. The tendency to judge according to the genus is at its most stubborn where we are concerned with differences of sex. Almost invariably man sees in woman, and woman in man,

too much of the general character of the other sex and too little of what is individual. (p. 200)

Steiner is arguing against essentializing, not against locating another person in cultural or physical circumstances. He continues:

> In practical life this does less harm to men than to women. The social position of women is for the most part such an unworthy one because in so many respects it is determined not as it should be by the particular characteristics of the individual woman, but by the general picture one has of woman's natural tasks and needs. A man's activity in life is governed by his individual capacities and inclinations, whereas a woman's is supposed to be determined solely by the mere fact that she is a woman. She is supposed to be a slave to what is generic, to womanhood in general. As long as men continue to debate whether a woman is suited to this or that profession "according to her natural disposition," the so-called woman's question cannot advance beyond its most elementary stage. What a woman, within her natural limitations wants to become had better be left to the woman herself to decide. If it is true that women are suited only to that profession which is theirs at present, then they will hardly have it in them to attain any other. But they must be allowed to decide for themselves. (p. 200)

Steiner finishes this denunciation of stereotyping with the following challenge to conservatives who might demur: "To all who fear an upheaval of our social structure through accepting women as individuals and not as females, we must reply that a social structure in which the status of one half of humanity is unworthy of a human being is itself in great need of improvement" (*Philosophy* 201).

That was in 1894. Readers (presumably male ones) immediately objected that women are able to shape their lives individually, in fact more freely than men, since men are socialized by such homogenizing institutions as schooling, military service, and the demands of various professions. Citing these criticisms in his 1918 addenda to *The Philosophy of Freedom* and acknowledging that "this objection will be urged today [in 1918] even more strongly," Steiner remarked drily that he wished to let his sentences stand and that he hoped at least some readers would understand his point (*Philosophy* 201). He was arguing that generic thinking disregards individuality; he was not focusing on social institutions like the army. (At that, the generic thinking he deplored can certainly be analyzed as an institution and feminist critics of science are among those who are doing so.)

Generic thinking erases individuality. The example of gender makes this clear. When sex is constituted as a genus, says Steiner, individuals of either sex become invisible as individuals and this is particularly true of women in societies where males dominate.

Steiner's idea that the individual and the generic are inversely related also produces a useful way to think about the standard objection to individualism—that it will create anarchy. Speaking about that objection, Steiner points out that when I perform a criminal act, I do so not from what is individual in me but precisely from shared instincts and urges that I have not as yet made individual by consciously interrogating my relationship to them and theirs to me. "Through my instincts and cravings, I am the sort of person of whom there are twelve to the dozen; through the particular form of the idea by means of which I designate myself within the dozen as "I," I am an individual" (*Philosophy* 134).

The "idea by which I designate myself as 'I'" is a "particular form" of the universal idea, "I." Here; we arrive at the crucial paradox in Steiner's epistemology: Individuality and universality are both spiritual realities; they belong equally and inseparably to that "purely spiritual content" that thinking intuits when thinking intuits its own intuitive nature. Thinking intuits "I"-ness; only "I"-ness can act freely, that is, individually, in the way described. How? Out of uncoerced desire to act in a particular way.

Part Four: Conclusion and Review—Connecting Individualism, Knowing, and Freedom

If the opposite of individuality is genus, for Steiner, a synonym for individuality is universality. All human beings are "I"-beings.[24]

---

24. The phrase is Georg Kühlewind's. See especially his *From Normal to Healthy: Paths to the Liberation of Consciousness*.

Our uniqueness is what we have in common. Paradoxically, the realities and processes by which we individuate are universal ones.

Understanding the paradox of this shared uniqueness is absolutely basic to Steiner's project. Steiner intends to demonstrate that human beings have a unique capacity that is largely unexercised. This capacity is freedom, and it takes the form of cognition or knowing, performed by a process of uniting concepts with perception in an experienced perceiving. That process is called thinking. In thinking, we individuate concepts and universalize percepts, to use Steiner's terms. In thinking we experience concepts and conceptualize experience. When we manage to observe this thinking in progress (as distinct from observing its results—our thoughts), we are intuiting our own individuality as a function of our universality. This intuiting-perceiving is a suprasensory, or spiritual, activity.

Steiner disdained Kant's categorical imperative and his worship of duty just as Steiner challenged Kant's idea of thinking. For Kant, thinking exists mainly to record reality. As Steiner presents matters, thinking's main purpose is to help create reality. In both his quarrels with Kantianism, Steiner advocated consciousness-raising. He called it spiritual activity and equated it with freedom, whereas Kant's view sponsored an insidious passivity that, Steiner felt, denied human agency and thus paralyzed human capacity for freedom.

For Steiner, thinking neither creates reality nor distorts a reality that exists independently of it. Thinking, as Steiner describes it, *completes* reality. It is that part of reality that our psychophysical organization removes from what we ordinarily experience as reality (recall part two). When we think, we unite what our organization has separated. Ordinarily we don't notice this activity, so we project onto reality the incompleteness that our own organization has put there (recall part one). But we can develop the capacity to notice our thinking. When we do, we intuit the intuitive nature of the process, and we are then also in a position to validate for ourselves the intuitive nature of our being—that is, we then know ourselves to be "I"-beings. There can be no principled limit to the knowledge of an "I"-being. "I"-beings are free beings because they—that is, *we*—know that there is no reality applicable to us in the making of which we do not, at least potentially, participate.

Steiner's ethical epistemology shows that cognition, freedom, and individuality are three aspects of one reality. It is a spirit reality, not a physical one, so it requires spiritual activity to cognize it. When such activity is practiced—it is intuitive in the way Steiner describes intuition—the practitioner's freedom becomes more and more available to her or him as its reality and its integrity with one's being become clearer and clearer.

Does being a feminist help one see the potential of Steiner's work? I am unsure. Feminists may be as likely as others are to overlook the fact that our thinking is always implicated in any allegations, including those we ourselves may make, about its limits. Thanks to hard-won insights, however, feminists are among those best equipped to detect and refuse the practices of othering, gendering, or universalizing. Furthermore, despite an informed mistrust of individualism, feminists may be less inclined to throw it out with the bathwater of patriarchal and bourgeois oppressions because they know not to construct it in opposition to society or community.

In any case, congeniality aside, feminist insights into both ethics and epistemology make room for Steiner's ethical epistemology. Feminist discourse creates categories to which Steiner's thought seems at least pertinent and possibly a crucial source of redirection. I think that whoever wants to try to understand cultures in order to work politically and otherwise for social changes would do well to heed both feminist analyses of oppressive practices and Steinerean indications for developing free individuality through what he sometimes called "a path of cognition." If thinking becomes increasingly a spiritual activity and political activism becomes more and more spiritually mindful, the combination could become powerful indeed. If the personal is political, so is the epistemological.

Bibliography

Abrams, M. H. *Natural Supernaturalism: Tradition and Revolution in Romantic Literature*. New York: Norton, 1973.
Adey, L. *C. S. Lewis's "Great War" with Owen Barfield*. Victoria, BC: University of Victoria, 1978.
Anderson, Victor. *Pragmatic Theology: Negotiating the Intersections of an American Philosophy of Religion and Public Theology*. Albany: SUNY, 1998).
Barfield, Owen. *The Rediscovery of Meaning and Other Essays*. Middletown, CN: Wesleyan University, 1977.
———. *Romanticism Comes of Age*. Middletown, CN.: Wesleyan University, 1967.
———. *Saving the Appearances; A Study in Idolatry*. New York: Harcourt, Brace, n.d.
Bateson, Mary Catherine. *Composing a Life*. New York: Grove, 2001.
Belyi, Andrei, Aasya Turgenieff, and Marfarita Voloschin. *Reminiscences of Rudolph Steiner*. Christy Barnes, ed. Ghent, NY: Adonis Press, 1987.
Bennett, Maxwell, et al. *Neuroscience and Philosophy: Brain, Mind, and Language*. New York: Columbia University, 2007.
Bordo, Susan. *The Flight to Objectivity: Essays on Cartesianism and Culture*. Albany: SUNY, 1987.
Brent, Joseph. *Charles Sanders Peirce: A Life*. Bloomington, IN: Indiana University Press, 1993.
Brooks, Gwendolyn. *Report from Part One*. Detroit: Broadside Press, 1972.
Buchler, Justus, ed. *Philosophical Writings of Peirce*. New York: Dover, 1955.
Buell, Lawrence. *Emerson*. Cambridge, MA: Belknap Press of Harvard University Press, 2004.
Judith Butler, *Gender Trouble: Feminism and the Subversion of Identity*. New York: Routledge, 2006.
Caws, Peter, ed. *Two Centuries of Philosophy in America*. London: Basil Blackwell, 1980.
Clendenning, John (ed.). *The Letters of Josiah Royce*. Chicago: University of Chicago Press, 1970.
———. *The Life and Thought of Josiah Royce*. Madison: University of Wisconsin Press, 1985.
Cobb, John. *The Structure of Christian Existence*. Lanham, MD: University Press of America, 1990.
Corbin, Henry. *The Concept of Comparative Philosophy*. Ispwich: Golgonooza, 1981.
Corrington, Robert S. *Ecstatic Naturalism: Signs of the World*. Bloomington: Indiana University, 1994.

———. *An Introduction to C. S. Peirce: Philosopher, Semiotician, and Ecstatic Naturalist*. Lanham, MD: Rowman and Littlefield, 1993.
Davis, Stephen, ed. *Encountering Evil*. Knoxville: John Know, 1981.
Dean, Bradley, ed. *Faith in a Seed: The Dispersion of Seeds and Other Late Natural History Writings*. Washington, DC: Island Press, 1996.
Dewey, John. *Art as Experience*. New York: Capricorn, 1958.
———. *A Common Faith*. New Haven, CT: Yale University, 1934.
———. *Experience and Nature*. London: George Allen and Urwin, 1929.
———. *Freedom and Culture*. New York: Capricorn, 1963.
———. *Human Nature and Conduct*. New York: Henry Holt, 1922.
———. *Philosophy and Civilization*. New York: Capricon, 1963.
———. *The Philosophy of John Dewey*, vol. 1, ed. John J. McDermott. New York: Putnam, 1973.
———. *The Public and Its Problems*. Chicago: Swallow, nd. (originally published 1927).
———. *The Quest for Certainty: A Study of the Relation of Knowledge and Action*. New York: Capricorn, 1960.
———. *The Sources of a Science of Education in John Dewey: The Later Works, 1925–1953*. JoAnn Boydston ed. Carbondale, IL: Southern Illinois University, 1984.
———. *Theory of Valuation*. Chicago: University of Chicago, 1939.
Dewey, John, and Albert Barnes, et al., *Art and Education*. Merion, PA: Barnes Foundation, 1929.
Drengson, Alan, and Yuichi Inoue. *The Deep Ecology Movement: An Introductory Anthology*. Berkeley: North Atlantic Books, 1995.
Eisenstein, Zillah R. *The Radical Future of Liberal Feminism*. New York: Longman, 1981.
Emerson, Ralph Waldo. *The Complete Works of Ralph Waldo Emerson*. Boston: Houghton Mifflin, 1865, 1876.
———. *Essays: First and Second Series*. New York: Vintage, 1990.
———. *Natural History of the Intellect: The Last Lectures of Ralph Waldo Emerson*. Chicago and Raleigh: Wrightwood Press, 2008.
Feder Kittay, Eva, and Licia Carlson, eds. *Cognitive Disability and its Challenge to Moral Philosophy*. Malden, MA: Wiley-Blackwell, 2010.
Feder Kittay, Eva, and Ellen K. Feder. *The Subject of Care: Feminist Perspectives on Dependency*. Lanham, MD: Rowman & Littlefield, 2003.
Ferre, Frederick. *Shaping the Future: Resources for the Post-Modern World*. New York: Harper and Row, 1976.
Flower, Elizabeth, and Murray G. Murphey. *A History of Philosophy in America*. New York: Putnam, 1977.
Freeman, Eugene, ed. *The Relevance of Charles Peirce*. La Salle, IL: Hegeler Institute, 1983.
Frommer, Eva. *Voyage through Childhood into the Adult World*. Oxford: Pergamon, 1969.
Fuss, Peter. *The Moral Philosophy of Josiah Royce*. Cambridge: Harvard University Press, 1965.

Bibliography

Gardner, John Fentress. *American Heralds of the Spirit: Emerson Whitman, Melville.* Hudson, NY: Lindisfarne Press, 1992.
Garry, Ann, and Marilyn Pearsall, eds. *Women, Knowledge, and Reality: Explorations in Feminist Philosophy.* Boston: Unwin, Hyman, 1989.
Gilligan, Carol, and Sara Ruddick. *Maternal Thinking: Toward a Politics of Peace.* Boston: Beacon Press, 1995.
Griffin, David Ray. *Evil Revisited: Responses and Reconsiderations.* Albany: SUNY, 1991.
———, ed. *Founders of Constructive Postmodern Philosophy: Peirce, James, Bergson, Whitehead, Hartshorne.* Albany: SUNY, 1992.
———. *God and Religion in the Postmodern World.* Albany: SUNY, 1989.
———. *God, Power, and Evil: A Process Theodicy.* Lanham, MD.: University Press of America, 1991.
———. *The Reenchantment of Science.* Albany: SUNY, 1988.
Hadot, Pierre. *Philosophy as a Way of Life: Spiritual Exercises from Socrates to Foucault,* trans. Michael Chase. New York: Blackwell, 1995.
Hall, David D. *Worlds of Wonder: Days of Judgment: Popular Religious Belief in Early New England.* Cambridge, MA: Harvard, 1990.
Harding, Sandra G. *The Science Question in Feminism.* Ithaca, NY: Cornell, 1986.
Harding, Walter. *The Days of Henry Thoreau.* New York: Knopf, 1965.
———. *A Thoreau Profile.* New York: Thomas Crowell, 1962.
Hartshorne, Charles. *Creativity in American Philosophy.* Albany: SUNY, 1984.
Harwood, A. C. *The Recovery of Man in Childhood.* Great Barrington, MA: The Myrin Institute, 1958.
James, William. 1986. "Essays in Psychical Research." In *The Works of William James.* Cambridge, MA.: Harvard University Press, 1977.
———. [1909]. "A Pluralistic Universe." In *The Works of William James.* Cambridge, MA.: Harvard University Press, 1977.
———. [1907]. "Pragmatism and the Meaning of Truth." In *The Works of William James.* Cambridge, MA.: Harvard University Press, 1975.
———. [1902]. "Varieties of Religious Experience." In *The Works of Wiliam James.* Cambridge, MA.: Harvard University Press, 1985.
———. [1897]. "The Will to Believe." In *The Works of William James.* Cambridge, MA.: Harvard University Press, 1979.
———. *Writings 1902–1910.* New York: The Library of America, 1987.
Jeager, Werner. *Aristotle: Fundamentals of the History of His Development.* New York: Oxford University, 1948.
Kolakowski. Leszek. *The Alienation of Reason: A History of Positivist Thought.* Garden City, NY: Anchor, 1968.
Kubie, Lawrence S. *Neurotic Distortion of the Creative Process.* New York: Farrar, Straus and Giroux, 1958.
Kuklick, Bruce. *Churchmen and Philosophers, From Jonathan Edwards to John Dewey.* New Haven, CT: Yale University, 1985.

Kühlewind, Georg. *From Normal to Healthy: Paths to the Liberation of Consciousness.* Hudson, NY: Lindisfarne Press, 1988.

———. *Stages of Consciousness: Meditations on the Boundaries of the Soul.* West Stockbridge, MA: Lindisfame Press, 1984.

Lachman, Gary. *Rudolf Steiner: An Introduction to His Life and Work.* New York: Tarcher, 2007.

Loewenberg, J. (ed.). *Royce's Fugitive Essays.* Cambridge: Harvard University Press, 1920.

Lowe, M., and R. Hubbard, ed. *Woman's Nature: Rationalizations of Inequality.* New York: Pergamon, n.d.

MacIntyre, Alasdair. *After Virtue: A Study in Moral Theory,* 3d ed. Notre Dame, IN.: Notre Dame University, 2007.

Macmurray, John. *Reason and Emotion.* London: Faber and Faber, 1935.

McDermott, John J., ed. *The Writings of William James: A Comprehensive Edition.* New York: Random House, 1967.

McDermott, Robert, ed. *The Essential Steiner: Basic Writings of Rudolf Steiner.* Lindisfarne Books, 2007.

———. *The New Essential Steiner: An Introduction to Rudolf Steiner for the 21st Century.* Lindisfarne Books, 2009.

Miller, Perry. *Errand Into the Wilderness.* Cambridge, MA: Belknap, 1956.

Misak, Cheryl, ed. *The Cambridge Campanion to Peirce.* New York: Cambridge University, 2004.

Naess, Arne. *Ecology, Community, and Lifestyle: Outline of an Ecosophy.* Cambridge: Cambridge University, 1993.

Nelson Garner, Shirley, Claire Kahane, Madelon Sprengnether, eds. *The (M)Other Tongue: Essays in Feminist Psychoanalytic Interpretation.* Ithaca, NY: Cornell University, 1985.

Neville, Robert C. *Reconstruction of Thinking.* Albany: SUNY, 1981.

Niebuhr, Richard H. *The Responsible Self.* New York: Harper and Row, 1963.

Noddings, Nel. *Caring: A Feminine Approach to Ethics and Moral Education,* 2d ed. Berkeley: University of California, 2003.

Olson, Richard. *Science Deified and Science Defied: The Historical Significance of Science in Western Culture, Vol. 1: From Bronze Age to the Beginnings of the Modern Era, ca 3500 BC to AD 1640.* Berkeley: University of California, 1982.

Oppenheim, Frank. *Royce's Mature Philosophy of Religion.* Notre Dame, IN: University of Notre Dame, 1993.

———. *Reverence for the Relations of Life: Reimagining Pragmatism via Josiah Royce's Interactions with Peirce, James, and Dewey.* Notre Dame, IN: University of Notre Dame, 2005.

———. *Royce's Voyage Down Under: A Journey of the Mind.* Lexington, KY: University Press of Kentucky, 1980.

Perry, Ralph Barton, ed. *The Thought and Character of William James.* Boston: Little, Brown, 1935.

Polanyi, Michael. *Personal Knowledge.* Chicago: The University of Chicago Press, 1962.

———. *The Tacit Dimension*. Garden City, NY: Anchor, 1967.
Powers, Johnathan. *Philosophy and the New Physics*. London and New York: Methuen, 1982.
Rabinow, Paul, and Nikolas Rose, eds. *The Essential Foucault*. New York: New Press, 2003.
Rich, Adrienne. *The Dream of Common Language: Poems 1974-1977*. New York: Norton, 1978.
Richards, M. C. *Toward Wholeness: Rudolf Steiner Education in America*. Middletown, CN: Wesleyan University, 1980.
Rorty, Richard. *Contingency, Irony, and Solidarity*. Cambridge: Cambridge University, 1989.
———. *An Ethics for Today: Finding Common Ground Between Philosophy and Religion*. New York: Columbia University, 2011.
———. *Philosophy and the Mirror of Nature*. Princeton, NJ: Princeton University, 1979.
Rosenstock-Huessy, Eugen. *The Christian Future, or the Modern Mind Outrun*. New York: Harper Torchbooks, 1966.
Royce, Josiah. *The Basic Writings of Josiah Royce*, 2 vols. (ed. J. McDermott). Chicago: University of Chicago Press, 1969.
———. *The Hope of the Great Community*. New York: Macmillan, 1916.
———. "Mind," in *Hastings' Encyclopaedia of Religion and Ethics*. New York: Scribner's, 1916.
———. *The Philosophy of Loyalty*. New York: Macmillan, 1908.
———. *A Primer of Logical Analysis*. San Francisco: A. L. Bancroft, 1881.
———. *The Problem of Christianity*, 2 vols. New York: Macmillan, 1913.
———. "The Relation of the Principles of Logic to the Foundations of Geometry." *Transactions of the American Mathematical Society* 24 (1905).
———. "Royce's Last Lectures on Metaphysics." Harvard University Archives, Richard C. Cabot Papers, n.d.
———. *Royce's Logical Essays* (ed. Daniel S. Robinson). Dubuque, IA: Wm. C. Brown, 1951.
———. *The Sources of Religious Insight*. New York: Charles Scribner's Sons, 1912.
———. *Studies of Good and Evil*. New York: D. Appleton, 1898.
———. *War and Insurance*. New York: Macmillan, 1914.
———. *The World and the Individual*, 2 vols. New York: Macmillan, 1899-1901.
Saatkamp, Herman J., ed. *Rorty and Pragmatism: The Philosopher Responds to His Critics*. Nashville: Vanderbilt University, 1995.
Salih, Sarah, ed., *The Judith Butler Reader*. Malden, MA.: Blackwell, 2004.
Sanborn, F. B. *Henry David Thoreau: American Men of Letters*. Charles Dudley Warner, series ed. Cambridge, MA: The Riverside Press, 1883.
Santayana, George. *Interpretations of Poetry and Religion*. New York: Harper, 1957.
Sheldrake, Rupert. *A New Science of Life: The Hypothesis of Formative Causation*. London: Blond & Briggs, 1981.

———. *The Presence of the Past: Morphic Resonance and the Habits of Nature*. New York: Times Books, 1988.

Sloan, Douglas, ed. *The Computer in Education: A Critical Perspective*. New York: Teachers College, 1985.

Smith, John E. *Purpose and Thought: The Meaning of Pragmatism*. London: Hutchinson. 1978.

———. *Themes in American Philosophy: Purpose, Experience, and Community*. New York: Harper Torchbooks, 1970.

Steiner, Rudolf. [1924]. *Anthroposophical Leading Thoughts; Anthroposophy as a Path of Knowledge: The Michael Mystery*, London: Rudolf Steiner Press, 1998.

———. [1924]. *Autobiography: Chapters in the Course of My Life, 1861–1907*, Great Barrington, MA: SteinerBooks, 2006.

———. *Building Stones for an Understanding of the Mystery of Golgotha*. London: Rudolf Steiner Press, 1972.

———. [1902]. *Christianity as Mystical Fact: And the Mysteries of Antiquity*. (trans., intro. by Andrew Welburn). London: Rudolf Steiner Press, 2006.

———. *Cosmic Memory: The Story of Atlantis, Lemuria, and the Division of the Sexes*. Great Barrington, MA: SteinerBooks, 2006.

———. [1924]. *The Course of My Life*. Hudson, NY: Anthroposophic Press, 1951.

———. [1984]. *The Essential Steiner: Basic Writings of Rudolf Steiner* (ed., intro. R. McDermott). Great Barrington, MA: Lindisfarne Books, 2007.

———. *The Gospel of St. John*. Spring Valley, NY: Anthroposophic Press, 1962.

———. [1904]. *How to Know Higher Worlds: A Modern Path of Initiation* (trans. by Christopher Bamford). Hudson, NY: Anthroposophic Press, 1994.

———. [1894]. *Intuitive Thinking as a Spiritual Path: A Philosophy of Freedom* (trans. by Michael Lipson). Hudson, NY: Anthroposophic Press, 1995.

———. *Knowledge of the Higher Worlds and Its Attainment*. Hudson, N.Y.: Anthroposophic Press, 1947.

———. [1901]. *Mystics after Modernism: Discovering the Seeds of a New Science in the Renaissance*. Great Barrington, MA: Anthroposophic Press, 2000.

———. *The New Essential Steiner: An Introduction to Rudolf Steiner for the 21st Century* (ed., intro. R. McDermott). Great Barrington, MA: Lindisfarne Books, 2009.

Bibliography

———. *Nietzsche: Fighter for Freedom*. Blauvelt, NY: Garber, 1960.

———. [1909]. *An Outline of Esoteric Science* (trans. C. E. Creeger). Hudson, NY: Anthroposophic Press, 1997.

———. [1909]. *An Outline of Occult Science* (trans. rev. by Lisa Monges). Spring Valley, N.Y.: Anthroposophic Press, 1972.

———. [1894]. *The Philosophy of Freedom: The Basis for a Modern World Conception* (trans. Michael Wilson). London: Rudolf Steiner Press, 2012.

———. *The Philosophy of Spiritual Activity* (trans. Rita Stebbing). Hudson, N.Y.: Anthroposophic Press, 1986.

———. *The Redemption of Thinking: A Study of the Philosophy of St. Thomas Aquinas*. Spring Valley, NY: Anthroposophic Press, 1956.

———. [1914]. *The Riddles of Philosophy: Presented in an Outline of Its History*. Great Barrington, MA: SteinerBooks, 2009.

———. *A Theory of Knowledge Implicit in Goethe's World Conception* (1894; rev. 1924). Spring Valley, NY: Anthroposophic Press, 1978; new ed.: *Goethe's Theory of Knowledge: An Outline of the Epistemology of His Worldview*. Great Barrington, MA: SteinerBooks, 2008.

———. [1904]. *Theosophy: An Introduction to the Spiritual Processes in Human Life and in the Cosmos* (trans. by Catherine E. Creeger). Hudson, NY: Anthroposohic Press, 1994.

———. [1892]. *Truth and Knowledge: Introduction to Philosophy of Spiritual Activity* (trans. by Rita Stebbing). Great Barrington, MA: SteinerBooks, 2007.

Stout, Jeffrey. *Democracy and Tradition*. Princeton: Princeton University Press, 2004.

Sugarman, Shirley. (ed.). *Evolution of Consciousness: Studies in Polarity*. Middletown, CN.: Wesleyan University, 1976.

Taves, Ann. *Religious Experience Reconsidered: A Building-Block Approach to the Study of Religion and Other Special Things*. Princeton: Princeton University, 2009.

Taylor, Bron, ed. *The Encyclopedia of Religion and Nature*. New York: Continnum, 2005.

Thoreau, Henry David. *American Men of Letters*. Charles Dudley Warner, series ed. Cambridge, MA: The Riverside Press, 1883.

———. *Nature/Walking*. John Elder, ed. Boston: Beacon Press, 1991.

———. *Walden*. Boston: Ticknor and Fields, 1854.

———. *Walden: A Fully Annotated Edition*. Jeffrey S. Cramer, ed. New Haven, CT: Yale University, 2004.

Urban, Wilbur Marshall. *Beyond Realism and Idealism*. London: George Allen and Unwin, 1949.

———. *Language and Reality: The Philosophy of Language and the Principles of Symbolism*. London: George Allen and Unwin, 1939.

Warren, Karen J., ed. *Ecofeminism: Women, Culture, Nature*. Bloomington: Indiana University Press, 1997.

Weizenbaum, Joseph. *Computer Power and Human Reason: From Judgment to Calculation*. San Francisco: Freeman, 1976.

West, Cornel. *The American Evasion of Philosophy: A Genealogy of Pragmatism*. Madison: University of Wisconsin Press, 1989)

———. *Keeping Faith: Philosophy and Race in America*. New York: Routledge, 2009.

Whicher, Stephen E., ed. *Selections from Ralph Waldo Emerson: an Organic Anthology 1803–1882*. Boston: Houghton Mifflin, 1957.

Whitehead, Alfred North. *Adventure of Ideas*. New York: Macmillan, 1933.

———. *The Function of Reason*. Boston: Beacon Press, 1958.

———. *Process and Reality: An Essay in Cosmology* (corr. ed., ed. D. R. Griffin and D. W. Sherburne). New York: The Free Press, 1978.

———. *Religion in the Making*. Cleveland: World Publishing, 1960.

———. *Science and the Modern World*. New York: Macmillan, 1926.

Wohlgelernter, Maurice, ed. *History, Religion, and Spiritual Democracy*. New York: Columbia University, 1980.

About the Contributors

Rebecca Kneale Gould is Associate Professor of Religion and Environmental Studies at Middlebury College in Vermont. Gould's first book, *At Home in Nature: Modern Homesteading and Spiritual Practice in America* (University of California, 2005) is an ethnographic and historical study of back-to-the-land experiments based on research she conducted while living and working at the homestead of Helen and Scott Nearing. Gould's more recent publications (in Jon Isham's, *Ignition;* Whitney Bauman's *Grounding Religion;* Cecile Andrew's *Less is More;* and Tufts University Press/Mildred's Lane Press, *Renovating Walden*) reflect two of her current research and writing projects: religiously based environmental action and the impact "time-famine" on physical, spiritual, and ecological wellbeing. Gould is the co-creator and coproducer (with director Phil Walker) of the documentary film, *The Fire Inside: Place, Passion, and the Primacy of Nature* (2012), which premiered in at the Yale Divinity School. She lives in Vermont, with her partner and six well-loved sheep.

David Ray Griffin is Professor of Philosophy of Religion and Theology, Emeritus, Claremont School of Theology and Claremont Graduate University in Claremont, California, where he remains a co-director of the Center for Process Studies. He is a major exponent of the thought of Alfred North Whitehead and Constructive Postmodernism. He has published (as author or editor) thirty-four books, primarily in theology, philosophy, and philosophy of religion, with special emphases on the problem of evil and the relation between science and religion, including *The Reenchantment of Science* (1988); *Unsnarling the World-Knot: Consciousness, Freedom, and the Mind-Body Problem* (1998); *Religion and Scientific Naturalism: Overcoming the Conflicts* (2000); and *Reenchantment without Supernaturalism: A Process Philosophy of Religion* (2001). He is also a major critic of the official version of the 9/11 attack: *Debunking 9/11 Debunking: An Answer to Popular Mechanics and Other Defenders of the Official Conspiracy Theory* (2007); *The New Pearl Harbor Revisited: 9/11, the Cover-up, and the Exposé* (2008); and *9/11 Ten Years Later: When State Crimes against Democracy Succeed* (2011).

Gertrude Reif Hughes is Professor Emerita of English and Women's Studies at Wesleyan University, where she served as Chair of her Department and of the Women's Studies Program. The author of *Emerson's Demanding Optimism* (1984), she has published essays on American poets, including Emily Dickinson, Gwendolyn Brooks, H.D., and Adrienne Rich, as well as essays on Rudolf Steiner and feminist thought and on Steiner's *Calendar of the Soul*. A lifelong student of Anthroposophy, she is a former chair of the Board of Anthroposophic Press (Steinerbooks) and former president of the Rudolf Steiner (summer) Institute, where she taught meditation for many years and served on its board. Her degrees are from Yale University and Mount Holyoke College. As a child, she attended the New York City Rudolf Steiner School.

Robert McDermott is president emeritus, California Institute of Integral Studies (CIIS) and chair of the CIIS Program in Philosophy, Cosmology, and Consciousness (PCC). He was Secretary of the American Academy of Religion. He was a senior Fulbright professor at the Open University, U.K., and has received several NEH grants. He directed the NEH project for the review of the audio-visual materials for the study of Hinduism and Buddhism. He has published in *International Philosophical Quarterly*, *Philosophy East and West*, *Journal for the American Academy of Religion*. He wrote the "Introduction" to William James, *Essays in Psychical Research* (1986). His other publications include *Radhakrishnan* (1970); *The Essential Aurobindo* (1987); *The Bhagavad Gita and the West* (Steinerbooks 2009); *The New Essential Steiner* (2009); and *Six: Pillars: Introductions to the Major Works of Sri Aurobindo* (2012). He is series editor of *Classics from the Journal for Anthroposophy* (10 vols., 2005–2011). He is currently writing *Unique, Not Alone: Steiner and Others*.

Dan McKanan is Ralph Waldo Emerson Unitarian Universalist Association Senior Lecturer in Divinity at the Harvard Divinity School. Before coming to Harvard in 2008, he served as department chair and associate professor of theology at the College of Saint Benedict/Saint John's University, where he began teaching in 1998. He studies religious movements for social transformation in the United States from the abolitionist era to the present. His first book, *Identifying the Image of God: Radical Christians and Nonviolent Power in the Antebellum United States* (2002), explores theological understandings of violence and nonviolence among abolitionists, pacifists, and temperance activists. *Touching the World: Christian Communities Transforming Society* (2007) and *The Catholic Worker After Dorothy: Practicing the Works of Mercy in a New Generation* (2008) deal with the Camphill and Catholic Worker networks of intentional communities. Professor McKanan's newest book, *Prophetic Encounters: Religion and the American Radical Tradition*, is a general history of religion and the Left in the United States.

Frank Oppenheim, S.J., is Research Professor at Xavier University (Cincinnati). Ordained to priesthood in 1955, he began teaching at Xavier in 1961 in its department of philosophy (philosophical anthropology, ethics, history of modern philosophy, business ethics). He specializes in American philosopher of community, Josiah Royce (1855–1916), and in other American philosophers. Besides numerous articles, Oppenheim's published books include *Royce's Voyage Down Under: A Journey of the Mind* (1980); *Royce's Mature Philosophy of Religion* (1987); and *Royce's Mature Ethics* (1993). He coedited Royce's 1915–1916 *Metaphysics* (1999) and edited two volumes of *Josiah Royce's Late Writings* (2001). His magnum opus, entitled *Reverence for the Relations of Life: Re-imagining Pragmatism via Josiah Royce's Interactions with Peirce, James and Dewey*, was published by the University of Notre Dame Press in 2004. He lives in Clarkston, Michigan, where he continues his research on Josiah Royce.

 **Douglas Sloan** is Professor of History and Education Emeritus at Teachers College, Columbia University, where he taught for more than thirty years. During this time, he was also Adjunct Professor of Religion and Education at Union Theological Seminary and The Jewish Theological Seminary, New York, and Director of the Center for the Study of the Spiritual Foundations of Education at Teachers College. From 1992 until 2000, he was also Director of the Master's Program in Waldorf Education at Sunbridge College. His books include *Insight-Imagination: The Emancipation of Thought and the Modern World* (1983) and *Faith and Knowledge: Mainstream Protestantism and American Higher Education* (1994). He and his wife Fern live near Harlemville, New York.

www.ingramcontent.com/pod-product-compliance
Lightning Source LLC
Chambersburg PA
CBHW030611230426
43661CB00053B/1930